T0247657

'A new book by Jerome McGann is an event, though there have been many such events over his long career. But a new book by him about Byron is a special kind of event. No other scholar has done as much for Byron as McGann has, and few living scholars as much for any single author as he has done for Byron. This book marks a kind of return to origins since, like McGann's first book, Fiery Dust, this one focuses on Byron's work before Don Juan. The new emphasis, however, falls on Byron's relationship to language and poetic craft and on how it differs from that of his major contemporaries. Playful, allusive, and itself 'adverse,' McGann's style in this book, like Byron's own, means to set our language free.'

James K. Chandler, William K. Ogden Distinguished Service
Professor, University of Chicago

'This is a book written with much of Byron's own intelligence, wit, and passion. It pays particular and welcome attention to the 'dark' poems which Professor McGann sees as 'in some ways more impressive than the ottava rima masterpieces'. It moves between very wide perspectives and sustained, often dazzling, close reading helped by his unrivalled knowledge of the textual history.'

Bernard Beatty, Senior Fellow in English, Liverpool University and
Editor of The Byron Journal 1987–2004

'Take physic, cant. The words are nowhere, the command everywhere in Byron and McGann. The physic is philology: a word-loving that embraces the cunning, ambivalence, and enthrallments of language along with its beauties and benevolences. If words are actions (and who today could doubt that), McGann's 'inner standing point' (D. G. Rossetti) on Byron is as a sword that divides, setting fiction against factitiousness, expressive contradiction against the suavities of doublespeak. McGann's 'little book,' as he calls it, is a work of pity and rage; its perfectly measured disorders a min(e)d-field to blast the pieties of the present. Go litel book… '

Marjorie Levinson, F. L. Huetwell Professor,
University of Michigan

'Combative, liberatory, and dazzling, Byron's poetics receive the close attention they deserve in McGann's beautiful book. Byron and the Poetics of Adversity illuminates the full sweep of Byron's poetic experimentation and ruthless unveiling of his culture's cherished illusions in poems such as Manfred, The Giaour, Lara, and Cain, difficult poems often undervalued in favor of the poetic pyrotechnics of the epic Don Juan. McGann's scholarly and playful close readings of the full range of Byron's 'perversifications' and their 'disastered heroes' reveal new dimensions of what made these poems both scandalous and brilliant, and how they engaged with leading writers of the age like Blake and Goethe.'

Adriana Craciun, Emma MacLachlan Metcalf Chair of Humanities,
Boston University

Jerome McGann shows that Byron's "treasonous" attitude to poetry, his "perversification," his unfit and shifty tones, his Blakean refusal of invariable aesthetic systems, his "spoiler's art" is as pertinent now as it was 200 years ago. By repeatedly exposing the shibboleths of lyric and Romantic verse culture, McGann's sweeping advocacy of Byron's inventive, performative, rhetorical, and adversive genius is a defense of poetry for our time as well.

Charles Bernstein, Donald T. Regan Professor, Emeritus, of English
and Comparative Literature, University of Pennsylvania

'Byron and the Poetics of Adversity is a genuinely revolutionary book in which Professor McGann returns to the textual entanglements of Byron's prosody and looks afresh at the two phases of Byron's poetic career in 1808–16 and 1817–24. Seven brilliant, compelling essays trace the poetic offensives that connect The Giaour, The Corsair, Lara, The Siege of Corinth, shorter lyrics and Manfred with the offensive poetics of Don Juan. Identifying practical criticism as the vital, oppositional act which Byron's poetry commits on its readers and demands from them, this bold and provocative study goes back to where all the ladders start – in close readings of some of the most perverse lines in Romantic period poetry.'

Jane Stabler, Professor of Romantic Literature,
University of St Andrews

Byron and the Poetics of Adversity

A long line of traditional, often conservative, criticism and cultural commentary deplored Byron as a slipshod poet. This pithy yet aptly poetic book, written by one of the world's foremost Romantic scholars, argues that assessment is badly mistaken. Byron's great subject is what he called "Cant," the habit of abusing the world through misusing language. Setting up his poetry as a laboratory to investigate failures of writing, reading, and thinking, Byron delivered sharp critical judgment on the costs exacted by a careless approach to his mother tongue. Perspicuous readings of Byron alongside some of his Romantic contemporaries – Burns, Blake, Wordsworth, Coleridge, Shelley – reveal Byron's startling reconfiguration of poetry as a "broken mirror" and shattered lamp. The paradoxical result was to argue that his age's contradictions, and his own, offered both ethical opportunities and a promise of poetic – broadly cultural – emancipation. This book represents a major contribution to ideas about Romanticism.

Jerome McGann is Professor Emeritus in the Department of English at the University of Virginia. He is the editor of Byron's *Complete Poetical Works* (seven volumes, 1980–1993) and is one of the leading authorities on Romanticism and its aftermath. This book is a major addition to his influential argument for a "Literature of Knowledge," which he first outlined in his 1989 Clark Lectures (Trinity College, Cambridge) and Carpenter Lectures (University of Chicago).

Byron and the Poetics of Adversity

JEROME MCGANN

University of Virginia

CAMBRIDGE
UNIVERSITY PRESS

CAMBRIDGE
UNIVERSITY PRESS

University Printing House, Cambridge CB2 8BS, United Kingdom

One Liberty Plaza, 20th Floor, New York, NY 10006, USA

477 Williamstown Road, Port Melbourne, VIC 3207, Australia

314–321, 3rd Floor, Plot 3, Splendor Forum, Jasola District Centre,
New Delhi – 110025, India

103 Penang Road, #05–06/07, Visioncrest Commercial, Singapore 238467

Cambridge University Press is part of the University of Cambridge.

It furthers the University's mission by disseminating knowledge in the pursuit of
education, learning, and research at the highest international levels of excellence.

www.cambridge.org
Information on this title: www.cambridge.org/9781009232951
DOI: 10.1017/9781009232968

Printed in the United Kingdom by TJ Books Limited, Padstow Cornwall

A catalogue record for this publication is available from the British Library.

ISBN 978-1-009-23295-1 Hardback

For Bernard Beatty, Geoffrey and Dianora Bond, and Drummond
Bone and
implora eterna quiete
Marilyn Butler, Peter Cochran, Elma Dangerfield, Michael Foot,
Doris Langley Moore, Jock Murray, Andrew Nicholson, William St
Clair

The ethical responsibility to object.

Barry Lopez, *Horizon*

CONTENTS

Acknowledgments   *page* x

    INTRODUCTION   1
1 DON JUAN AND THE ENGLISH LANGUAGE   9
2 BYRON AGONISTES, 1809–1816   38
    Philology, Pope, Poetics   38
    Byron's Perversifications   64
3 MANFRED: ONE WORD FOR MERCY   82
4 BYRON AND THE "WRONG REVOLUTIONARY
    POETICAL SYSTEM"   103
5 BYRON, BLAKE, AND THE ADVERSITY OF POETICS   119
6 THE STUBBORN FOE: BAD VERSE AND THE POETRY
    OF ACTION   154

Notes   183
Index   207

ACKNOWLEDGMENTS

I have dedicated this book to a company of men and women who must stand in for many who helped me from the first year (1965–1966) I came to the United Kingdom to work on Byron. These people make up a special group who looked after me again and again, even to the present. I was a stranger and they took me in.

My deepest thanks too for long years of conversation and comradeship with my friends in the collegial company of the Byron Society and the Keats-Shelley Memorial Association, and a special salute to friends and colleagues Steve Arata, Tom Berenato, Charles Bernstein, Adriana Craciun, Morris Eaves, Bob Essick, Cheryl Giuliano, Peter Graham, Jonathan Gross, Jeffrey Herrick, Susan Howe, Jon Klancher, Alice Levine, Marjorie Levinson, Peter Manning, Marsha Manns, Morton Paley, Michael Pickard, Jeffrey Robinson, Jim Soderholm, Jane Stabler, Andrew Stauffer, Sarah Storti, Annie Thompson, Chip Tucker, Joseph Viscomi, and Susan Wolfson, all of whom have kept a divine vision of the human world, even our tight little scholarly island, in a time of trouble.

While Jim Chandler is a distinguished member of that company, I set him apart here because he has had, like Bernard Beatty, a direct influence on this book. He read it in its first state and then, *mirabile dictu*, kept rereading as I went about revising.

Finally, my deep gratitude goes to Bethany Thomas, who encouraged me in the work at every stage, and to George Laver, for his meticulous attention to the book in its final stages.

Introduction

The Eastern Gate, fourfold: terrible & deadly its ornaments:
Taking their forms from the Wheels of Albions sons; as cogs
Are formd in a wheel, to fit the cogs of the adverse wheel.
                                    William Blake, *Jerusalem*, Chapter 1

While no one has ever questioned Byron's immense historical and cultural significance – though many have deplored it – the eminence of his poetry and poetics has been controversial. Wordsworth and Keats were among the first distinguished witnesses for the prosecution just as Blake, Scott, and Shelley had a different view.

Understandably, *Don Juan* has shaped the recovery of Byron the Poet over the past fifty and more years. But the poetic character of the rest of the work is regularly obscured by *Don Juan*'s celebrity. This is unfortunate, especially for the poetry that established his international influence – the verse from *Childe Harold's Pilgrimage: A Romaunt* (1812) through the Oriental Tales to *Manfred* (1817). In key respects, those works are more impressive than the *ottava rima* masterpieces: for better and for worse, more driven, perhaps more dangerous, mostly less urbane.

Indeed, *Don Juan* is such a spectacular performance one might take it for that "thing of words" Byron most despised, poetical Cant, written merely to "tak[e] the tone of the time."

The truth is that in these days the grand "primum mobile" of England is *Cant* – Cant political – Cant poetical – Cant religious – Cant moral – but always *Cant* – multiplied through all the varieties of life. – It is the fashion – & while it lasts – will be too powerful for those who can only exist by taking the tone of the time – I say *Cant* – because it is a thing of words – without the smallest influence on human actions – the English being no wiser – no better – and much poorer … than they were before the prevalence of this verbal decorum.[1]

Of course *Don Juan* can be and has been read as such, and of course it most definitely takes the tone of its time. But its seductive charms are cunning and even dangerous because, though a mere "thing of words," it threatens an "influence on human actions."

That is why, though he could not know it at the time, from 1809 to 1817, Byron was in training for *Don Juan*'s insidious ways. It is also why, if we want to see what is happening in the earlier work, we have to pay the same kind of close attention to the language and versification of those years as we do to that of *Don Juan*. Early and late, as Bernard Beatty has suggested, Byron's verse is "addressed to the understanding."[2] By that he did not mean, any more than Goethe meant when he urged the same view, that Byron is a poet of ideas. He is not; he is rather what G. Wilson Knight once called him, a poet of action, of engaged performance.[3] His language and versification are not deployed to deliver ideas but to provoke and unsettle his readers.

Unworking (and mixing and confusing) a set of foundational literary forms – satire, lyric, narrative, and finally drama – Byron's poetry from 1812 forward was announcing a tectonic shift in what literature and especially poetry could or might do. With *Don Juan*, readers could see that no subject or language was out of bounds and, more pointedly, that both should be ready to take on any point of view, including views that Byron opposed. Under the regime of *Don Juan* – "born for opposition" – poetic forms had to answer the calls of Contradiction. So one directive takes the measure of the game's rules and moves:

> In play there are two pleasures for your choosing,
> The one is winning and the other, losing.
>
> (*Don Juan*, XIV. 12)[4]

The poetry of the Years of Fame laid the foundation for that poetical agenda, but it laid in a stony poetics of loss and defeat. Not that *Don Juan* tells a different story: flashing its way "o'er a waste and icy clime" (*Don Juan* VII. 2), the poem was dancing Juan to his execution during the Reign of Terror, an ending he may have forecast in the death of Haidee. Childe Harold's first pilgrimage is a tale of more urgent failures – from its outgoing fiasco, linguistic and personal, to its final home desolations – and the following five tales are all flights to disaster. But they are also pleasure domes and romantic chasms because their afflictions are laid in meticulous if also bewildering prosodies. The reader's mind is affected – pleasured – by being led through fields of carefully measured disorder.[5]

This is not verse composed as a mirror or a lamp, though it does both represent and reveal the world. It is rather a "mental net" poetics (*Lara* I. 381), its language woven and then broadly cast to snare and take minds "bred in darkness [and] unprepared" (*Childe Harold's Pilgrimage* IV. 127) to deal with their condition. Rigorously alienated throughout its content and medium, the verse proposes a new contract based in ruthless sympathy. It assumes that the available poetic resources, the mirrors and the lamps, regularly fail to bring themselves to more than sentimental judgment about what they do.

Sentimental judgment would lead Keats though a long poem that tries to persuade us "A thing of beauty is a joy for ever." Hearing him recite from it in 1818, Wordsworth called the effort – cruelly, if

not untruly – "a pretty piece of paganism," and soon enough Keats
would himself be glossing it "forlorn."[6] That judgment – it will
pervade Keats's verse – would perhaps never have achieved its
depth or complexity had he not put his dream of deathless beauty
to the sore trial of *Endymion*.

Because Wordsworth's sentiment of beauty underwent (much
earlier) a similar trial, he might have been less carping about Keats.
From 1797 forward, this was the poetic tale that dominated nearly
everything he wrote:

> We poets in our youth begin in gladness,
> But thereof come in the end despondency and madness.
>   ("Resolution and Independence," 48–49)

We marvel at the many poignant ways he found to play out that
story just as we marvel at the famous summary he gave them all:
"Not without hope we suffer and we mourn" ("Elegiac Stanzas,"
60). That turned out the refrain of a song Wordsworth sang "As if
that song could have no ending" ("The Solitary Reaper," 26). "As
if"; "Not without hope": those uncertain codes get reconceived
each time they are run, from "Michael" through *The Prelude* to
The White Doe of Rylstone and beyond.

I summarize this familiar myth of Romantic passage because
Byron's is so different: from despondency and even madness,
Byron moves to the gay science of *Don Juan*. Now we regularly
use the latter to take the measure of what came before, as if Byron
spent ten years trying to unlearn an inheritance of spurious versifying. But if we take that line, we will start at a deficit of attention
that his contemporaries – admirers and detractors both – did not
have because Byron's art – *Beppo* and *Don Juan* as much as *Childe
Harold* or *The Giaour* – gave them no peace. Whatever else we
might think of Byron's poetry of 1809–1816, it is plainly every bit
as deliberated as *Don Juan*. Early and late, Byron never lets his

readers forget that he has them in his sights and writes to demand
their attention.

Take a notable passage from *The Giaour*. Byron wrote poetry as
fine as this, but he rarely wrote anything better, and, in *Don Juan*,
very little as powerful. It pays if you pay attention.

* *

> The Mind, that broods o'er guilty woes,
>   Is like the Scorpion girt by fire,
> In circle narrowing as it glows
> The flames around their captive close,
> Till inly search'd by thousand throes,
>   And maddening in her ire,
> One sad and sole relief she knows,
> The sting she nourish'd for her foes,
> Whose venom never yet was vain,
> Gives but one pang, and cures all pain,
> And darts into her desperate brain. –
> So do the dark in soul expire,
> Or live like Scorpion girt by fire;
> So writhes the mind Remorse hath riven,
> Unfit for earth, undoom'd for heaven,
> Darkness above, despair beneath,
> Around it flame, within it death!

* *

(*The Giaour*, 422–438)

Start with the evidence of those asterisks, which interrupt *The
Giaour*'s narrative twenty-six times.[7] The poem is a notoriously
difficult read and the asterisks are largely responsible, signaling as
they do the presence of a catastrophic textual loss pervading
Byron's "Fragment of a Turkish Tale." What we are reading –
we only learn this in the poem's last note – is his (invented)
memorial reconstruction of a modern epic he heard by chance in
a Levantine coffeehouse in 1810–1811. This passage is a parody of
an epic simile – as it happens, one of three in the poem – and *The*

Giaour is a narrative elegy for the loss of poetry in England and Europe, with Homeric verse offered as the emblematic measure of the loss.

Because these two sets of asterisks are the seventh and eighth the poem has thrown out, we are familiar with the incomprehension they come to declare. But we are not reconciled to it. On the contrary, each time they appear, they serve to unnerve us once again, a remorseless reminder and revival of the poem's long-drawn-out torment of reading. Most immediately, these two become typographical signs of a specific disfunction, reflecting the reflection of the disordered "Mind" – brooding, remorseful, guilty – that the simile considers. But as all *The Giaour*'s asterisks strip the poem of crucial explanatory context, we are here dislocated from the simile's point of reference.

The passage follows immediately upon a long section (398–421), also asterisk-framed, that introduces the first of the poem's epic similes, a meditation on what Byron's note identifies as "The blue-winged butterfly of Kashmeer." Only as we get further into the poem do we recall both similes as fractured figurations of the star-crossed lovers Leila and the Giaour, but then we also come to realize they resonate much further. Leila and that butterfly are explicitly a seductive "Beauty" (396), and the subject of the scorpion passage is more than precisely the Giaour. The poem's paratactic structure – think of *The Waste Land* – sends us prying much further into its textual abyss. This Mind is equally Byron's in his tale's first-person introduction, bent over the corpse of Greece. It is also the narrator's of the original Turkish Tale, and it is the minds of all the speakers that narrator ventriloquizes. And perhaps most of all it becomes a simile of the reader's mind who has been drawn into a sympathetic relation with a poem explicitly organized to bewilder us with questions that are raised up and left hanging. (Why is Mind gendered female? For that matter, and thinking forward to *Don Juan*, why is Truth [*Don Juan* XV. 88]?)

Or consider closely the legendary figuration that is the focus of the passage. The scorpion has not been tossed into the ring of fire by some sadic agent. The tormented Mind is not the scorpion; it is the fire-ringed scorpion being "inly searched" by its own fiery pain. But when that figure lifts its thought to the desperate hope of suicidal relief (428–433), the verse turns sharply away, closing with a pair of couplets that shut off the remarkable music (422–434) that plays with its three repeating rhymes: woes, fire, vain. That finale designs for this closing Mind a closed placeless space ("above, beneath, around, within"), "Unfit for earth" (clearly) but also – what could it mean? – "undoomed for heaven." "Undoomed"?

The prosody is turning an adverse wheel against the poem's obdurate figurations, unbuilding it for his readers from a thoughtful music perhaps more dreadful – certainly more sharply defined – than Tennyson's city built to music. Setting an example of thoughtfulness for his reader, Byron steps away to add an explanatory prose note:

Alluding to the dubious suicide of the scorpion, so placed for experiment by gentle philosophers. Some maintain that the position of the sting, when turned toward the head, is merely a convulsive movement; but others have actually brought in the verdict "Felo de se." The scorpions are surely interested in a speedy decision of the question; as, if once established as insect Catos, they will probably be allowed to live as long as they think proper, without being martyred for the sake of an hypothesis.

(*CPW* III. 418)

Oddly – subtly – that enlightened pose has recharged Byron's dark simile. In *Don Juan*, Byron will lift that kind of footnote-aside out of prose *recitative* and recompose it as digression. Each of those two kinds of poetic move is very different and many now would judge *Don Juan*'s digressive style more artful, as perhaps it is. But *The Giaour*'s resort to this ironical prose note leaves the reader in a far more disturbed poetic field. Because that enlightened commentary is clearly – too clearly – posed, the poetic tale itself is set more free to display and explore its sinister ways.

It is a nice question which to prefer: the beauty of *The Giaour*'s inflections, or the beauty of *Don Juan*'s innuendoes. That is the question I want to raise in this little book. I'll confess right now that, on Mondays, Wednesday, and Fridays, I incline one way, on Tuesdays, Thursdays, and Saturdays, another. I rest on Sundays.

I

Don Juan and the English Language

Virginia Woolf's reflections on *Don Juan* in her diary of 1918 forecast the dramatic recovery of Byron's cultural importance since the 1960s.

It is the most readable poem of its length ever written, I suppose; a quality which it owes in part to the springy random haphazard galloping nature of its method. This method is a discovery in itself. It's what one has looked for in vain – a[n] elastic shape which will hold whatever you choose to put into it.[1]

That assessment of the poem's "method" has framed the discussion ever since, whether the focus has been on poetic form or on poetic argument.[2] But in an interesting swerve some twenty years later, T. S. Eliot used the work's "readability" to recover the very first line of critical judgment brought against Byron, and in particular *Don Juan*. Though Eliot's terms are philological, the rationale is clearly moral:

Of Byron one can say, as of no other English poet of his eminence, that he added nothing to the language, that he discovered nothing in the sounds, and developed nothing in the meaning, of individual words. (201)

That is not so far from Robert Southey's 1820 charge that *Don Juan* was "an act of high treason on English poetry."[3] In Eliotic

9

idiom, Byron was a great individual talent whose negligence abused the poetic tradition he had made his vocation. This happened, Eliot judged, because Byron had a "defective sensibility" – an "imperceptiveness to the English word" and a mere "schoolboy command" of his mother tongue. Briefly, Byron corrupted the language, doing "for [English] very much what the leader writers of our journals are doing day by day" (201).[4]

I used to struggle with that passage: it seemed so patently, perversely, mistaken. But I've come to see it differently. Indeed, both Southey and Eliot bring real clarity to the character of Byron's work, especially the work after he left England. When Byron attacked what he called the "wrong revolutionary poetical system" of contemporary poetry, his target was the contemporary (Romantic) refiguration of the ancient theory of poetry as an ideal discourse, with Imagination serving as both the index and the vehicle of ideal encounter. But for Byron, rhetorical address, not Imagination, was the determining element in poetic discourse.[5]

Few scholars or critics regard Byron as a significant poetic theorist because he never wrote or even attempted extended prose reflections on poetry or poetics. Perhaps even worse, and in contrast to all his contemporaries, he maintained a firmly skeptical view of poetry and the idea of the poet, nor did he exempt himself and his own work from that aporetic view. But his great significance as a poetic "theorist" rests in both of those intellectual postures. He theorizes poetry only when he is actually carrying out a poetic practice. By contrast, he sees prose explanations as conceptual moves – generalizing and abstract – that necessarily miss the essential point of poetic practice, which is a human intercourse not of ideas but of words and language. In that respect, the practice is always falling short or getting waylaid – "Failure stalks in every word" the poets deploy – but not because of some deficiency in the language as such.[6] The deficit is human; the poets are as fallible as the people they address and the worlds they mirror.

For Byron, the objective and sociomaterial character of language – its relation to the volatile world of fact and event – puts him at odds with both Coleridge's and Wordsworth's Romantic theories of poetry and Imagination. Byron's poetry – not his "ideas" – is perhaps the period's most Romantic work because it executes the period's most radical critique of Romanticism. It both practices and provokes "contradiction" in order to hold up a mirror to the truth of the human world and its asymmetrical exchanges, of which poetry – as an imitation of its life – is (and ought to be) one of the most resolutely asymmetrical.

The differential of Byron comes out clearly when we look at his relation to what may be the period's most seriously consequential event, Wordsworth and Coleridge's *Lyrical Ballads*. The focus of that work was the poetic importance of English vernacular – "the language really used by men" – and its explicit context was a "general evil" threatening culture and society.[7] Byron returned to that primal scene of English Romanticism in 1817 when he began to explore the project that soon became *Don Juan*. He too made English vernacular the focus of his attention. But because he took a very different approach to the language, he saw the project of *Lyrical Ballads* in a critical light.

A brief sketch of some literary historical commonplaces provides a clearer view of what was at stake here. The period from about 1760 forward involved two major and related upheavals, one called Romanticism, the other, Modernism.[8] I start from the second since Eliot's view of Byron is such a clear function of his particular Modernist poetry and poetics. It is a Modernism quite unlike other Modernist forms. Futurism, dada, and surrealism did not much concern him, being primarily non-English phenomena, and he barely dipped into the American lines that descend from Whitman: Charles Reznikoff, Hart Crane, William Carlos Williams, Gertrude Stein, Muriel Rukeyser, even Wallace Stevens.

Yet despite his notorious neoclassicism, Eliot's Modernism was built from a consequential Romantic tradition. Parsing Eliot's severe judgment on Byron, Peter Manning forty years ago pointed out that Eliot's work was grounded in "the Romantic-Symbolist tradition" (231) of poetry and poetics.[9] Drawing upon Romantic theories of Imagination, that line of thought stressed "metaphoric, symbolic concentration" – an ideal of linguistic precision and *le mot juste*. "Little Gidding" closes with a poetic vision where "the end and the beginning" round in upon themselves. For poetry, this is the place "where every phrase/ And sentence that is right" is exactly "where every word is at home,/ Taking its place to support the others." Reprising the theory of the Romantic symbol, Eliot all but echoes Coleridge's famous formula for the action of the Secondary Imagination: "the balance and reconciliation of opposite and discordant qualities." In the final figure of "Little Gidding," this is the symbolic place where "The fire and the rose are one."[10]

As Manning pointed out, Eliot did not think about language and poetry the way Byron did. Because Byron's "characteristic" poetic mode was "excursive, associative, [and] metonymic" (Manning 223), not symbolic, its energies do not covet Eliotic resolutions – the still points in the turning world. Rather, they live in a dream of perpetual motion: "Then let the Winds howl on! their harmony/ Shall henceforth be my music" (*Childe Harold* IV. 106). Because this involves a prodigal take on Language, the imaginative action Byron draws from it is exorbitant, profuse, and reliably capricious, like the river Po, Byron's river of love. Dangerous and powerful, it was yet for him a "congenial" river whose springtime floods brought both nourishment and wreckage as it drove "wildly to the wilder main" ("To the Po" 19).[11]

Byron's verse, like "To the Po," focuses on quotidian life in what Wordsworth called "the very world which is the world/ Of all of us" (*The Prelude* X. 725–726). That is Eliot's and Byron's chief interest as well. But the life and language of Byron's world are distinctively different from Wordsworth's and Eliot's. Consider these famous passages from *Four Quartets* where Eliot recounts his struggles with a resistant medium:

> Words strain,
> Crack and sometimes break, under the burden,
> Under the tension, slip, slide, perish,
> Decay with imprecision, will not stay in place.
>
> ("Burnt Norton" V)

"And so," he writes in "East Coker,"

> each venture
> Is a new beginning, a raid on the inarticulate,
> With shabby equipment always deteriorating.
>
> ("East Coker" V)

That would have been for Byron a preposterous view of his preeminent resource. Byron had small interest in making Language behave properly. Nor did he see it as a piece of "shabby equipment, always deteriorating." Even when he hardly knew how to manage it, as in the wonderfully mismanaged first two cantos of *Childe Harold*, Byron approached language as a gift, never more so than in *Don Juan*. Recollecting Dryden, he set down his "moderate-minded" (I. 118) procedural rule: "Good workman never quarrel with their tools" (I. 201). So his view of Language was less fretful than Eliot's, less captious than Wordsworth's, more gratulant. He had no quarrel with his mother tongue. Quite the contrary.

Eliot's uncertainties about the state of English in the twentieth century recall Wordsworth's concerns at the turn of the nineteenth. *Lyrical Ballads* registered a broad crisis of cultural sensibility. "For a multitude of causes, unknown to former times, are now acting with a combined force to blunt the discriminating powers of the mind" ("Preface" 249). Wordsworth launched *Lyrical Ballads*, as his "Preface" argued, to move against "degraded" literary conditions that had "the magnitude of [a] general evil." Like Eliot later,

Wordsworth's was a program to "purify the language of the tribe" ("Little Gidding" II) at a moment when language seemed in peril.

Crucially, the language that Wordsworth promotes in *Lyrical Ballads* is the spoken vernacular, not literary English (whether poetical or prosaic). He celebrated "the language really used by men" because it was, he judged, the "natural" language of human feeling. The "experiment" of *Lyrical Ballads* argued that poetic expression might be, even ought to be, grounded in a simple and even prosaic English style and diction. The poems were his proofs.

Lyrical Ballads was setting its face against two English language practices, both of them literary. Scholars almost always focus only on one: the much-deplored "poetic diction" of late eighteenth-century poetry, fiction, and drama. For Wordsworth, the feeling developed in such work was simply factitious, a mere game of feeling. To counter it, he made his momentous proposal: "between the language of prose and metrical composition . . . there neither is, nor can be any essential difference." What contemporary poetry most needed was "the language of prose," not literary works that "indulge[d] arbitrary and capricious habits of expression" ("Preface" 253, 246).

But Wordsworth's poetic program sensed an even greater challenge from a different quarter: the powerful nonfiction prose of natural and moral philosophy that came from men he often admired, like Priestley, Beddoes, Darwin, Godwin, and Davy. The philosophical prose of "The Man of Science," as Wordsworth called him, posed an unusual threat to language and society. For Science – Natural and even Moral Philosophy – used languages so "remote" from "the language of the heart" that they might even be called "barren leaves," as Wordsworth explicitly did in "The Tables Turned." "Far more truly philosophical" than such literatures, Wordsworth argued, was a poetry that drew on the "plainer and more emphatic language" of ordinary vernacular English as regularly practiced by men in "low and rustic life" ("Preface" 259, 245). What he called "the philosophic mind" emerged from carefully cultivated habits of human sympathy: the "soothing thoughts that spring/ Out of human suffering" ("Intimations Ode" 189–191).

Perhaps the *Lyrical Ballads* experiments added nothing significant to the English language, but their contribution to English poetry and poetics was immense nonetheless. Setting poetry to the rhythms of English vernacular prose was a revolutionary move with consequences Wordsworth could not have foreseen and, had he been able, would probably have disapproved. If he resisted, as he did, John Thelwall's more radical approach to the relation of prose and verse, what would he have thought of Whitman or, worse yet, Williams?[12] What would Coleridge have made of Stein?

In that context of Modernist and Romantic poetics, the question of what (if anything) Byron's poetry, *Don Juan* in particular, contributed to the English language – or for that matter to English poetry – is deeply pertinent. Indeed, it catches at the express purpose Byron himself advanced for his work in 1817. As he began closing down the project of *Childe Harold's Pilgrimage* and, with *Beppo*, opening up the project of *Don Juan*, he declared that "I twine/ My hopes of being remembered in my line/ With my land's language" (*Childe Harold* IV. 9). This determination proved doubly paradoxical and singularly consequential. Byron moved to establish his English-language credentials by putting himself to school to another language, Italian, and to a "line" of its most distinguished poets. It was a move he had begun to make in 1809 when he wrote *Childe Harold's Pilgrimage: A Romaunt* under the auspices of Ariosto.[13] But by 1817–1818 he was making a much deeper investment in all the classic works of Italian literature.[14] What came of this, *mirabile dictu*, was a prosaic and vernacular verse that ran a shocking parallel with the *Lyrical Ballads* program and what might well be called a "treasonous" posture toward English poetry itself.

Like Wordsworth in 1800, Byron in 1817 found himself half in love with easeful prose.

> I've half a mind to tumble down to prose,
> But Verse is more in fashion – so here goes!
>
> ("Beppo" stanza 52)

"Tumble down" signals a very different "Revolution of the Word" from Wordsworth's.[15] Byron's was explicitly a kind of counterrevolution. As he began composing *Beppo*, his forecast of *Don Juan*, he wrote his letter of Romantic apostasy to Murray.[16] It is certain that he shifted from his soberly framed purpose of June to this emphatic September pronouncement against the contemporary "wrong revolutionary poetical system – or systems" because he had just read *Biographia Literaria*, which appeared in July. There Coleridge set Wordsworth and the event of *Lyrical Ballads* as the standard for measuring the important shift that English poetry had taken in 1798. But it was not the work of "the simple Wordsworth" that was decisive for Coleridge.[17] It was the Wordsworth of such poems as "Tintern Abbey," the "Intimations Ode," and, most important of all, the still-unpublished *Prelude*. These demonstrated Coleridge's view of the "revolutionary" turn toward what Wordsworth in 1814 announced as his "high argument" for poetry.[18] They expressed "the philosophic mind" of an Enlightenment that had not been corrupted by what Coleridge called "Jacobin" secularities.[19]

As the first draft of the *Don Juan* "Dedication" shows, that polemical context remained in force when he began writing his masterpiece a year later, in July 1818.[20] Confirming Wordsworth as the founder of the poetical "system" he was opposing, he took Southey's 1813 laureateship as an official endorsement of Lake School poetics, and he identified Coleridge as its principal theorist. Significantly, the catalyst for Byron's "Dedication" was neither Southey's laureateship, which was five years gone, nor the four-year-old failure of Wordsworth's *Excursion*. It was Coleridge once again, this time his (to Byron) forbidding discussions of poetry and "metaphysics" in *The Friend*, which Byron had just read in Coleridge's reissued 1818 augmented three-volume edition.

Scholars often judge that Byron contributed little of importance to the vigorous contemporary discussions of language and poetry. That is a fair assessment of Byron's formal prose criticism, though his dismissal of Bowles's attacks on Pope's character was well managed and, most of all, his commentary on the language of Cant was as profound as anything ever written at the time in England.[21] But it is in his inimitable letters and, most of all, in his verse where we should take Byron's measure as a critic and even as a poetic theorist. *Beppo* and *Don Juan*'s ideas about poetry are important exactly because they are framed in verse, in poetic rather than conceptual terms. Hence Byron's commitment to Horace and especially, given his English position, to Pope. If a poet is to take on philosophic issues, Byron is arguing, make the moves in verse – *An Essay on Criticism, An Essay on Man*.

Beppo and *Don Juan* did not rise up to denounce the verse of *Lyrical Ballads*, though some of it Byron – like Coleridge – deplored. Before Wordsworth's involvement with Byron's personal scandals in 1816, Byron even expressed a "reverence" for Wordsworth and his work.[22] His admiration for Coleridge's greatest poetry is well known. So if by 1819 Byron judged *The Excursion* a "drowsy frowzy poem ... Writ in a manner which is my aversion" (III. 94), still he acknowledged, even insisted, "'Tis poetry" ("Dedication" 4). QED, or as he added, "The field is universal, and allows/ Scope to all such a feel the inherent glow" ("Dedication" 7).

What was "wrong" for Byron was the conceptual brief for a "poetical system" being set down in *Biographia Literaria* and *The Friend*, or in Wordsworth's related 1800–1802 "Preface" and the "Preface" and "Essay Supplementary" in his 1815 *Poems*. Like Byron, Blake sneered at promoting art through what he called "systematic reasoning," and Byron took the same line when he famously averred that "When a man talks to me of system" – he was thinking explicitly about poetry and poetics – "his case is hopeless."[23] Contemporary verse went "wrong" when it proceeded on "system": Coleridge's "principles" or, worse yet, Bowles's "invariable principles."[24] It was the road – the strait gate – to a prison house of language.

Because Byron was such an admirer of his poetry, Coleridge's case is perhaps even more illuminating than Wordsworth's. Scholars and critics regularly turn to Coleridge's prose writings, especially *Biographia Literaria*, to elucidate his poetics. This conceptual approach is understandable since Coleridge himself put such stress on his philosophic argument for poetic "principles." But we want to remember that *Biographia Literaria* offers an account of the *operation* of imaginative action, not a *conception* of imaginative action. The account is the focus of chapter 18, where he locates the "ideal" of poetry's imaginative action in a poem's nonconceptual music – its metrical and phonic disposition. It is a systematic critique of Wordsworth's remarkable thought that "between the language of prose and metrical composition ... there neither is, nor can be any essential difference." When Coleridge ends his long analysis, he simply writes: "there may be, is, and ought to be, an *essential* difference between the language of prose and of metrical composition."[25]

"I write in metre," Coleridge argues, "because I am about to use a language different from that of prose" (*BL* II. 69). Briefly, "metre is the proper form of poetry" (*BL* II. 71). Glancing back at his discussion of the "synthetic" work of poetic imagination in chapter 14, Coleridge argued that meter represents the action of that

high instinct of the human being impelling us to seek unity by harmonious adjustment, and thus establishing the principle, that *all* the parts of an organized whole must be assimilated to the most important and essential parts.

(*BL* II. 72)

It is "the very act of composition itself," its effort to "produce, an unusual state of excitement, which of course justifies and demands [the] correspondent difference" between poetry and prose. In metrical composition, then, "The wheels take fire from the mere rapidity of the motion" of the verse. The key object, "harmonious adjustment," is a function of poetry's distinctively Ideal, nonconceptual feature, its rhythmic movement. Whatever the poem takes up in its "descriptions or declamations ... reflections, forms, or incidents" – in general, its conceptual "subject and materials" – prosody represented its most important and essential synthesizing action (*BL* II. 72).

Reading the "Rime," "Christabel," and "Kubla Khan," Byron had no difficulty recognizing the remarkable character of Coleridge's poetry.[26] Indeed, he was so impressed by the prosodic argument Coleridge executed in "Christabel" that he attempted to exploit and imitate it in *The Siege of Corinth* (1816). But shrinking from the studied philosophic prose of *Biographia Literaria* and *The Friend*, Byron mischievously asked Coleridge to "explain his explanation[s]" of the "new system" that had been "perplex[ing] the sages" of poetry since 1798 ("Dedication" 2, 4). It was mischievous because Coleridge had recently published, at Byron's urging and with his help, two exemplary verse demonstrations of his poetics, "Christabel" and "Kubla Khan."[27] So Coleridge's turn from poetry to prose was unfortunate.

Byron may not have known what we now know, that the turn began in mid-1800 and that Coleridge himself felt it grievously. After he was forced to withdraw "Christabel" from the 1800 volume over which Wordsworth had taken complete charge, Coleridge wrote to James Tobin that he meant to "abandon poetry altogether." Wordsworth's poetic enterprise between 1797 and 1800 had been prodigious, throwing Coleridge's efforts into eclipse. Worse, Coleridge's masterpiece, "The Rime of the Ancyent Marinere," had been a special object of attack, even derision, among the hostile reviewers of the 1798 volume. So he told Tobin that "I leave the higher & deeper Kinds [of poetry] to Wordsworth ... & reserve for myself the honorable attempt to make others feel and understand [his] writings."[28]

Coleridge's three great poems – the "Rime," "Christabel," and "Kubla Khan" – each in different ways illustrated how poetry's imaginative action was driven by the "symphony and song" ("Kubla Khan" 43) of the verse. In 1798, the demonstration of this view in the "The Rime of the Ancyent Marinere" baffled nearly everyone except Charles Lamb. Coleridge wrote the metrical "experiment" of "Christabel" as an even more emphatic perform- ance for an "Ideal" rather than a prosaic – Wordsworthian – imaginative action. In 1800, the truncated state of the narrative in "Christabel" may have persuaded Wordsworth, perhaps even Coleridge, that, after the public failure of the "Rime," another performative argument for Coleridge's Ideal poetics might prove counterproductive. As Wordsworth put his stamp on the character of the 1800 *Lyrical Ballads*, "Christabel" was withdrawn and Coleridge wrote his dismal letter to Tobin.

Coleridge's misfortune proved a misfortune for the history of poetry as well. "Christabel" is one of the period's supreme demon- strations of an Ideal poetry and poetics: briefly, that vernacular language might be enlisted to expose the music of "the love that moves the sun and the other stars."[29] While that is the ultimate theme of "Kubla Khan," "Christabel's" prosodic experiment made it a real presence in the movement and physique of the verse. Like the "Rime" – and in contrast to "Kubla Khan" – "Christabel" also foregrounded a Christian rendering of the ancient Pythagorean "music of the spheres."

This brief survey of Wordsworth's and Coleridge's Romantic poetics returns us to Byron. If he "duly seated [Wordsworth and Coleridge] on the immortal hill" of poetry ("Dedication" 6), he knew he was working another side of the mountain. Most important, he saw different opportunities in English vernacular. Wordsworth wrote his poetry to help purify the language, Coleridge to demonstrate its sacred, Ideal office. Byron worked to set it free.[30]

Perhaps no passage in *Don Juan* provides a more arresting example of where he wanted to take poetry than the notorious stanzas about Catherine of Russia (Canto IX. 55–59). He opens the passage by addressing neither queen nor sex organ but an old word, "cunnus," that he then quickly and impishly edits out of his text: "Oh, thou 'teterrima Causa' of all 'belli.'" But by airbrushing that Latin word, Byron fills our ears with its English cognate, perhaps even reminding us how it has been kept alive by such eminences as Chaucer and Shakespeare.

English has one other forbidden word, and Byron makes sure his poem calls it out. But once again he moves obliquely. In this case, he makes a different word – the word "serious" – his initial focus of attention. The context is the language of "serious" writing, with William Wilberforce and Thomas Malthus as Byron's exemplary cases (XII. 20). The one emerges as a serious and splendid public figure, the champion of human freedom, the other as seriously forbidding, the champion of abstract reasoning and moral restraint.

So the word "serious" emerges in the verse as seriously ambivalent. Wilberforce and Malthus having served to bring out the initial distinction, Byron moves to a further one. He's a "serious" writer too:

> I'm serious – so are all men upon paper;
>> And why should I not form my speculation,
> And hold up to the sun my little taper?
>> Mankind just now seem wrapt in meditation
> On constitutions and Steam-boats of vapour;
>> While sages write against all procreation,
> Unless a man can calculate his means
> Of feeding brats the moment his wife weans.

> That's noble! That's romantic! For my part,
>   I think that "Philo-genitiveness" is –
> (Now here's a word quite after my own heart,
>   Though there's a shorter a good deal than this,
> If that politeness set it not apart,
>   But I'm resolved to say nought that's amiss) –
> I say, methinks that "Philo-genitiveness"
> Might meet from men a little more forgiveness.
>
> (XII. 21–22)[31]

So may a "meditation" on Language be as serious a business as discourses on abolition or demography, constitutions or steamboats. Or phrenology for that matter, Spurzheim having supplied Byron with a spiffy new word for an old vulgar word.[32] Byron is seriously, wittily concerned to show that both are signs of creativity. Gaming the catchphrase "after my own heart," Byron plays off Spurzheim's technical term to pay an old debt to his Scots heritage, where a ubiquitous vulgate word, "shorter," stronger, if not sweeter than Spurzheim's, was kept in cultural and linguistic memory. From Dunbar and Lindsay to Robertson and Burns, and of course well beyond, the word is alive and well. Fuck yes.

So far as Byron's commitments to Language is concerned, this passage has even further significance. Wilberforce, Malthus, and Spurzheim index the "barren leaves" of the languages of science that concerned Wordsworth, who hoped for the day when it would be available "to us as enjoying and suffering beings" ("Preface" 258–259). But in *Don Juan* it was already available. Byron's greatest example of such an unattempted, unpoetical language is surely Canto X stanza 41 – a passage that has to be seen to be believed:

> But here is one prescription out of many:
> "*Sodæ-Sulphat. 3vj.3fs. Mannæ optim.*
> *Aq. fervent. f. 3ifs. 3ij. tinct. Sennæ*
>   *Haustus*" (And here the surgeon came and cupped him)

"R Pulv. Com. gr. iij. Ipecacuanhæ"
  (With more beside if Juan had not stopped 'em).
"Bolus Potassæ Sulphuret. sumendus,
Et Haustus ter in die capiendus."

Do not be fooled by the stanza's startling panache. This is one of *Don Juan*'s richest and most complex passages and has to be carefully unpacked. First of all, then, the prescription itself. Its first move was to administer ("F[iat] ... Haustus") a draft of soda sulfate and the laxative manna, mixed in boiling water with a tincture of senna. After the patient was "cupped," he was to take three grains of ground ipecac and, three times a day, a large pill of sulfurated potash. This remedy is a no-nonsense set of "doubled" purgatives (10. 39) – so severe, in fact, that it could either "mend or end" the patient (X. 42), as Byron's gloss on the passage observes.

The stanza's cancelled first line – "But here is Doctor Rogerson's prescription" – is notable. Had it stayed, the poem would have kept its focus on the story of Juan, grown "sick" from "the fatigue of [his] last campaign" with Catherine (X. 39, 40). Dr. John Rogerson was the Scots doctor who became the official physician to the Russian court in 1769.[33] But when Byron dropped that topical reference – it happened right away – he greatly extended the ironical range of the passage. The stanza turned to a synecdoche for *Don Juan*'s attempt to medicate a whole set of interrelated social, literary, and political maladies: "one prescription" – the wordplay is now obvious – to index the "many" written up for Byron's poem.

Then look closely at the stanza strictly as poetry – or, rather, as *verse*. That Byron intended it to be seen as verse is clear from its shape on the page and its correct rhyme scheme. But does it scan? Can it be recited? Well, as a matter of fact, yes, as two scholars pointed out more than fifty years ago.[34] While I'd slightly modify their proposal, its general correctness is clear, so that a recitation of the abbreviated terms would go like this:

> Soda sulfate six drams half dram mann' optim
> Ak fervent ef saysay two drams tinkt sennay
> Howstus (and here the surgeon came and cupped him)
> R pulv com three grains ipececuanay

Note too that Byron is quoting, not inventing, the prescription. The document might even be lying right there on the table before him. That is a key point for *Don Juan*'s argument about language and poetry. Casting the prescription into perfect *ottava rima* is a dazzling poetic feat, true, but only because of the prescription's objective and personal character. Byron is either copying or remembering documents he knew at first hand.

The stanza's decisive feature, then, is its aggressive physicality, oral, visual, and referential. It throws up what Eliot called an objective correlative for *Don Juan*'s fundamental commitment to "facts." Because the poem's morals and politics address mulish reality, objective conditions both set and take *Don Juan*'s measure, according to the poem's key procedural rule: "'tis the part/ Of a true poet to escape from fiction" (VIII. 86).

I highlight those words because no passage in *Don Juan* reveals more clearly its radical position within the ethos of Romanticism. Besides Crabbe – a poet of real consequence, though not a Romantic poet – who else at the time imagined that a "true poet" should seek to escape the fictions of the Imagination, understanding that those lands of hope and glory were equally the "unreached paradise of our despair" (*Childe Harold* 4.122)? "Few men dare show their thoughts of worst or best" (XV. 3), he observed in an important late passage, a timidity he thought disgraceful to poets especially – "they are such liars (III. 87) – since only truthful talk, whether merciful or merciless, shameful or shameless, justified their vocation. Purely aesthetic

simulations, affirming and denying nothing, he calls *dis-*
simulations, since

> Dissimulation always sets apart
> A corner for herself; and therefore Fiction
> Is that which passes with least contradiction.
>
> (XV. 3)

But "contradiction" is exactly what *Don Juan* pursues and provokes. So the poem holds little back. Has it lapsed into
a grammatical solecism, a bad rhyme or metrical blunder, an
indecent, a tasteless, or a spiteful comment?[35] Does some passage
seem little better than schoolboy verse? Such things are all there
and they are all left standing. Indeed, in a poem born for the
opposition it flaunts, *Don Juan* has to bear with, even bear witness
to, the aversions it has quickened, like Southey's and Eliot's.[36]

Indeed, *Don Juan* was born for the opposition even of Byron's
friends. His editor and publisher in London not only expurgated
four stanzas in Canto I, removing two of them entirely. They
published *Don Juan* with disfigurations like this on full display.[37]

Every time I look at this page, I think of Marianne Moore's
comment: "It is a privilege to see so much confusion." Batteries
of asterisks signal pushbacks against a poetry that had provoked
them in the first place. If an escape from his own fictions was
Byron's highest aspiration, it is happening here, where the great
moral of *Don Juan* is perfectly exposed:

> I wish men to be free,
> As much from mobs as kings – from you as me.
>
> (IX. 25)

But those are just spectacular examples of Byron's project to
liberate rather than to purify his language. Byron's signature move
in his Progress of Poesy was, in a sense, to do nothing – or, rather,
to write so that the vernacular's rich, natural resources are not

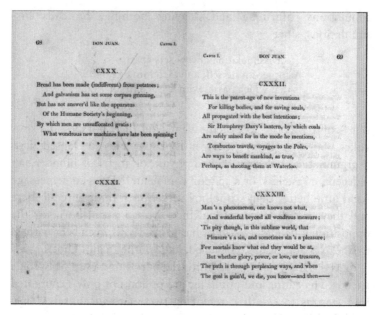

Figure 1 Image of Canto I, stanzas 130–131, in the first edition, second issue of the 1819 edition of *Don Juan*. Image in the public domain, sourced through the Internet Archive (https://archive.org/details/donjuano3byro/page/68/mode/2up). The copy is located in the Special Collections Library, Duke University.

dammed up. What Byron "adds" to the language is an across-the-board allegiance to the borderless condition of *vox populi*. *Don Juan* feeds off a stock of familiar, even trivial idioms and many kinds of commonplace expressions. These are so pervasive that one scarcely pays them any attention, though if you pause to look, you'll see them everywhere. They are slipped into other familiar expressions throughout the poem: anecdotes, maxims, and every kind of literary allusion from nursery rhymes to the Bible, Homer, Horace, Shakespeare, Milton, Pope, even Southey. Angel hosts, they are legion, what Poe later called "The good and the bad and the worst and the best" ("The City in the Sea" 4).

Everyday expressions organize the rhythms of the opening stanzas of Canto I, as if his language had made Byron her mouthpiece. "I should not care to," "Sent to the devil" (1); "in their turn" (2); "as we know" (3); "the tide is turn'd" (4); "A good deal like" (5); "by way of," "whene'er you please," "at his ease" (6); "if you'd rather" (7). Such talk then slips naturally into stanza 8:

> In Seville was he born, a pleasant city,
> Famous for oranges and women – he
> Who has not seen it will be much to pity,
> So says the proverb – and I quite agree.

The proverb is "Quien no ha visto Sevilla/ No ha visto maravilla," which Byron catches up, transliterates into English, cites two reasons for Seville's fame, and then folds in three everyday vernacular phrases. As he will tell us later, the "narrative" of Juan's history will actually be no more than "a mere airy and fantastic basis" set in motion in order "To build up common things with [English] common places" (XIV. 7).

Though Coleridge demurred from Wordsworth's theory of poetic diction in *Biographia Literaria*, he was reaffirming the original project – writing the *Biographia*, as it were, to purify the argument of Wordsworth's too prosaic "Preface." The standard for a properly "philosophical" poetry – Wordsworth's object as well as Coleridge's – could not be "a rustic's language," Coleridge argued, but the language of an "educated man" whose intellectual faculties, being more "developed," were able to "discover and express [the] *connections* of things" and their "general law" (*Biographia Literaria* chapter 17).

But unlike Wordsworth and Coleridge, or Eliot for that matter, Byron was pushing a radical extension of poetry's materials. *Don Juan* proposed virtually no limit to the "things" to be taken up or

the kinds of "connections" they might involve. Its poetry comes
not to balance and reconcile opposite and discordant things and
qualities. It comes to magnify their profusion and multiply the
kinds of profusion to be discovered when your linguistic horizon
is "De rebus cunctis et quibusdam aliis" (XVI. 3). Wordsworth had
an abusive term for the contemporary literature he despised,
"capricious," but that is one of *Don Juan*'s keywords. Love,
poetry, and fame – Byron's three great subjects – are all explicitly
marked "capricious" in *Don Juan* (II. 22, IV. 74, VII. 15).

Byron's Romanticism is a poetic centrifuge built from *Beppo*'s
carnival of language:[38]

> And there are dresses splendid, but fantastical,
>   Masks of all times and nations, Turks and Jews,
> And harlequins and clowns, with feats gymnastical,
>   Greeks, Romans, Yankee-doodles, and Hindoos;
> All kinds of dress, except the ecclesiastical,
>   All people, as their fancies hit, may choose,
> But no one in these parts may quiz the clergy,
> Therefore take heed, ye Freethinkers! I charge ye.

This little assortment – a reimagining of poetic numbers – will
proliferate in *Don Juan* from relatively brief word runs ("sheets,
shirts, jackets, bales of muslin," II. 28) to more detailed arrays, like
the litany on the word "sweet" (I.122–127). These medleys prize
variation and odd shifts:

> A Beauty at the season's close grown hectic,
>   A genius who has drunk himself to death,
> A rake turned methodistic, or Elcectic . . .
> But most, an Alderman struck apoplectic. . . .

(III. 66)

In the stanza I quoted from *Beppo*, note the asymmetric turn it takes
with the caveat "except the ecclesiastical."[39] Byron's inventories, like
his poetry tout court, operate what Alfred Jarry would later call "a

science of exceptions," a calculus of differences.[40] Because the Venetian carnival is a Lenten event, the "Clergy" is everywhere present even if their outward and visible signs are not. So the world of *Beppo* reflects a "Catholic persuasion" (*Beppo* 1) and Byron's wordplay is crucial. The Venetian "seat of all dissoluteness" is a "mix'd company" (*Beppo* 58) tolerant enough to include – to invite even – Byron's mirror world, the audience he imagines of "Freethinkers," "foreign[ers]," and "Protestant[s]" (*Beppo* 3, 9), even Southey, even Wellington, even Castlereagh and Sir Samuel Romilly.

In this generous, treasonous imagination, the *poetry* is determined to "like all and every thing" (*Beppo*, 48), including everything it does not like or outright hates. Recall again *Don Juan*'s opening. In a quick move – speed is one of the poem's signature features – Byron chooses "our ancient friend Don Juan" (I. 1) as his hero, rejecting an extensive set of famous European contemporaries. The list is an important index of the poem's style:

> Vernon, the butcher Cumberland, Wolfe, Hawke,
>   Prince Ferdinand, Granby, Burgoyne, Keppel, Howe,
> Evil and good, have had their tithe of talk,
>   And fill'd their sign-posts then, like Wellesley now;
> Each in their turn like Banquo's monarchs stalk,
>   Followers of fame, "nine farrow" of that sow:
> France, too, had Buonaparté and Dumourier
> Recorded in the Moniteur and Courier.
>
> Barnave, Brissot, Condorcet, Mirabeau,
>   Petion, Clootz, Danton, Marat, La Fayette,
> Were French, and famous people, as we know:
>   And there were others, scarce forgotten yet,
> Joubert, Hoche, Marceau, Lannes, Desaix, Moreau,
>   With many of the military set,
> Exceedingly remarkable at times,
> But not at all adapted to my rhymes.

(I. 2–3)

The hero "Fit for my poem" is not a great sage, statesman, or warrior but a "new one" altogether, a storied libertine. Byron's choice entails two decisive procedural moves, one general, one very particular. First, the presentation of the hero will not begin *in medias res* after the Don's bad eminence had been long established. Like the tale of Tristram Shandy, it will "begin with the beginning" and track his untold early history in notable detail.

The second, particular move is strictly metrical. The hero's Spanish name gets "adapted to [Byron's English] rhymes" by simple linguistic fiat: "true one ... new one ... Juan." That English pronunciation, so simple on its face, represents one of *Don Juan*'s normative acts of poetic allegiance. Though all these great men are repudiated as heroes, "not at all adapted to my rhymes," here they are anyway, well adapted from the start, thank you very much. As the poem moves along, many more even less attractive characters and materials will be adapted to Byron's purposes. The catalogue of dismissed heroes and the anglicized Spanish reprobate provide *Don Juan*'s initial declaration that anything can be "adapted" to Byron's devotional English exercise, whose tutelary spirit and muse is Aphrodite: "Alma Venus Genetrix" (VIII. 119).

The social discourse that organizes the opening of *Beppo* shifts to a personal register at its close, where the eclectic catalogue at the start reemerges as the speech rhythms of Laura, another familiar name for Byron's fecund muse:

> "And are you *really*, *truly*, now a Turk?
>   With any other women did you wive?
> Is't true they use their fingers for a fork?
>   Well, that's the prettiest shawl – as I'm alive!
> You'll give it me? They say you eat no pork.
>   And how so many years did you contrive

To – Bless me! did I ever? No, I never
　Saw a man grown so yellow! How's your liver?

"Beppo! that beard of yours becomes you not;
　It shall be shaved before you're a day older;
Why do you wear it? Oh! I had forgot –
　Pray don't you think the weather here is colder?
How do I look? You shan't stir from this spot
　In that queer dress, for fear that some beholder
Should find you out, and make the story known.
How short your hair is! Lord! how grey it's grown."

(*Beppo* 88–89)

Laura talks the way Ornette Coleman directed his free jazz improvisations.[41] Coming at you initially as random thoughts with irregular transitions, the passage builds up a rare ensemble – the sign of a language promising poetic moves unattempted yet in prose or rhyme.

Annotated lists abound: a roll call of warriors, a tally of country guests, an Italian theatrical troupe, a menu. If Byron "like[d] to be particular in dates" (I. 103), he liked even more to be particular in his descriptions: Juan and Julia's consummated flirtation, the feast on Lambro's island, the sketches of Haidee and of Norman Abbey. Most elaborate of all are the digressions. While they can come as brief interruptions in the narrative, they often run at length – more than twenty or even thirty stanzas.

Especially notable are Byron's similes – his favorite verse figure. Unlike metaphor, which collapses and synthesizes, similes court expansion and draw, as well as draw out, distinctions. The "graceful ladies" of Cadiz have such an arresting carriage that "I can't describe it, though so much it strike,/ Nor liken it – I never saw the like." But he tries anyway, probably recollecting a famous sonnet by Guido Cavalcanti: "An Arab horse, a stately stag, a barb/ New broke, a cameleopard, a gazelle,/ No – none of these will do" (II. 56). Or here's another set of failed comparisons. He tries them out to answer a question: who feels a "rapture" as much as someone watching a sleeping beloved?

> An infant when it gazes on a light,
>   A child the moment when it drains the breast,
> A devotee when soars the Host in sight,
>   An Arab with a stranger for a guest,
> A sailor when the prize has struck in fight,
>   A miser filling his most hoarded chest. . . .

(II.196)

The failure of the comparisons turns out the success of verse that is celebrating its lavish resources.

Perhaps the most famous of Byron's heaped similes is the set he throws at "The evaporation of a joyous day":

> The evaporation of a joyous day
>   Is like the last glass of champagne, without
> The foam which made its virgin bumper gay;
>   Or like a system coupled with a doubt;
> Or like a soda bottle when its spray
>   Has sparkled and let half its spirit out;
> Or like a billow left by storms behind,
> Without the animation of the wind;
>
> Or like an opiate which brings troubled rest,
>   Or none; or like – like nothing that I know
> Except itself; – such is the human breast;
>   A thing, of which similitudes can show
> No real likeness. . . .

(XVI. 9–10)

The eight similes shift gears six times. The third shift ("like a soda bottle") flips back briefly to catch at the first ("the last glass of champagne") while the sixth and seventh – "like nothing that I know/ Except itself; – such is the human breast" – focus on something so complex and variable, "the human breast," that it defies all comparison.

Having reached that climactic impasse, however, the stanza is hanging fire in its fifth line. What to do? Well, how about this?

> – like the old Tyrian vest
> Dyed purple, none at present can tell how,
> If from a shell-fish or from cochineal.
> So perish every tyrant's robe piece-meal!

What is the object of this final comparison? The evaporating day, the human breast? More, what exactly is the *point* of the comparison? The "old Tyrian vest/ Dyed purple" has tossed us into a field of "arbitrary and capricious" associations. As Whitman might say, Byron is afoot with his language. At first the comparison works from the old controversy – now settled – about the source of this famous dye. But the final line entirely drops that point of reference, pivoting sharply to recall how the dye, indelible and fadeless, became identified with robes of royal power. In the ancient world, Tyrian dye was more valuable even than gold.

Note that by the final line the simile has mutated to a synecdoche – the "tyrant's robe" that recollects the torn and bloody "mantle" of Shakespeare's Julius Caesar (Act 3 Scene 2), the first and most famous of the Caesars to don the Tyrian *toga purpurea*. But because that association too does not seize control of the language's wavering movement, the final line – and especially its final word, "piece-meal" – drops into the stanza out of nowhere, a motiveless and free signifier left to drift back through the passage like a ghost haunting "The evaporation of a joyous day" where it all began.

What necessity called up that word? Prosodic demand? But no dearth of rhymes for "cochineal" might have served once the political theme was decided – which, we can see, did not happen until the final line.[42] Do not all tyrants have an Achilles' heel, might they be forced to kneel? Give way to a commonweal? Imperial war being one of tyranny's chief occupations, is Byron playing on the word, thinking of a "peace" meal to come? Or is the suggestion that the end of tyranny can only come in "piece-meal" stages? Or perhaps not at all, since the final line is a curse, not a prophecy or a prayer. Because all three of those unstable convictions run through the poem's "irregular design" (I. 120), the passage models its struggles through many reliably uncertain climates.

In its grand, downbeat arrangements, *Don Juan* – hyped on language – traffics in multiple languages ancient and modern, foreign and domestic. Though English is the poem's processing data set, its flexibilities set an example for Language in general. So anglicization, off rhymes, and torqued phonologies are the recurrent, demonstrative focal points for the account of Language that the poem brings forward. Latin, French, and Italian provide the bulk of the inter-language connections. But its heart is a mash-up drawn from a congeries of British vernacular usage. It assembles different specialized idioms – legal, naval, culinary, and couture; slang ranging from urban Flash to Silver Fork *patois*; technical terms and specialized currencies ("philo-genetiveness," "R"); poetical diction and literary usage; and contemporary advertising and newspaper jargons. It quotes verbatim, it parodies, it echoes, it fashions pastiche documents of many kinds. Notably and given Wordsworth's dismissal of poetic diction, *Don Juan* covets and plays with it, rummaging even its basement terms: "eke," "lo," "forsooth," "methinks." Finally and crucially, all of that is poured into an encyclopedic assortment of proverbs, maxims, catchphrases, and dicta that are *Don Juan's* normative "common places."[43] It is a poem organized, like Murray's dictionary to come, "on historical principles," the languages in question spread across largely Western domains three thousand years in the making. *Don Juan* is a time-lapse snapshot taken in 1817–1823 by an itinerant and very worldly Englishman. Its clear inheritor is *Finnegans Wake*, though *Don Juan* avoids the insolence of that semiprecious academic masterpiece.

I make this comparison because Joyce had long abandoned the tormented world of *Dubliners* when he undertook *Finnegans Wake*. But the dark backward and abysm of Byron's time – the world of Childe Harold, the tales, and the plays – is never far from the language games of *Don Juan*. Byron proposed his gambling trope as a congenial proverb for the lavish argument of his poem: "In play, there are two pleasures for your choosing – / The one is winning, and the other losing." While that splendid couplet folds into *Don Juan's* prismatic glories, the poetic spectacle is finally an "Aurora Borealis/ *Which flashes o'er a waste and icy clime*" (VII. 2, my italics). In a note on his future plans for the poem, Byron said that Juan would die, like Anacharsis Cloots, on the guillotine in the Reign of Terror. What a remarkable idea. Who would have thought it? Like Byron, our chief surrogate in the poem, we are driven through the unexpected world of language. The poem does not know what its Language knows. Setting forth on its discovery mission, it keeps bringing itself – and us – up surprisingly short.

So *Don Juan* imagines Language as an unimaginable, and perhaps most of all an unmasterable, gift, like God's grace. We miss the point, I think, both when we glorify Byron's spectacular language games or when, like Eliot, we deplore what we judge deplorable. Eliot disapproved Byron's "ambitious attempts to be poetic [that] turned] out, on examination, to be fake" (195). But he misunderstood *Don Juan's* foremost argument. Or perhaps Southey saw the matter more clearly when he called the poem an act of high treason, refusing legitimacy to Byron's project. *Don Juan* judges that all of poetry's simulations, perhaps especially its "ambitious" simulations, incorporate fakery and "dissimulation" that ought, as much as possible, to be taken into account. "The dog-star [that] rages" ("Dedication" 4) above *The Excursion* rages as well above *Don Juan*, and both set loose "all Bedlam, or Parnassus" – or in Byron's revision of his master's voice, all Bedlam *and* Parnassus.[44]

But the stanza that Eliot most disapproved, the final stanza of Canto XV, is not what he thought it was, an "ambitious attempt to be poetic" that turned out "on examination, to be fake" poetry. You do not need expertise to catch this stanza's counterfeit art. It is hiding in plain sight, like virtually everything else in *Don Juan*'s ambitious assault on poetic pretension.

> Between two worlds life hovers like a star,
>> 'Twixt night and morn, upon the horizon's verge:
> How little do we know that which we are!
>> How less what we may be! The eternal surge
> Of time and tide rolls on, and bears afar
>> Our bubbles; as the old burst, new emerge,
> Lash'd from the foam of ages; while the graves
> Of Empires heave but like some passing waves.

The commonplaceness of the passage is about as plain as day (so to speak). It rides to nowhere on a series of weary poetical figures and threadbare expressions that are being kept in circulation at a clearly marked discount. The passage is a fine example of what Paul West years ago called Byron's "spoiler's art."[45] Played in that key, *Don Juan* practices a more extravagant art of sinking than Wordsworth's, an act of high poetic treason determined to ransack "the foul rag and boneshop of the heart" of our language.

In what key has *Don Juan*'s polyglot music been written? Is it elegiac? Is it satiric? In the tintamarre of the poem, where everything is illusion except the helpless drive to escape from illusion, neither poet nor reader can be sure. "Note or text, I never know the word that will come next" (IX. 41), nor what it will entail. Apparitions of "le mot juste" are everywhere dancing with "le mot vulgaire." So *Don Juan*'s empires are all lower, ironical, literary empires. His verse is saved, sometimes even glorified, by being brought lower even than Wordsworth's "low and rustic life." As Eliot ought to have remembered, "The way up and the way down are the same," at least if you have the sense to recognize "How little do we know that which we are" (XV. 99).[46]

To have "l'abito dell' arte," as Dante remarked, is to live with "le man che trema" (*Paradiso* 13. 78) from all the circumstantial forces that made the hand "tremble" in the first place, "as magnetic needles do" (I. 198). That is why Byron did not judge the Language taken up in *Don Juan* a tool kit of "shabby equipment always deteriorating" and why we, reading it, should not see it that way either. Like great creating Nature, like Shelley's clouds, the Language of *Don Juan* is both a Tower of Babel and a roar of many waters. Out of that chaos and confusion, debility and glory, one hears, or suspects one hears or hopes to hear, the still small voice of Language whispering: "We change, but we cannot die."

A friend of mine recently called my attention to the online Urban Dictionary's definition of the English language circa 2000: "A language that lurks in dark alleys beats up other languages and rifles through their pockets for spare vocabulary." That would be a language mad, bad, and dangerous to know: *Don Juan*'s language, highly treasonous only in the perspective of a laureate's vision of poetry. But for the "waste and icy clime" of Byron's (and our) modern world, where "Plato" rhymes so happily with "potato," Byron made an aurora borealis by keeping perfect faith with his mortal mother tongue.

2

Byron Agonistes, 1809–1816

PHILOLOGY, POPE, POETICS

Unlike the poetry of all the other major Romantics, Byron's is regularly discussed as if it had no relation to a poetics. The famous comment on canting language already quoted is an important exception because it makes the general question of language a front-and-center issue for poetics. As we've seen, language was as much the paramount focus and concern for Byron as it was for Wordsworth. But because Wordsworth held out an ideal of a "philosophic" language for poetry, his work was shaped as "overheard" self-reflection. By sharp contrast, Byron practiced a rhetorical poetics: a voiced address to multiple audiences, from the most intimate to the most public, and modulated in registers ranging from a Longinian high style to easy conversation to the street profanities of his splendid, irreverent epigrams. That is why even his most personal poems are theatrical, like *Childe Harold's Pilgrimage*, or dramatic, like *Manfred*, and why his turn to "mental theatre" made such significant contributions to poetic drama.[1]

And yet while all that is clear enough, Byron's poetics remains elusive. The difficulty is partly due to the preponderant influence of

Wordsworthian/Coleridgean poetic theory on academic thinking and, more generally, the "lyricization" of Romantic and post-Romantic aesthetics, especially the "wrong revolutionary poetical system – or systems" of Romantic theory. Even more consequential, that perspective throws into eclipse one of the most important cultural movements of the long eighteenth century: the emergence of the ethnographic and anthropological approaches to language and culture that would be one of the great achievements of the long nineteenth century.

The case of Wordsworth throws Byron's poetics into sharp relief. Odd as it may seem and different as were their cultural commitments, both were pursuing a root-and-branch reconsideration of poetry's relation to their mother tongue. But whereas Wordsworth had in view a normative vernacular – what he called a "philosophical language" – Byron's frame of reference was philological.[2] His wide reading in ancient and modern history, antiquarian studies, and cultural anthropology set the context for his famous trip to the Levant, which fed his craving for firsthand experience with bygone and/or unfamiliar people, places, and, most important, with their vocable languages. Equally consequential were the literary works that fed off those studies: most immediately the long verse narratives published between 1798 and 1810, especially Scott's. Earlier eighteenth-century narrative experiments were also important, like the Spenserian poems of Thomson, Shenstone, Mickle, and, in particular, James Beatty's *The Minstrel* (1771).

Finally and decisively there is Pope. The Romantic critique of poetic diction obscured for many of Byron's contemporaries what he recognized and respected: the catholic range of Pope's diction and vernacular usage.[3] But most important was Pope's prosodic example. For his extended narrative and didactic verse of 1809–1816, Byron studied closely Pope's four- and (heroic) five-stress couplet verse. To appreciate what Byron achieved in his radically innovative verse tales, you have to watch how he appropriated and transformed his master's voice.

For Byron, then, Wordsworth's epochal pronouncement – that "There is no essential difference between the language of prose and that of metrical composition" – was not a normative philosophical thought but the plainest factual truth. The world history of poetry, even the special history of English poetry, proved that "metrical compositions" were built out of every kind of usage, from the most philosophical and hieratic to the most specialized and vulgar. In an important sense – it was particularly important for the crisis that fairly defined the Romantic movement – the poets of the period, certainly Wordsworth and Byron, assumed a vocational mission to rethink the relation of language to culture and society, and to make poetry the determining agent for carrying out the mission. As it happened, both prepared the way for a remarkable, unintended literary consequence: the emergence of prose poetry and free verse.

II

Byron's work between 1812 and 1816 tells the story of his fight for a nonnormative vernacular poetry and poetics. The combative achievement of *Don Juan* and his exilic years is the second coming of the struggle he began during the Years of Fame. But that double history was forecast by an earlier event: the publication of *English Bards and Scotch Reviewers* (1809). This work gave Byron his first lesson in the need, the difficulty, and the cost of trying to break with normative preconceptions about what poetry can and cannot do, should or should not do. When you speak about social and cultural defeatures from an inner standing point – as Byron did, as anyone and everyone must – how can you frame reliable judgments? That is the poem's central question. How it responds to but does not answer the question is what makes the poem important.

English Bards became possible when Byron, addressing an audience of what Blake called "corporeal friends," published

Hours of Idleness. An eminent example of "a thing of words [and] verbal decorum," Byron's canting book provoked Henry Brougham's merciless and salutary review. In 1812, Byron woke to find himself famous when he published a poem – *Childe Harold's Pilgrimage: A Romaunt* (1812) – that was fundamentally his first version of *The Waste Land* (he wrote several). In 1808, awaking to find himself shamed, he flung himself into a version of *The Dunciad*.

But for all its explicit echoes of Pope, the headlong undertaking of *English Bards and Scotch Reviewers* turned out something very different.

> A man must serve his time to every trade
> Save Censure; Critics all are ready made.
> Take hackneyed jokes from MILLER, got by rote,
> With just enough of learning to misquote;
> A mind well skilled to find, or forge a fault,
> A turn for punning, call it Attic salt;
> To JEFFREY go, be silent and discreet,
> His pay is just ten sterling pounds per sheet:
> Fear not to lie, 'twill seem a sharper hit,
> Shrink not from blasphemy, 'twill pass for wit;
> Care not for feeling – pass your proper jest,
> And stand a Critic hated, yet caressed.
>
> (*English Bards*, 63–74)

> Now thousand tongues are heard in one loud din:
> The Monkey mimics rush discordant in;
> 'T was chatt'ring, grinning, mouthing, jabb'ring all,
> And noise and Norton, brangling and Breval,
> Dennis and Dissonance, and captious art,
> And Snipsnap short, and Interruption smart,
> And Demonstration thin, and Theses thick,
> And Major, Minor, and Conclusion quick.
> 'Hold (cried the Queen), a Cat-call each shall win;
> Equal your merits! equal is your din!
>
> (*Dunciad* (B) II. 235–244)[4]

Byron's couplet prosody and diction are more than respectable, though Pope's dazzling performance takes their limited measure. It would be years before Byron could manage, as he would, that kind of brilliant conversational facility. Like Pope, Byron's couplets shape a poetry of direct address, but this address, while nervy, is not confident or quite free enough. Any number of examples would show how often he talks at us rather than to us or for us. Indeed, one of the virtues of Byron's poem is that its uncertain agitation is on such full display.

> The time hath been, when no harsh sound would fall
> From lips that now may seem inbued with gall;
> Nor fools nor follies tempt me to despise
> The meanest thing that crawled beneath my eyes:
> But now, so callous grown, so changed since youth,
> I've learned to think, and sternly speak the truth;
> Learned to deride the critic's starch decree,
> And break him on the wheel he meant for me.
> (*English Bards*, 1053–1060)

That is quite affecting because it is so irritably posed and personal. Because *English Bards* is often an annoyed and an annoying – and, sometimes, an ugly – poem, an extended investment exposes how scatterbrained it can be, as if it were caught up in its own mayhem. Having internalized and mastered Horace's poise, Pope is a severe but not a reckless poet.

> Satire's my Weapon, but I'm too discreet
> To run a Muck, and tilt at all I meet.
> (*Imitations of Horace, Satire I*, Book II, lines 69–70)

For his part, Byron will never be so coolly reserved, which does not mean – though some have thought so – that he was not artful. *English Bards*, like Keats's late and very Byronic "The Cap and Bells," is definitely satire run amuck, though it makes a show of different appearances.

But Byron's irritated verse brought him to an unusual discovery. When he disqualifies himself as a poetic monitor because he is *morally* derelict, he has left "verbal decorum" in the dust.

> Even I – least thinking of a thoughtless throng,
> Just skilled to know the right and chuse the wrong.
>
> (689–690)

The debt to Pope's balanced concisions is obvious. What is less obvious is the insidious import of the second line. Even if you fill out the initial phrase to imply "just skilled enough," what is the perverse logic by which choosing wrong follows upon knowing even a modicum of "the right"? Worse, what poetic conscience monitored another, even more immediate choice – the word "skilled"? This is nothing less than Byron unfurling the banner of "the spoiler's art" that so appalled and fascinated Paul West. Byron's less-than-zero admission is shocking because it is exactly *not* the canting, conventional gesture of poetic modesty Brougham had pilloried in *Hours of Idleness*. Byron's truculent frankness has announced the arrival of a voice to be reckoned with, a "stubborn foe" (1052) in the culture wars. Without license or authority, a stranger – perhaps even a reprobate – calls contemporary art and judgment to judgment.

Had Byron issued that declaration in the poem's finale, he could have managed a sentimental *cri de coeur*. But placed here, with almost half the poem still to come, and played in an aggressive minor key, it is unsettling. In a single couplet Byron has called his entire poem, including his own judgments, to judgment. Like Samson, he is pulling down the English palace of art.

> Truth! rouse some genuine Bard, and guide his hand
> To drive this pestilence from out the land.
>
> (687–688)

Is there a genuine bard alive in England who might drive away the pestilence, "GIFFORD perchance" (702)? Byron's poem has left that a forlorn hope and, having sounded off, he ends by begging off. His pestilential self is bound for the Levant and "beauty's native clime/ Where Kaff is clad in rocks, and crowned with snows sublime" (1021–1022). If he cannot clean up the mess – would anyone reading his poem expect him too?! – he can head for the hills.

But those lines are also unsettling. Naming Kaff as his destination, and then glossing it as "Mount Caucasus," Byron throws an oblique light on the desperate idealism that will preoccupy his work for the next ten years and beyond. Anglicizing the legendary Persian Mount Qaf, said to be located at the end of the earth, Byron is heading where Baudelaire always thought he really wanted to go: "Anywhere Out of the World."[5]

It is a nice question, fairly pressing even, why anyone would go on reading a poem that has so brazenly declared itself at odds with itself. Yet readers did and still do, and at the time they were especially eager for it: the poem went through five editions (one suppressed) and multiple piracies. A rhetoric and a prosody is poised to emerge from the attitude that *English Bards* took toward the writing and the reading of poetry. Between 1812 and 1816, it would blossom as the dark aporetic verse that forced the world to give it a name: Byronism.

III

At this point I take my bearings from a set of topics brought forward by three impressive literary minds: Scott (on Byron's diction), Goethe (on his "Invention"), and Poe (on his versification). I start with Scott.

Writing an "Introduction" to *Rokeby* for the eleven-volume 1830 edition of his poetical works, Scott recalled hesitating to venture yet another octosyllabic narrative, especially because "a mighty and unexpected rival was advancing on the stage – a rival not in poetical powers only, but in that art of attracting popularity, in which the present writer had hitherto preceded better men." With the whole of Byron's career in his mind, and not least the coming series of Byronic tales, Scott continued a long discussion of how Byron in 1812 had "immediately placed [himself] on a level with the very highest names of his age." What most struck him in Byron's verse "was a depth of thought, an eager abundance in his diction, which argued full confidence in his inexhaustible resources."[6]

Because of his own investment in philology and ethnolinguistics, Scott recognized the relation between Byron's "depth of thought" and the eager abundance of his diction and usage. With the first two cantos of *Childe Harold* Byron began his lifelong commitment to throw open the doors of poetic expression. Like the tales and, later, *Don Juan*, *Childe Harold* is at once and by turns narrative poem, didactic satire, and lyrical effusion. Of course Byron was ranging far from "the depth of thought" or the purified "diction" that Wordsworth had made the watchwords of his reserved poetic address.

Here is a small sample of the dramatic variations of style that follow upon *Childe Harold*'s depth of thought and abundance of diction.

> Oh, thou Parnassus! whom I now survey, *
> Not in the phrenzy of a dreamer's eye,
> Not in the fabled landscape of a lay,
> But soaring snow-clad through thy native sky,
> In the wild pomp of mountain majesty!

(I. 60)

* These stanzas were written in Castri (Delphos), at the foot of Parnassus, now called Λιακυρα – Liakura.

> Such be the sons of Spain, and strange her fate!
> They fight for freedom who were never free,
> A Kingless people for a nerveless state;

> Her vassals combat when their chieftains flee,
> True to the veriest slaves of Treachery:
> Fond of a land which gave them nought but life,
> Pride points the path that leads to Liberty;
> Back to the struggle, baffled in the strife,
>   War, war is still the cry, "War even to the knife!" *

(I. 86)

* "War to the knife." Palafox's answer to the French general at the siege of Saragoza.

> And oh, the little warlike world within!
> The well-reev'd guns, the netted canopy, *
> The hoarse command, the busy humming din,
> When, at a word, the tops are mann'd on high:
> Hark to the Boatswain's call, the cheering cry!
> While through the seaman's hand the tackle glides.

(II. 18)

* The netting to prevent blocks or splinters falling on deck during action.

> Dusky and huge, enlarging on the sight,
> Nature's volcanic amphitheatre, *
> Chimæra's alps extend from left to right:
> Beneath, a living valley seems to stir;
> Flocks play, trees wave, streams flow, the mountain-fir
> Nodding above: behold black Acheron! †

(II. 51)

* The Chimariot mountains appear to have been volcanic.
† Now called Kalamas.

The appended philological notes are important. They populate the tales of 1813–1816 where they can run to extravagant lengths. But as often as not Byron leaves his readers to their own resources, as in this snapshot of Giaffir (in *The Bride of Abydos*) at an ordinary moment in an ordinary day.

> Thrice clapped his hands, and called his steed,
>   Resigned his gem-adorned Chibouque,
> And mounting featly for the mead,

> With Maugrabee – and Mamaluke –
> His way amid his Delhis took,
> To witness many an active deed
> With sabre keen – or blunt jereed.
> The Kislar only and his Moors
> Watch well the Haram's massy doors.
>
> *(The Bride of Abydos I. 232–240)*

The whole point of this is to show off an everyday language "really used by men" in a quotidian life beyond Byron's England. If "featly" and "mead" were in uncommon usage in 1813 London, so much the better, particularly since both were still as much a vulgate in parts of Great Britain as the living Ottoman diction Byron was foregrounding. Byron's ethnolinguistic stance prods the reader to stop, look, and listen to language as such, to this language he is using right here. Like Scott, Lewis, and Southey, and from Bishop Percy forward, that kind of writing, that cultural mindset, was arguably the chief consequence of the ballad revival and the antiquarian movement.

Strictly in terms of English diction and usage, *The Giaour* and especially *The Siege of Corinth* stand apart among the early tales for the "abundance" of their English diction and usage. None of the others has anything like this:

> From a Tartar's skull they had stripped the flesh,
> As ye peel the fig when its fruit is fresh;
> And their white tusks crunched o'er the whiter skull, †
> As it slipped through their jaws, when their edge grew dull,
> As they lazily mumbled the bones of the dead,
> When they scarce could rise from the spot where they fed;
> So well had they broken a lingering fast
> With those who had fallen for that night's repast.
> And Alp knew, by the turbans that rolled on the sand,
> The foremost of these were the best of his band:
> Crimson and green were the shawls of their wear,
> And each scalp had a single long tuft of hair, ‡
> All the rest was shaven and bare.
>
> *(The Siege of Corinth, 413–425)*

To which Byron appended a pair of notes:

†This spectacle I have seen, such as described, beneath the wall of the
Seraglio at Constantinople, in the little cavities worn by the Bosphorous in
the rock, a narrow terrace of which projects between the wall and the
water. I think the fact is also mentioned in Hobhouse's Travels. The bodies
were probably those of some refractory Janizaries.
‡ This tuft, or long lock, is left from a superstition that Mahomet will draw
them into paradise by it.

But lexicon and usage are by no means the only source of Byron's
linguistic abundance or depth of thought in this kind of work.
Indeed, when Scott linked Byron's thought and language, his
frame of reference was very close to Goethe's extended conversations about Byron with Eckermann. His judgment that "I never
saw the true poetical power greater in any man than in him" is
grounded in his view that Byron's work had "Erfindung und
Geist," "invention and intellect."[7] Goethe's comments are still
sometimes misrepresented as Matthew Arnold misrepresented
them in 1880 when he quoted Goethe as saying "when [Byron]
thinks he is a child" ("Lord Byron ist nur gross wenn er dichtet,
sobald er reflectirt, er ist ein Kind"). For Goethe as for Scott,
Byron's intellectual power – his "depth of thought" – was
a function of his poetry: he is only great when he is writing poetry
("nur gross wenn er dichtet"). To translate "Sobald er reflectirt" as
"When he thinks" is quite indefensible since Goethe makes his
meaning perfectly clear. He is specifically criticizing Byron's public
replies to the ignorant attacks ("unverständige Angriffe") made on
his work by his English critics. He ought to have taken a much
stronger line, Goethe says: "er hätte sich stärker dagegen
ausdrücken sollen".

Goethe's phrase "Erfindung und Geist" is important because it
shows that Goethe's poetic categories were shaped in classical
and neoclassical terms. When Goethe wrote "Erfindung," he was

recalling the traditional rhetorical concept "inventio," invention. Romantic theorists would work to reconceive "inventio" as "imagination," but Goethe (like Byron and, before him, Pope) preserved the traditional distinction. "Erfindung" would be wrongly rendered as Romantic "imagination" because "Erfindung" refers to a consciously deployed poetic act.[8] In classical and neoclassical terms, imagination is the power of making images and verbal figures, whereas invention is the power of conceiving and versifying dramatic scenes and actions. Goethe had particular praise for *The Deformed Transformed*. So for Goethe, Byron's tales and plays had "Erfindung und Geist" to a surpassing degree.

The Giaour, as a whole and in its fractured parts, is exemplary. As a poetical work it exhibits great intellectual invention: in *literal* fact, the representation of the survival of heroic values in tormented modern conditions. Here is the Giaour telling the friar about the deaths of Leila and Hassan:

> Still, ere thou dost condemn me – pause –
> Not mine the act, though I the cause;
> Yet did he but what I had done
> Had she been false to more than one;
> Faithless to him – he gave the blow,
> But true to me – I laid him low;
> Howe'er deserved her doom might be,
> Her treachery was truth to me;
> To me she gave her heart, that all
> Which tyranny can ne'er enthrall;
> And I, alas! too late to save,
> Yet all I then could give – I gave –
> 'Twas some relief – our foe a grave.
>
> (*The Giaour* 1060–1072)

This shocking admission captures the poem's bleak psychopolitical landscape. But step back and notice the voicing. The

core of *The Giaour* is modeled on actual oral narrative –
latter-day epic performances – that Byron had heard in the
coffeehouses. So Byron's couplet verse, as here, sets a matrix
for exposing the poem's spoken address.

But making out the voiced language of *The Giaour* is famously
difficult. Though you are forced to pay careful attention, you
cannot always tell who is talking or where you are. And yet
often, indeed most of the time, you do know. The Giaour
(971–1328) sounds nothing like the Moslem fisherman or the
unnamed person from Hassan's court (747–786) or the friar
(883–915), or the coffeehouse poet who was reciting the tale
(655–674, 689–746), and even less like Byron in his verse introduction (1–167) to the tale proper.[9]

Those introductory passages are especially important. Like
Keats in "The Fall of Hyperion," Byron sets himself apart at the
beginning as a secondary tale-teller. Unlike Keats, however, Byron
uses the conventions of Enlightenment philology – especially the
asterisked signals of textual lacunae – to create a dream of primary
epic in secondary conditions. But Byron invents the poem not as
a dream but as an actual memory. Recalling his experience of the
coffeehouse singers, bringing Homer to his mind, leads him to
invent a work of oral recitation. The central action (invention) of
The Giaour is not the invention of the story of Leila, Hassan, and
the Giaour; it is the poetic recital that Byron can only manage to
recover in pieces. Between the asterisks we catch clear glimpses –
fleeting and broken memorial reconstructions – of that most famous quality of Homeric verse: a drama of human speech and action
projected from the recitational "Invention" of a "cameleon
poet."[10]

The disjointed organization produces a recurrent double-
voicing that is particularly evident in the sections of lines
655 to 786. That kind of prosodic inventiveness, where
Byron projects a glimpse of the bardic performer, shines

most in the outstanding epic similes, which add another layer
of prosodic formality to the verse. Because the narrative
account of the Giaour's and Hassan's death-battle is buried
in the poem's asterisks, we witness it only in this explicitly
poetical mirror.

> As rolls the river into ocean,
> In sable torrent wildly streaming;
> As the sea-tide's opposing motion
> In azure column proudly gleaming,
> Beats back the current many a rood,
> In curling foam and mingling flood;
> While eddying whirl, and breaking wave,
> Roused by the blast of winter rave;
> Through sparkling spray in thundering clash,
> The lightnings of the waters flash
> In awful whiteness o'er the shore,
> That shines and shakes beneath the roar;
> Thus – as the stream and Ocean greet,
> With waves that madden as they meet –
> Thus join the bands whom mutual wrong,
> And fate and fury drive along.
>
> (620–635)

As in the dramatic passages, the oral tale-teller here enters into the
emotional condition that the action has precipitated – in this case,
the "fate and fury driv[ing]" two machines of implacable mascu-
line desire, each the other's double, each at once a person and
a social ethos.

Now compare that remarkable passage with the lines in Scott's
Rokeby (1813) that Byron was clearly recalling:[11]

> The battle's rage
> Was like the strife which currents wage
> Where Orinoco in his pride
> Rolls to the main no tribute tide,
> But 'gainst broad ocean urges far

> A rival sea of roaring war;
> While, in ten thousand eddies driven,
> The billows fling their foam to heaven.
>
> (Canto I. section 13)

Although Bertram – the darkest of Scott's antiheroes – speaks these lines, his rhetoric is indistinguishable from the measured voice that pours through the narrative sections of Scott's tale. In the strictly bardic fragments of *The Giaour* – they comprise most of the poem from line 168 to line 970 – the voicing can seem not that much different from Scott's. But, as we see in the two passages already cited, Byron's prosodic pace is much quicker and more urgent. That is because Scott's narratives, even *Marmion* and *Rokeby*, always know – and let us know – that everything will come out right in the end. But from their outset and throughout, Byronic tales tell us we are rushing to disasters that the poems will "dare you to forget" (*Lara* I. 382).

When the violent "stream and Ocean" simile closes, its mimetic affect persists through the tour de force rhetoric of the interpretive verses that follow. With that interpretive shift the Homeric pastiche disappears. Byron's secular homily launches itself with an unusual Scots colloquialism ("The bickering sabres' shivering jar") and a brief general report on the fight.

> The bickering sabres' shivering jar;
>   And pealing wide – or ringing near,
>   Its echoes on the throbbing ear,
> The deathshot hissing from afar –
> The shock – the shout – the groan of war –
>   Reverberate along that vale,
>   More suited to the shepherd's tale.
>
> (636–642)

Because this "vale" is in fact "Parne's vale" (528, i.e., Parnassus), sacred to poetry and culture, the poet called to report finds himself, in the concluding passage, cursed to report.

> Though few the numbers – theirs the strife,
> That neither spares nor speaks for life!
> Ah! fondly youthful hearts can press,
> To seize and share the dear caress;
> But Love itself could never pant
> For all that Beauty sighs to grant,
> With half the fervour Hate bestows
> Upon the last embrace of foes,
> When grappling in the fight they fold
> Those arms that ne'er shall lose their hold.
>
> (643–652)

All that is pure Byron, far from Homer or the coffeehouse performers who inspired him to his modern inventions. A bold wordplay underscores the forbidding "strife" Byron's imitative "numbers" are executing.[12] From that initial couplet, the verse builds up its grimly ironic, indeed blackly comic, comparison. Then comes the desolated wit of a closing and unforgettable final couplet – something sorely thought and perhaps never expressed in such exacting terms.

> Friends meet to part – Love laughs at faith;–
> True foes, once met, are joined till death!
>
> (653–654)

The couplet draws a summary moral reflection on a narrative action that has caught up the Giaour, Hassan, and Leila. But in doing that it is drawing from, and bleakly drawing down, a fund of cultural commonplaces. In the last line we hear fading away "True loves once met are joined till death," and in the second half Byron uplifts the figure of Aphrodite, the Laughing Goddess, as an ironical revenant.[13] The first four words are similarly deconstructive and even more explicitly Byronic, recalling as they do, and reversing, the proverbial expression – the title of an early Byron lyric – "L'amitié, c'est l'amour sans ailes" (*CPW* I. 22–25).

I give these specimens of Byron's verse to draw a rarely noticed contrast between Byron's poetics and other well-recognized Romantic forms of address. Byron's first tale is especially important because its explicit imitation of a "modern" oral epic is performing as distinctive a poetics as "Michael" or "The Fall of Hyperion." But Byron's tale-telling leaves behind "troubled Memory" (*The Giaour*, 205), not tranquil recollection (Wordsworth) or the "delights [of] the cameleon poet" (Keats).[14] The poem's severe address neither spares nor speaks for life (or love) because, like Byron in his introduction, it is "bent ... o'er" (68) what Coleridge called Death-in-Life. In *The Giaour* and its associated tales we witness the birth of that ubiquitous post-Romantic figure, the cursed poet (*poète maudit*).

We also witness the emergence of a distinctive prosody that Poe first brought to attention in his underappreciated satire of traditional treatises on scansion, "The Rationale of Verse." A controversy over the "correctness" of the celebrated opening passage of *The Bride of Abydos* led Poe to a comic send-up of the dispute between the "Grammars" and the "Prosodies," eye scansion versus ear scansion. The premise of Poe's verse theory (scansion) and practice (prosody) is that the rhythmic expression must not violate "the customary accentuation of the word in conversation." This is no more and no less than what Harry Partch argued one hundred years later, when he was reimagining musical tones, that "Language *is* Music."[15]

The dispute would never have happened, Poe argues, "had this court of inquiry been in possession of even the shadow of the philosophy of Verse." To be understood, the opening lines of *The Bride of Abydos* required "scanning ... without reference to lines, and, continuously" because in verse "the length of a line is entirely an arbitrary matter," a decision poets will make about how they want to control the tempo of the articulate language they deliver. It is crucial to recall that Poe, like Wordsworth and

Byron, assumed poetry was made of vocable language. He also assumed – *pari passu* – that the primal interpretive act was recitation.[16]

When Poe went on to prove his point by printing the passage margin to margin, and then drove it home by offering other possible lineations, he exposed a quality of Byron's verse that would become obvious when he launched into his conversational *ottava rima*. If prose is not verse, and verse is not merely prose (*English Bards*, 242), the language they have in common is itself musical, though its rhythms need form, measured or unmeasured, to make it show and tell itself. A new arrangement of the music of *Beppo* and *Don Juan* can reveal much about his prosody and his language:

> If ever I should condescend to prose, I'll write poetical commandments, which shall supersede beyond all doubt all those that went before; in these I shall enrich my text with many things that no one knows, and carry precept to the highest pitch: I'll call the work 'Longinus o'er a Bottle, or, Every Poet his *own* Aristotle.'

> *(Don Juan* I. 204)

Reflecting on the music of Milton's blank verse, Johnson argued that the poet needed "skilful and happy readers ... to perceive where the lines end or begin."[17] Something like that might be said of the couplet verse of Byron's tales. Their artifice needs careful attention.

A close look at the description of Lara in Canto I (section 18) is instructive. Consider (see below) the first part of the manuscript Byron sent to his publisher. Lightly pointed, it leaves itself open to editorial intervention(s). In this case we know the result was worked out in proof between Byron and his publisher's editor, the poet William Gifford. It happens that Byron actively solicited that kind of early reader response, though he was also quick to resist suggestions he did not approve.

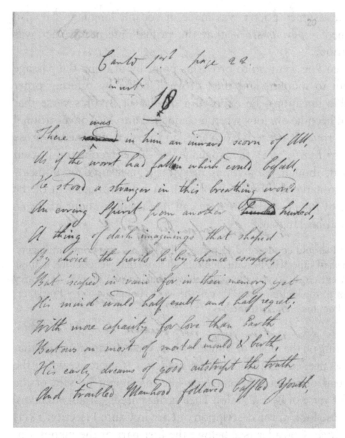

Figure 2 Image of Byron's fair copy of *Lara* Canto I section 18.
Reproduced with the permission of the National Library of Scotland, John
Murray Archive.

Here is the result – the opening lines of section 18 as Gifford
persuaded Byron to print them. Wrangling the manuscript, Gifford
tries to compose an arrangement for the text's slipshod grammar,
rhetoric, and prosodic rhythms.

> There was in him a vital scorn of all:
> As if the worst had fall'n which could befall
> He stood a stranger in this breathing world,
> An erring spirit from another hurled;
> A thing of dark imaginings, that shaped
> By choice the perils he by chance escaped;
> But 'scaped in vain, for in their memory yet
> His mind would half exult and half regret:
> With more capacity for love than earth
> Bestows on most of mortal mould and birth,
> His early dreams of good outstripped the truth,
> And troubled manhood followed baffled youth;
> With thought of years in phantom chace misspent,
> And wasted powers for better purpose lent;
> And fiery passions that had poured their wrath
> In hurried desolation o'er his path,
> And left the better feelings all at strife
> In wild reflection o'er his stormy life.

> (*Lara* I. 313–330)

The punctuation of this passage is so odd that later editors have regularly supplied their own. One can readily see that a different pointing would yield a dramatically different grammar and rhythmic/prosodic significance. Aside from the periods that close each section and the one exclamation point that comes a bit later (355), Gifford works with four punctuation marks: comma, semicolon, colon, and the empty space of enjambment. The result is at once bizarre and telling. Gifford's arbitrary precisions – the colons in 313 and 320 are especially notable – lay in a system of punctuation that exposes the "mental net" (I. 381) Byron wove from his loosely hung couplets. Gifford's punctuation is a monstrous reflection – in truth, an eccentric and brilliant interpretation – of the manuscript text's rhythmic puzzles. As the urgent tempo of each line wanders and waylays, we find ourselves struggling in a passage of arrested development and fruitless action.

The grammar of Byron's verse tales is often even looser than what we see here: *The Giaour*'s celebrated "trailing anacoluthon" is emblematic, as we shall find.[18] In this case from *Lara*, observe closely Byron's first three couplets. Prosody and grammar cunningly turn "A thing of dark imaginings" loose on the reader. Whose mind are we observing here, whose dark imaginings? Lara's, yes, but the amazed reader's as well. Byron is hiding in plain sight the dangerous rule of this verse – first announced explicitly in *The Corsair*:[19]

> He had the skill, when Cunning's gaze would seek
> To probe his heart and watch his changing cheek,
> At once the observer's purpose to espy,
> And on himself roll back his scrutiny,
> Lest he to Conrad rather should betray
> Some secret thought, than drag that chief's to day.
>
> (*The Corsair* I. 217–222)

Or again:

> His features' deepening lines and varying hue
> At times attracted, yet perplexed the view,
> As if within that murkiness of mind
> Worked feelings fearful, and yet undefined.
>
> (*The Corsair* I. 209–212)

Lara's murkiness of mind is the dark mirror of the reader's "perplexed ... view." Byron's signature invention, the Byronic Hero, is like Ahab's doubloon – a device for rolling readers' scrutiny back on themselves. Lara and *Lara* both fixate and bewilder a reader's attention, letting him know – it is first and foremost a "him" – what he knows and does not want to know: "Man as himself," Conrad/Lara as Man as reader, "Stranger" (I. 315) and "Stranger" (I. 243).

> Then – Stranger! if thou canst, and tremblest not
> Behold his soul – the rest that soothes his lot!

> Mark – how that lone and blighted bosom sears
> The scathing thought of execrated years!
> Behold – but who hath seen, or e'er shall see,
> Man as himself – the secret spirit free?
>
> (*The Corsair* I. 243–248)

Pope's couplets taught Byron how to construct this kind of verse, but it was Byron who learned to bewilder it. The prosody creates a poetic world of convertible signs by throwing off a cascade of discrete figures and expressions that Byron's prosody quickly attenuates. This verse – it is true for all these early tales – is neither clearly narrative, didactic, nor lyrical but a kind of "mixed company" (*Beppo*, 58) of language operating from a "secret spirit" now being set free both by and within customary poetic rules and recognizable poetic language. "Addressed to the understanding" of the reader, like virtually all of Byron's work, these passages dramatize the language of a poetry of resistance. It is composed against the backdrop of the airbrushed language of a canting world.

I V

Tactics of digression serve the tale-telling of *Beppo* and *Don Juan*. The early tales deploy tactics of fragmentation and distraction, which are quite as various and inventive. The most obvious come when Byron swerves into his prose notes, often as extensive and amusing as anything in Byron's *ottava rima* digressions. But when narrative is interrupted or driven off course in the early tales' verse, the breaks are far from charming or frictionless, even when they are comical. While no one doubts the serious difficulties *Don Juan* puts to its readers, the early tales are on the whole more aggressive, disturbing, even horrid.

The Giaour is once again a fine test case because it presents itself as a work that is missing parts of itself. It is not just *a* fragment poem; it is a series of fragment poems, each one a more complete but still defective edition of the ones before. Between March and December 1813, it went through eight distinct versions. The first was a privately printed work of 453 lines; the last was the seventh edition (1,334 lines).

Although *The Siege of Corinth* is, by contrast, a finished work from the get-go, its narrative organization is abrupt and irregular. The central action is compact, two days flanking a night, but the organization, more spatial than temporal, veers through a set of sharply framed, discontinuous events, some tightly focused, some much wider, even panoramic. Besides, the brooding presence of a world-historical fate links the siege to the fratricide at the founding of Corinth and invokes The Matter of Troy as a mythic paradigm. But most bewildering is the fracture between the presentation of the tale's historical ground (in the poem's "Advertisement") and the climactic event in the narrative, which blithely reinvents what Byron knew and believed – correctly – to be true.

But *The Corsair* and *Lara* present what may be the strangest dislocated narrative. Working ironically from Byron's remark that "the reader may probably regard [Lara] as a sequel to [The Corsair]," Peter Cochran found these tales so poorly executed that he subjected *The Corsair* to a ludic reimagining. As he acknowledged, that kind of deformation is a form of interpretive move I have strongly endorsed, especially when it illuminates entrenched misconceptions.[20] But Cochran's travesty, spun from his sense of the poems' contradictions, was meant to confirm, not counter, an established academic judgment.[21]

To my mind, however, the contradictions he was responding to have never been taken seriously enough. For example, the epigraphs from Dante that head the three cantos of *The Corsair* are strikingly bizarre: as Cochran justly remarked, "It is hard to see the[ir] relevance … to the action of *The Corsair*." But being so foregrounded and deliberate, surely the onus is on the reader to respond more seriously to their provocation. Or consider the small contradiction that set Cochran off: the fact that Gulnare's hair is auburn in *The Corsair* but dark black in *Lara*. He takes this as evidence of a general carelessness.

On the contrary, it seems to me an objective correlative for a perversity that is such a studied quality of both poems. A few months after *Lara* had been published (August 1814), Byron added an arresting note to the seventh edition of *The Corsair*. To show that Conrad "entering as a spy [was] not out of nature," which some early readers felt, Byron quoted a salient passage from Gibbon. But even more remarkable than the note's application to Conrad is its oblique gloss on Gulnare/Kaled's hair: "Anxious to explore with his own eyes the state of the Vandals, Majorian ventured, after disguising the colour of his hair, to visit Carthage in the character of his own ambassador" (*CPW* III. 447).[22] As Gibbon's note went on to observe, if such things may be "rejected as … improbable fiction," they are fictions appropriately "imagined … in the life of a hero."

A wicked irony plays through the note because these linked tales deliver a searching study of the idea and the life of a hero through the presentation of an unstable heroic world. As Cochran suggested, it is a darker and a colder man – and woman – who rise up from Conrad's poem into Lara's, though all four are, like their poetic worlds, dark and cold enough. *The Corsair*'s closing couplet is the defining event for both poems because it puts the question of love, Conrad's "one (apparent) virtue," at the center of the violent action. But from *The Giaour* through *The Siege of Corinth* and even *Parisina* we are immersed in "Fierce loves and faithless wars" (*Don Juan* VII. 8) because love and violence are the heads and tails of their life-world, the coin of the realm.

The Giaour's love for Leila – an intense, sexless, and most of all a violent passion – is the model for all the tales, even *Parisina*. It is true that *Parisina*'s opening lines (1–48) are notably erotic: indeed, lines 29–48 are virtually a condensed forecast of the Juan/Haidee idyll. But the lethal devotion of the afflicted Byronic hero lives on to precipitate the tragic finale of both these tales of love. As Byron made clear, the Giaour would have murdered Leila had she been as "faithless" to him as she was to Hassan. So, when Byron gives a long catalogue of the signs of Conrad's love (I. 285–304), he organizes it within an equivocal, even deplorable, grammar: "Yes, it was love . . . If there be love in mortals, this was love" (287, 304). The poem finishes by suggesting that the "one virtue" of Conrad – and Lara (and Kaled), and all the heroes of the tales – is not love at all. A case might be made that his "one virtue" was the "impenetrable spirit" ("Prometheus" 42) Byron associated with Prometheus and Lucifer, who were missioned souls, not lovers. That would be a secular and pagan imagination of the meaning of *The Corsair*'s famous final couplet. In Christian terms, their one virtue might be their virtually Calvinist awareness of guilt. But surely most of all Byron left us with the task of honestly facing the unreliability of our moral judgments.

In an important sense, Peter Cochran's effort to reimagine these tales and their uncertain connections gets to the heart of their power. He might have tried to imagine what Byron was doing with those Dante epigraphs. Why did Byron put key passages from Dante's story of Paolo and Francesca at the head of *The Corsair*'s cantos after he'd finished the narrative text? Everyone who cares to know now knows that *The Bride of Abydos*, *The Corsair*, and *Lara*, all written between November 1813 and June 1814, are in some sense Byron's tormented meditations on – he called them "distractions" from – Byron and Augusta's guilty love.[23]

But while readers since the publication of *Astarte* (1905) sometimes try to code and decode the poems from that book's revelations, the tales are precisely *not* telling that story. Rather, they are Byron's first attempt to tell, or retell, the primal human story of forbidden knowledge, whose Western source texts were Genesis and Plato's *Apology*, both key reference points for Byron. In an important sense, that was the governing subject of everything he wrote from 1812 forward – *Manfred*, *Don Juan*, and *Cain* being the key works. *Sapere aude* was a brave watchword of Enlightenment, but *dicere aude* (or *scribere aude*) was a line written even in Enlightenment sand. Like Kaled at the end of *Lara*, Byron rewrote that line but did not cross it – or cross it out. He did make us see more clearly the fearful, even tragic, prohibition it involved. As William Blake was the first of the Romantic poets to let us know, the Genesis story is very far from telling the whole truth. Like Byron, its authors told what they could and their contradictions, like Byron's, made a strait gate of a crooked record.

Two things make these three works, all written in less than a year, such a remarkable innovation: first, they explicitly filled out the story of forbidden knowledge as a complex and historically ramified social dynamic; second, the narratives themselves – that is to say, their writer and their readers – were thrust forward as the principal characters in the tales. In each instance, Byron had to punctuate his narratives with distractions and fracture an attention that he was obligated, at the same time, to promote. Readers were to be troubled to realize – it was fully realized in Byron's day – that much was being said that was not being said.[24] So while the three epigraphs from *Inferno* Canto V – the tale of Paolo and Francesca – have small relevance to the surface narratives, they are greatly relevant to what Byron was doing with those narratives. Recollecting forbidden love and the dangerous book the lovers were reading, the epigraphs are dire instructions, literal and performative, for reading Byron's tales' tale of forbidden speaking and hearing, writing and reading.

BYRON'S PERVERSIFICATIONS

A thing of beauty is annoyed forever.

Charles Bernstein, *Recalculating*

"I leave the thing a problem, like all things:–" (*Don Juan* XVII. 13): coming just before *Don Juan* breaks off, unfinished, the line has always seemed a fit comment on the unusually satisfying poetics of failure Byron set loose to celebrate "The World, which at the worst's a glorious blunder" (XI. 3). But leaving his readers in 1823 to deal with those problems – to see them as his problems and take them for our problems – has been Byron's way since at least 1809, and it might be the very definition of Byronism. That continuity of fifteen years is why Byron could also truthfully write in *Don Juan*'s last gasp that he is "Changeable too – but somehow '*Idem semper*'" (XVII. 11).

Don Juan is managed differently than the spectacular tales of 1813–1816. While both leave Byron's readers with their hands full of problems, the poetics of adversity and failure in the tales is unmitigated by *Don Juan*'s urbanity and cynical candor. What difference does that difference make? That becomes a serious question – in both cases – as soon as we begin to take the tales as seriously as we take *Don Juan*. That would be as seriously as virtually every important nineteenth-century writer, musician, artist, and philosopher in Europe did. But because *Don Juan* is now our touchstone, as it was not in the nineteenth century, the question only becomes visible *as* serious if we approach the tales the way we approach *Don Juan*: through the prosodic character of the verse and the entire range of its poetic action.

Let me get down to a few salient cases: for starters, the amazing – at once famous and infamous – "trailing anacoluthon" in Byron's prelude to the tale of the Giaour.

He who hath bent him o'er the dead
Ere the first day of death is fled;
The first dark day of nothingness,
The last of danger and distress,
(Before Decay's effacing fingers
Have swept the lines where beauty lingers)
And mark'd the mild angelic air –
The rapture of repose that's there –
The fixed yet tender traits that streak
The languor of the placid cheek,
And – but for that sad shrouded eye,
  That fires not – wins not – weeps not – now –
  And but for that chill changeless brow,
Where cold Obstruction's apathy
Appals the gazing mourner's heart,
As if to him it could impart
The doom he dreads, yet dwells upon –
Yes – but for these and these alone,
Some moments – aye – one treacherous hour,
He still might doubt the tyrant's power;
So fair – so calm – so softly seal'd,
The first – last look – by death reveal'd!
Such is the aspect of this shore –
'Tis Greece – but living Greece no more!
So coldly sweet, so deadly fair,
We start – for soul is wanting there.
Hers is the loveliness in death,
That parts not quite with parting breath;
But beauty with that fearful bloom –
That hue which haunts it to the tomb –
Expression's last receding ray,
A gilded halo hovering round decay,
The farewell beam of Feeling past away!
Spark of that flame – perchance of heavenly birth –
Which gleams – but warms no more its cherish'd earth!

                         (*The Giaour*, 68–102)

The passage invites us to pay close attention – no easy task given the turns and counterturns of a syntax that is simultaneously arresting and baffling. But if you do follow closely you discover that there *is* no anacoluthon. Like the beautiful corpse being composed for us – and it is just a composition, a figure for the contemporary condition of poetry (72–73) and Greece (90–91) – the grammar is finished: "He who hath bent him o'er the dead and marked the rapture of Repose that's there, he still might doubt the Tyrant's power" (68, 74, 87).

Lines 72–73 ought to make clear that the passage is a prosodic *tour de force*, a symbol that stands for its own performance, since the couplet declares that a poet's hand is at work in the lines we read. But because the signal is as figurative as the corpse, it throws off a brief glimpse of the true subject of this ghostly action: the unfolding verse itself. Watching Byron watch his figurations, we become secret sharers in one of poetry's most enduring and unendurable subjects: the fadeaway ways of living beauty, whose flight is momently arrested by the artful ways of verse failing to arrest it.

So does everything between and after the three moments of grammatical order move through an exacting set of observations and reflections. Lines 69–73, 75–86, and 88–89 raise up and take down, draw out and then erase their actions. They veer and drift as certain words and parts of words deflect to glimpses of other words that contribute yet further tangential or parenthetical moves. The convoluted syntax, in particular the two adverse interruptions (72–73, 78–84), weaves a haunting body upon the syntactic spine of the passage.

That everything is an "aspect" of everything else is made explicit when the passage turns at lines 90–91: "Such is the aspect of this shore –/ 'Tis Greece – but living Greece no more!" But the precise confusions and sense transfers grounding this simple comparison also shatter it.

> Even as a broken mirror, which the glass
> In every fragment multiplies; and makes
> A thousand images of one that was,
> The same, and still the more, the more it breaks.
>
> (*Childe Harold* III. 33)

No matter where you set your focus in *The Giaour* passage, you discover the radically anamorphic character of the verse. For instance:

> And but for that chill changeless brow,   8
> Where cold Obstruction's apathy
> Appals the gazing mourner's heart,
> As if to him it could impart
> The doom he dreads, yet dwells upon –

Clearly declared uncertainties – "But for," "as if" – usher in what is perhaps the passage's most decisively unnerving, if also barely noticeable, word: "it." Parsing its ambiguity – is the reference to "heart" or to "apathy"? – is as simple as its implications are not. The silent form of the corpse, the silent forms of this verse, tease us into bewildered thought, as does mortality.

All of that produces the poetry's splendid closing movement, the "fearful bloom" of its lamentable final figures of itself: a haunting hue, a receding ray, a gilded halo, a farewell gleam of cold light that, if of "heavenly birth," would be even more lost in that loss. But note the prosody of those seven lines, and in particular the striking triplet that marks the passage as an undying fall of sorrow and cherishing. Crucially, it is delivered here not as the lingering promise of a forlorn hope but as a long-accepted mortal fate.

So spectacular a passage as this commands attention. But Byron's verse is often most unnerving when it catches us out in brief and fugitive moments. Some are well known, like the perfidious participle at the start of "Fare Thee Well!"

> Fare thee well! and if for ever –
>   Still for ever, fare *thee well* –
> Even though unforgiving, never
>   'Gainst thee shall my heart rebel. –

Or the comic double take he springs on us when "Another Spirit" observes that Manfred "would have made/ An awful spirit" (*Manfred* II. 4. 187).

One of his earliest and most limpid poems, "Written Beneath a Picture," has two notable glitches:

> 1.
> Dear object of defeated care!
>   Though now of Love and thee bereft,
> To reconcile me with despair
>   Thine image and my tears are left.

> 2.
> 'Tis said with Sorrow Time can cope;
>   But this I feel can ne'er be true:
> For by the death-blow of my Hope
>   My Memory immortal grew.

In its most outward and visible signs the poem could scarcely be more conventional. Though we might – should – stumble briefly to think that those traditional tokens of love and loss are given "to *reconcile* me with despair," the tokens, not the despair, lead us gently on to the second stanza. But we are brought up short once again by "of my Hope." Write it "to my Hope" and there would be no problem. But the preposition tilts everything, suggesting that Hope is a complicit agent in this loss, which changes the "Time" of loss to a deathless death-in-life, "Memory immortal."

This simple poem is the earliest and one of the clearest representations of that strange ethos – the "Dear object" – that would trouble the cultural imagination of Europe for decades: not despair but reconciled, Byronic despair, a love and "faith whose martyrs are the broken heart" (*Childe Harold* IV. 121). It also forecasts the kinds of prosodic moves Byron will continually make to stymie readers who have learned by seeing not to see and by hearing not to understand.

Love, one of Byron's great preoccupations, is continually put under pressure and scrutiny exactly because it seems so transparent – what perhaps Joyce was thinking he did not have to name when he wrote in *Ulysses* of "the word known to all men." But, for Byron, it is a treacherous word, its meanings certainly uncertain. Consider the famous passage in *The Corsair* that explicates Conrad's "one (apparent) virtue" (III. 696), his love for Medora.

It is important that *The Corsair* never explains how this love came about, especially because Conrad, we are told, regarded love as a "passion worthy of a fool or child" (I. 284). Despite that, his attachment to Medora is so intense and devoted that it "asks the name of Love." So the poem replies to that request:

> Yes – it was love – if thoughts of tenderness,
> Tried in temptation, strengthened by distress,
> Unmoved by absence, firm in every clime,
> And yet – Oh more than all! – untired by time;
> Which nor defeated hope, nor baffled wile,
> Could render sullen were she ne'er to smile,
> Nor rage could fire, nor sickness fret to vent
> On her one murmur of his discontent;
> Which still would meet with joy, with calmness part,
> Lest that his look of grief should reach her heart;
> Which nought removed, nor menaced to remove –
> If there be love in mortals – this was love!
>
> (*The Corsair* I. 293–304)

Those launching couplets, if more loose than Pope's, are yet clearly Popean. But with the third couplet the balanced pacings drop into a periodic grammar desperate for a completion it only barely achieves after twelve plunging lines. As usual, Byron's dashes are breathtaken. The single enjambment (299) signals the true character of all the end-stopped lines, which struggle to drive forward on their paratactic grammar ("which . . . which . . . which"). And at the heart of it all is an action of subtractions, what Byron later called "fixedness without a place."[25] *If* there is such a thing as mortal love, then this menaced devotion, we are told, is it. But is it? The question nags because Conrad's love seems less *amor* or even *caritas* than fidelity, and Medora seems less an object of love than a means for Conrad to fix upon an ideal commitment.

Like "He who hath bent him o'er the dead," that kind of verse, a common feature of Byron's early poetry, strikes the reader more as a troubling than a threatening problem. But – as with the third line in "Fare Thee Well!" – Byron can subject his readers to far more aggressive moves, like this knotted couplet:

> His soul in youth was haughty, but his sins
> No more than pleasure from the stripling wins.
>
> (*Lara* I. 61–62)

Now that is not easy to parse. Although the only possible subject of "wins" is "His soul," the couplet initially invites us to take "sins" as the subject, and with that taking to "hear" in the expression "wins from" the more common usage "wins for" (OED v.1, 9b). Byron thus installs a collision between a correct but very difficult grammar and an errant syntax that delivers a relatively familiar thought (sensual pleasure is the only thing you get from sin).

"His soul was haughty in his youth, but it does not win the stripling from his sins any more than it wins him from pleasure."

or:

"His soul was haughty in his youth, but his sins win from the stripling nothing more than sensual pleasures."

But neither translation is quite satisfying, partly because both are haunted by the echo of "wins for" that we hear in "wins from," and partly – perhaps mostly – because of the adversative logic of that "but."

The difficulties multiply if you look for clarity from the surrounding passage, which has introduced its own anomaly: a striking shift into the present tense. The turn leads to the final thought and couplet: that Lara's sins, "if not yet harden'd in their course,/ Might be redeem'd, nor ask a long remorse" (63–64). But because "haughty" and "harden'd" have more than an acoustic relation and because "might be" is not much of a promise, the force of the "but" persists.[26] When the narrative quickly reverts to the past tense (65ff.), the prosody restores the work to its foregone condition, and winning "from" and winning "for" turn out perfectly imperfect rhymes.

All of the early tales are riddled with such knots of verse, whether brief or extensive, that force readers to puzzle out what is involved. Discussing the "concise, energetic, and impetuous" character of Byron's tales in 1814, Francis Jeffrey observed that Byron's difficult prosody was "not always very solicitous about being comprehended by readers of inferior capacity" (206).[27] In *Parisina*, Hugo's long apology before his execution opens with a good example:

> "It is not that I dread the death –
>   For thou hast seen me by thy side
>   All redly through the battle ride;
> And that not once a useless brand
> Thy slaves have wrested from my hand,
> Hath shed more blood in cause of thine,
> Than e'er can stain the axe of mine.
>
>   (234–240)

Byron has tortured the fourth line (237) into two very different syntaxes, each in itself hard to make out. The parallel structure put into play – "It is not that ... And that not once" – is difficult enough in itself, but it runs into another syntax where the phrase "not once a useless" is essentially a single adjective describing

Hugo's sword when he fought for Azo. But that adjectival phrase only works if it steals the words "not once" from the other syntax.[28]

The passage throws off a further difficulty because the last couplet's rhyme draws a perplexing comparison. The axe Hugo refers to is only his in the ironic sense that it is the one that will soon decapitate him (403), though when we read the couplet that reference – and (so to speak) the point of it – is puzzled. It will soon become clear that the axe is more Azo's ("thine") than Hugo's ("mine"), a true rhyme that throws a devious light on the central argument of Hugo's final speech: he and his father are doubles of each other, violent men and sinful lovers.

This passage also harbors a subtle forecast of Hugo's last words to his father, who has passed a judgment of death on him.

> Begot in sin, to die in shame,
> My life begun and ends the same:
> As erred the sire, so erred the son,
> And thou must punish both in one.
> My crime seems worst to human view,
> But God must judge between us too!
>
> (*Parisina*, 312–317)

Added very late to the poem, these lines deliver a striking wordplay. Byron originally wrote "God must judge between us two." When he replaced "two" with "too" he brought Azo's judgment, and now Hugo's, to a further judgment.

But Byron's most shocking poetic acts in his Years of Fame came with the tale he finished last, *The Siege of Corinth*, where he brought European history under sharp scrutiny. Adding a lexicon drawn from recondite European events to an involute or uncertain syntax, Byron turns key passages into trials by reading, as here:

> Sent by the state to guard the land,
> (Which, wrested from the Moslem's hand,

> While Sobieski tamed his pride
> By Buda's wall and Danube's side,
> The chiefs of Venice wrung away
> From Patra to Eubœa's bay)
> Minotti held in Corinth's towers
> The Doge's delegated powers,
> While yet the pitying eye of Peace
> Smiled o'er her long-forgotten Greece;
> And ere that faithless truce was broke
> Which freed her from the unchristian yoke.
>
>   (167–178)

The passage delivers a cryptic account of the sixth Ottoman–Venetian War (1683–1699) and its immediate aftermath, when Jacopo Minotti was installed by the Holy League as governor of Corinth after the Treaty of Karlowitz (1699), shifting control of the city to Venice.[29] Elliptical references and a digressive grammar lay a stringent demand on reading comprehension. Unless it is met, however, you will miss the dark ironies that play throughout the passage – "Faithless truce," for instance. The Ottomans broke the truce arranged at Karlowitz when they opened the war that precipitated the 1715 siege of Corinth. But that was the seventh Ottoman–Venetian War (1714–1718). In the previous six, peace treaties were made and truces broken by both sides, a "faithless" habit learned since the earliest of the Venetian–Ottoman conflicts were initiated by the European Crusade of Nicopolis in 1396. "Peace" was "long forgotten" in Greece by all the powers fighting to possess and exploit it, and if Minotti had been sent after Karlowitz "to guard the land," it was not to protect Greece but Venice's diminishing mercantile resources. Indeed, the climax of Byron's poem will make Minotti's dreadful perversion of his mission – "Sent by the state to guard the land" – a virtual index of what all foreign investment had brought – and was still bringing (1815) – to Greece.

A similar network of ironies plays through the discussion of martial glory (96–105). Although Byron clarified his point with an historical note on the Turkish general Ali Coumourgi, he left it to readers to deal with his provocative syntax:

> Coumourgi – can his glory cease,
> That latest conqueror of Greece,
> Till Christian hands to Greece restore
> The freedom Venice gave of yore?
>
> (102–105)

"Till" makes the syntax of the sentence – is it a sentence? – uncertain as how to answer, how to understand the point of the question being posed. Western readers – Byron's readers – are invited to shift the question mark to line 103 and hear line 104 begin "Not till." Because that is not what we get, "Christian hands" and Venetian "freedom" – at home (see line 85) as well as in their Greek dominions – are as treacherous as the rest of the poem make them out to be.

But the most instructive lines of all come next:

> A hundred years have rolled away
> Since he [i.e., Ali Coumourgi] refixed the Moslem's sway,
> And now he led the Mussulman,
> And gave the guidance of the van
> To Alp, who well repaid the trust
> By cities levelled with the dust;
> And proved, by many a deed of death,
> How firm his heart in novel faith.
>
> (106–113)

You have to double-shift that first line to realize the point of view is not 1715. Because "A hundred years have rolled away" can mean only one thing – 1815, the date when Byron finished *The Siege* (published in 1816) – it carries the greatest significance for the poem and, most immediately, for the ambiguous deictic "now."

This is the passage where Byron slyly lets us know that if in the poetic fiction Coumourgi "gave the guidance" of the siege to Alp, Byron is guiding *The Siege* as a poetic action in the real world.

To explicate the importance of that, we have to recover some of the salient points of the work's composition history. Byron began *The Siege* in 1812, worked at it sporadically in 1813 and 1814, and then began the last half in January 1815.[30] He spent most of that year working over the poem. In its initial conception, the Hugo/Azo/Parisina triangle was plotted in *The Siege* as Alp/Francesca/Minotti. But in 1815, he spun off *Parisina* as a separate, largely psychological tale, finished that, and then turned to sharpen and finish off the aggressive documentary argument of *The Siege*. The decisive compositional event was one of the last: in November 1815, Byron sent the "Advertisement" to his publisher for the proof printing. That would turn out *The Siege*'s signal documentary feature, making the work a literal act of positive negation.

There is no doubt that the climactic years of the Napoleonic Wars hang over the poem, though *The Siege* does not draw specific contemporary parallels. Rather, it invokes the Venetian–Ottoman Wars to project a universal cyclic history of nations caught up in repeating and violent zero-sum political conflicts, "doomed to inflict or bear" (*Childe Harold* III. 71). The fourth canto of *Childe Harold* made that subject the center of its grievous lamentations. *The Siege* takes a different and far more unusual approach.

The "Advertisement" quotes from David Jones's new 1719 edition of *A Compleat History of the Turks*.[31] Published four years after the actual siege, the 1719 edition updated Jones's very Western view of the Ottoman Empire. That Byron did not regard it as a "Compleat" history is apparent.[32] The lifted passage recounts the explosion in the Ottoman camp of "six hundred barrels of powder ... by accident" that killed "six or seven hundred men." Though Jones does not explicitly report it, the Turks believed the Venetians were responsible. In that conviction, they became "so enraged ... that they would not grant any capitulation." They raised the siege and "stormed the place with so much fury" that "most of the garrison, with Signor Minotti, the governor, [was put] to the sword."

The Siege's spectacular climax deliberately flies in the face of what Byron at the start presented as Jones's authoritative account. The explosion in the poetic narrative takes place in the Christian church on the Corinthian acropolis and it is not an accident. As Minotti and his forces are at their fierce last-ditch stand, the governor – rather than capitulate – sets fire to the powder magazine he had himself stored in the church. The result is a total calamity that Byron describes in meticulously horrifying detail (971–1034), summing it up in a brutal and laconic final line: "Thus was Corinth lost and won!"

Byron's move here is not what today we might call an "alternative history" of the 1715 siege. It is not trying to reimagine the past into the promise or threat of a future historical change. On the contrary, and as with *Cain* five years later, Byron endorses Jones's Augustan report as openly as he would later endorse the Old Testament's *textus receptus*. But unlike *Cain*'s dark and, in its second act, darkly comical handling of the sacred text, *The Siege*'s more naked and direct move is making at least two startling pronouncements.

First, presenting Minotti not as the victim of the Turks but the agent of destruction, Byron moves to right Jones's unbalanced account of the Venetian–Ottoman Wars. (If there is a victim, it would be Greece, though given the longer historical view Byron invokes – see later in the poem – Greece has its own self-destructive history to bear.) Byron's 1715 siege is more than an episode in the long-running Ottoman–Venetian Wars for control of the Levant, more than part of a conflicted history stretching back more than a thousand years. Byron's Corinth is "that too long afflicted shore"

(984): a quasi-mythic *figura* of endless violent conflict, its famous acropolis mounting a fortress rather than a Parthenon.[33]

That is why Byron starts his poem by linking the siege to the fratricide at Corinth's founding (13–14), and why, when he later recounts the arrival of the Venetian governor with his daughter Francesca, he invokes The Matter of Troy.

> With him his gentle daughter came;
> Nor there, since Menelaus' dame
> Forsook her lord and land, to prove
> What woes await on lawless love,
> Had fairer form adorned the shore
> Than she, the matchless stranger, bore.
>
> (179–184)

Francesca is *Helena rediviva* because her loss is the focus of Alp's hatred of his native country.

At once lovely and unmarried ("matchless"), Francesca here names a love made lawless by the operation of Venetian law (84–89), perhaps – because it was internecine – even more dreadfully "lawless" than the Turkish breach of the treaty. The hopeless estrangement of the lovers at Corinth is the ominous sign of woes that await the delivery of the poem's disastered finale.[34] In Byron's contemporary context, the undercurrent of the poem's final line would be "Thus was Europe lost and won."

Francesca's ghostly visitation with Alp before the final battle is thus pivotal. She comes from the land of the dead to persuade Alp to join her there and "be blest" (518–519). That macabre context decorates a final and fearful lovers' tryst where Francesca and Alp negotiate an intercourse that echoes the death and violence of their threatening world. She begs him to renounce his Ottoman allegiance and "sign/ The sign of the cross, and for ever be mine ... And to-morrow unites us no more to part" (532–533, 535). Alp refuses the life in death she offers, promising instead to destroy the Venetians and then marry her. Francesca replies that, if he does not do what she asks, he will be doomed to an "immortality of ill" (605) by "The curse of him [Christ? Venice?] thou didst forsake" (595). Her threat produces Alp's even more violent refusal (612–617) as well as the ironic revelation that he has not forsaken his mother country. "What Venice made me, I must be" (626), he says – "devoted to the grave" like all "Her sons" (615) and, it is clear, like Venice's ideal daughter, Francesca. When Alp makes his last request that Francesca "fly with me!" (628), she silently replays his deadly devotion, vanishing into her other world of the dead.

But the strictly poetic significance of what Byron did with and to Jones's *Compleat History* is more consequential than the historical revisions it holds out. After having acknowledged at the outset the truth of the *Compleat History*, Byron finished with a defiant act of poetic contradiction. Crucially, Byron's affirmation and negation are primary poetic acts, not secondary representations. An Everlasting Nay is declared against what was "averred, and known" in 1715 and then "daily, hourly seen" (*Childe Harold* IV. 95) one hundred years on. Byron's blatant act of contradiction leaves us less involved with the constellation of meanings that the poem sustains than with the gravity field of Byron's countermove – his contradictory act of verse-making – and how it works.[35]

To represent Minotti bringing wholesale destruction to Corinth completes Byron's critical account of a zero-sum economy of winners and losers. But it does not complete the poem because Byron has something else to do: overwhelm us with a spectacle of what the received histories edit from their accounts. While Minotti's act needs only three lines (968–970), Byron's account of the history summarized by his act is long drawn out and terrible (971–1034).

But Byron takes us no further, offering no hope and making no promises. We are left with a picture of "All the living things" of

Nature (1012–1033) in panicked flight from a scene of desolation made by "man, enamoured of distress" (*The Giaour*, 50).

> All the living things that heard
> That deadly earth-shock disappeared:
> The wild birds flew; the wild dogs fled,
> And howling left the unburied dead.
>
> (1012–1015)

Suspended now in Byron's verse, we wonder, where can all the living go? When Baudelaire proposed "Anywhere out of the World," he was implicitly admitting there is no such place. For Byron here, this poetic flight represents nothing more (or less) than a Samsonite act of blind faith in a human world that we have never known and never made and, indeed, never will. As we take in that fearful prospect, we may and surely should remember that the living will be returning, as always, to their same place, "the world/ Which is the world of all of us," "the foul rag and boneshop of the heart." So at the poem's end we are left facing a famous existential question: What is to be done? We are not told.

Coda

So effective was the dire closing section of *The Siege* that William Gifford, its first reader, recoiled. He (vainly) urged Byron to cut out the heart of it (985–1011) as well as the equally shocking forecast (411–433) Byron laid in before Francesca's appearance and the climactic battle.[36] The brilliance of these passages rests in their disturbing versification, which flirts seriously with comic figures, diction, and prosody. Here is Alp walking among the dogs scavenging the corpses of his dead troops:

> Gorging and growling o'er carcass and limb;
> They were too busy to bark at him!
> From a Tartar's skull they had stripped the flesh,

> As ye peel the fig when its fruit is fresh;
> And their white tusks crunched o'er the whiter skull,
> As it slipped through their jaws, when their edge grew dull,
> As they lazily mumbled the bones of the dead,
> When they scarce could rise from the spot where they fed;
> So well had they broken a lingering fast
> With those who had fall'n for that night's repast.

(411–420)

"As ye peel the fig"; "mumbled the bones"; "that night's repast": those striking phrases are only the passage's most eye-catching mockeries. Byron's feasting dogs are in witty, wickedly bad taste. But, like Swift, Byron did not shrink from a cynical address before the currish pieties of religion, love, and, as here, war.

Though he left his Mephisto humor behind in the universal darkness of the poem's close, an outlier couplet's singular perversification swings it briefly into view. In a "shower of rain[ing]" body parts (991),

> Some fell in the gulf, which received the sprinkles
> With a thousand circling wrinkles.

(992–993)

Byron rides that turn to a strictly metrical address across the next nine lines, a dark rhyming *tour de force* unlike anything else in his verse:

> Some fell on the shore, but, far away,
> Scattered o'er the isthmus lay;
> Christian or Moslem, which be they?
> Let their mothers see and say!
> When in cradled rest they lay,
> And each nursing mother smiled
> On the sweet sleep of her child,
> Little deemed she such a day
> Would rend those tender limbs away.

(994–1002)

With that drifted internal rhyme (rend/ tender) marking a prosody taken to the brink, a perfect rhyme (away/ away) shuts to final closure – but not without having executed a series of rhetorical and syntactic moves (995–998) that make pertinent play with the timing of both the verse and its references. These are the rhymes of a grim reaper singing as if his song could have no ending.

The following flight of the natural world from the human world is Byron's gloss on the positive negation his poem delivers. The contradiction it brings to received history might appear the very opposite of the "escape from fiction" that *Don Juan* will demand of every "true poet" (VIII. 86). While *The Siege* brings judgment to that kind of history, judgment comes by the actions, not the meanings, of its textual signs. Its final fiction delivers a taxing argument because it needs no explanation. It is severe because it is explicit, not a symbol to be searched out but a "hard saying" (John 6: 60): "clear but, oh how cold" ("Sun of the Sleepless!" 8). The dire fiction Byron invents simply turns from the dire fiction he refuses, leaving the reader at an existential not a hermeneutic impasse. What counts – and so what needs to be accounted for – is what the action, not what the fiction, represents. That is why everything of real consequence in Byron's verse, as Goethe was the first to let us know, happens in its prosodic and rhetorical arrangements, where Byron's poetic *inventio* (*Erfindung*), his poetic action, is laid out.

3

Manfred
One Word for Mercy

Enigma, made to be unresolved, affords the opposition of immer-
sion, of argument: it offers an opaque exterior; not offering entry or
exit [it is] cued only to itself, faces nothing. However, it is not
bracketed. It is merely less let loose among particles more active.
Though its delight is not extinguished, it has no tendency. Its argument is that, it, is, here.
                    Alan Davies, "Private Enigma in the Opened Text"

The aspects of things that are most important for us are hidden
because of their simplicity and familiarity. (One is unable to notice
something – because it is always before one's eyes.)
                    Ludwig Wittgenstein, *Philosophical Investigations*

Manfred is a very strange work, as Nietzsche, perhaps more than
anyone, well understood. Partly it is strange because it is a genre
mash-up, "A Dramatic Poem" that, like Goethe's *Faust*, cultivates
a medley of tones that constantly shift from grave and exacting
reflection to satire and comedy.[1] Those tonal shifts – they often
come abruptly – make *Manfred* difficult to follow just as the
asterisks make *The Giaour* difficult. Then Byron turns the screw
on *Manfred*'s reading problems by organizing the poem around
secrets that are most provoking because they are so openly

displayed. The strangest things lie everywhere in plain sight. What is going on, and how do we get a grip on it?

Let us start with *Manfred*'s signature problem, the poem's greatest open secret: the scandalous reference to "the Lady Astarte, his – " (III. 3. 55). Read biographically – privately – the missing word has always been supposed to be "sister" and Manfred's "half-maddening sin" (II. 1. 31), incest. Everything about the historical context of *Manfred*, not least its reception history, supports that reading, which can, and I think should, be glimpsed in *Manfred*'s keyword: Astarte.

We haven't studied that word, listened to it, closely enough. Say it: Astarte. A star. A star is one of the poem's most prominent motifs. Say the name again: Astarte. Augusta. Star. Gus. Byron called his sister Gus. Once you catch the echo, it never goes away, though it will always be going away. So we might think that Astarte becomes in *Manfred* one enigmatic word for estrangement. But it is far more than that because it is laid into a spectacularly open and public text. Astarte is not a symbol that stands for a meaning. Astarte is a word that dare not speak its name.

Astarte is a character in "A Dramatic Poem," not "A Poetic Drama." The subtitle suggests why the work is so difficult to stage. It also suggests that we might usefully approach it as a play of words, which is how we approach the plays of Gertrude Stein. The action is primarily in the ways the words are being made to behave in the language they are driven to execute. The simplicity of the poem's surface, its rehearsal of the all-too-familiar Faust legend, is seriously deceptive. *Manfred* is a play full of secrets and, as such, a work whose dangerous words need to be watched closely. When we do we discover that its object is to dismantle the authority of the myth of Faust, one of the two great myths of Western civilization. Byron would soon undertake *Don Juan* to subject that other great Western myth to a similar critical inquiry.

So let us look closely at *Manfred*. Consider three famous passages – first, this reflection on Astarte:

> What is she now? – a sufferer for my sins –
> A thing I dare not think upon – or nothing.

(II. 2. 196–197)

What do we think of the three alternatives Manfred gives for his question "What is she now?" In point of fact, "a sufferer for my sins – /A thing I dare not think upon – /or nothing" are far from the only possible alternatives. But that is all we get because that is all Manfred can think of at this point. If we pay attention to exactly what Manfred says here, we ought to be provoked.

Or consider this exchange with Nemesis:

NEMESIS　　　　What would'st *thou*?
MANFRED　　　　　　　　　　　Thou canst not reply to me.
Call up the dead – my question is for them.
NEMESIS　　　　Great Arimanes, doth thy will avouch
The wishes of this mortal?
ARIMANES　　　　　　　　　　　　Yea.
NEMESIS　　　　　　　　　　　　　Whom wouldst thou
Uncharnel?
MANFRED　　　　　　　One without a tomb – call up
Astarte.

(II. 4. 78–83)

What are we to make of the "dead" Astarte being described as "one without a tomb"? The remark gives us pause in at least two respects. First of all, in an obvious sense, it upends the question Nemesis asks. Uncharnel what? Uncharnel one without a tomb? But then we also have to wonder how Manfred knows she is tombless, and what exactly that could mean.

The problems multiply. Consider the action that immediately follows when Nemesis actually succeeds in calling up "The Phantom of Astarte." Commanding her to speak, neither he nor

Arimanes can manage it. Then Manfred tries with his spasmodic, insistent, and ultimately confused prayer since, as he admits, "I know not what I ask, nor what I seek:/ I feel but what thou art, and what I am" (II. 4. 131–132). When Astarte is finally induced – *prayed* – to speak, her words are cryptic, not least when Manfred makes his final desperate plea: "One word for mercy" (II. 4. 154). The word turns out to be Manfred's name. What does that word *mean*? (What does any proper noun mean?)

From the outset of the poem/play Manfred has come before us as a person of consummate power, knowledge, and decision. But that image of Manfred is also cunningly undermined from the very beginning. Recall, for instance, his move to summon the "spirits" in Act I, scene one. A sly comical tone pervades a scene where we watch this mage take three tries to succeed in his conjuration. He doesn't know exactly how to proceed. When he finally does hit on the correct formula, we discover something else interesting. We see that Manfred did not know how those "subordinate" spirits, especially the Seventh Spirit, would play tricks on him. That happens because Manfred is mistaken when he tells the spirit that there is no "form on earth" he *would* find "hideous or beautiful" (I. 1. 184–185). Manfred has unaccountably forgotten that the "form" he at once fears and desires isn't "on earth." So when the Seventh Spirit conjures "The shape of a beautiful female figure," Manfred falls down "senseless." This is the "shape" or image of Astarte, but it is not her phantom or ghost. "The Phantom of Astarte" won't appear until much later. The two are not the same.

Or remember that he knew he wanted to leap from the crag but hadn't imagined he would be prevented by a Chamois Hunter. Chance intervenes to prevent his suicide. But when he leaves the Chamois Hunter – let us call him Wordsworth, another of *Manfred*'s secrets – he was free to resume what he began. But he doesn't. So we wonder: does he *really* want "Forgetfulness" and

"Self-Oblivion"? Do we believe him when he says he does? Does he even want to die? What exactly is Manfred after?

Or remember that he says he can "call the dead/ And ask them what it is we dread to be" (II. 2. 178–179). But when he does this in Act II scene four, he doesn't ask Astarte that question at all. His prayer to Astarte's Phantom is largely a confession of his bewilderment ("I know not what I ask or what I seek") until he stumbles at last to his desperate request: "One word for mercy." What are we to make of the Phantom's merciless-merciful answer, "Manfred"?

Let us run through some further provoking passages:

```
NEMESIS              Hast thou further question
Of our great sovereign, or his worshippers?
MANFRED      None.
NEMESIS              Then for a time farewell.
MANFRED                              We meet then –
Where? On the earth?
NEMESIS                          That will be seen hereafter.
MANFRED      Even as thou wilt: and for the grace accorded
I now depart a debtor. Fare ye well!
```

                                        (II. 4. 162–167)

Consider how freighted that final sentence is with the language of Christian theology. But here the remark has wrung out the theology that stands behind the words. Manfred politely declares how deeply he is in debt "for the grace accorded" to him by Nemesis, Arimanes, and the demons. But such creatures are not the agents of grace. Grace is accorded by God through Jesus Christ, and this grace then frees us of the debt of sin. For anyone – like myself – who has been educated in the discourse of grace and debt and redemption, the passage is a piece of well-mannered blasphemy.[2] It anticipates the amusingly polite exchanges between Michael and Satan in *The Vision of Judgment*.

Or consider this remark in his final act of defiance against the authority of the demons who come to demand that he fulfill his bargain to live out the great myth of Faust. "I do not combat against death, but thee/ And thy surrounding angels" (III. 4. 112–113). That is surely an odd thing to declare. Had he said, or had Byron written "And thy surrounding *demons*," both the prosody and the myth would have been preserved intact. The word "angels" is seriously intrusive. Are the angels of God hanging around the action of *Manfred*? When the word comes in here, we are flung back in thought to the time when the demons were simply rebellious angels "hurl'd from heaven for sinning" (*Don Juan* IV. 1). That prehistorical event is much on *Manfred*'s mind throughout the action of the poem.

These striking passages invite us to think again about what is perhaps *Manfred*'s greatest passage, the "Incantation" that climaxes and closes Act I scene one. Though it begs for a line-by-line examination, I will confine my comments to a few of the most salient passages. First, recall how it is introduced to us: "A Voice is heard in the Incantation which follows." That is surely far more a direction for reading than what it is formally, a stage direction. But it is indeed a stage direction for the play of language Byron has mounted. One can easily miss the plain meaning of those words: that we should be listening for "A Voice" within the incantation that follows. We hear and read an incantation as we hear and read for the subtext that is working somehow or other inside. The Incantation is double-talk, both "a magic voice *and* verse" that – *mirabile dictu* – has "baptized [Manfred] with a curse" (I. 1. 223–224).

In its most obvious register the Incantation is a curse laid upon Manfred by Manfred himself, as the astonishing sixth stanza makes clear:

> By thy cold breast and serpent smile,
> By thy unfathom'd gulfs of guile,
> By that most seeming virtuous eye,
> By thy shut soul's hypocrisy;
> By the perfection of thine art
> Which pass'd for human thine own heart;

By thy delight in others' pain,
And by thy brotherhood of Cain,
I call upon thee! and compel
Thyself to be thy proper Hell!

(I. 1. 252–261)

Manfred is the ultimate authority for the curse, just as earlier we saw that he could command the spirits because his life has been ruled by "a star condemn'd" (I. 1. 44). That would be "Astarte," who "withered" when she "gazed on" Manfred's "heart" (II. 2. 119). It would also be Manfred, since Astarte is "The star which rules [his] destiny" (I. 1. 110).

"Wither" is the key, the final word in the "Incantation." But it is a word within which we hear another word, as becomes clear when we pluck each of them out of their pivotal locations in *Manfred*:

Lo! the spell now works around thee,
And the clankless chain hath bound thee;
O'er thy heart and brain together
Hath the word been passed – now wither!

(from "Incantation," I. 1. 258–261)

C. HUNTER.   When thou art better, I will be thy guide –
But whither?

(II. 1. 4–5)

MANFRED   I loved her, and destroy'd her!
WITCH   With thy hand?
MANFRED   Not with my hand, but heart – which broke her heart –
It gazed on mine, and withered.

(II. 2. 116–119)

MANFRED   Old man! 'tis not so difficult to die. [MANFRED expires.
ABBOT   He's gone, his soul hath ta'en its earthless flight;
Whither? I dread to think; but he is gone.

(III. 4. 151–153)

Wither/whither is one of the most provocative as well as one of the most decisive wordplays in *Manfred*. It is decisive because it is so plainly tied to the surface action, the plot as traditionally understood. Whither has the withered Astarte gone, whither is the wither-cursed Manfred going at the end of the poem? Unlike Manfred, who has pledged allegiance to *sapere aude*, the Abbot dreads to think about that because he can only imagine either heaven or hell. But an entirely different "Voice" may be heard in the unreferenced first-person pronouns that speak through the Incantation. It is the voice we can only call *Manfred*. Not Manfred, not Astarte, not even Byron. *Manfred*: the one word that matches the strange "mercy" being offered by the poem (or is it a play?).

Well, as we know, it *is* a play, a play of language that we are called to pay attention to. Some of the moments announce themselves with an outrageous, comedic directness, as when a spirit says of the "convulsed" Manfred after Astarte departs at the end of Act II: "He would have made an awful spirit" (II. 4. 162). Of course, that word means, first of all, "awe-inspiring," like God Almighty. But a ludic voice is heard in the spirit's language that Byron would soon let loose (1818) when he published *Beppo*, written shortly after *Manfred*. It is a vulgate meaning of "awful" that he received out of his Scots linguistic heritage and that is now the primary meaning of the word.[3] In *Beppo*, Byron again puns upon that word, or rather torques and *works* it, to skewer the pious poet Sotheby as "A stalking oracle of awful phrase" (LXXIV).

Or consider the three times that *Manfred* calls up the image of a desert, the psychic place referenced in the contemporary lyric "Stanzas to Augusta": "In the desert a fountain is springing" (45). In *Manfred*, the word is carefully manipulated in order to effect its

striking final transformation and transvaluation. Here is the word
in its first two appearances:

MANFRED   Think'st thou existence doth depend on time?
It doth; but actions are our epochs: mine
Have made my days and nights imperishable,
Endless, and all alike, as sands on the shore,
Innumerable atoms, and one desart ...

                                                    (II. 1. 51–55)

MANFRED   Like the Wind,
The red-hot breath of the most lone Simoom,
Which dwells but in the desart.

                                                    (III. 1. 127–129)

That spelling, unusual now, was still a common orthographic form
in Byron's time. But the word could be – and was by Byron –
spelled both ways, and in *Manfred* Byron exploited the optional
spelling to fine effect. The third usage comes in Manfred's climactic
act of defiance in the final scene. I shall quote the relevant passage
at some length because it has some further, equally remarkable and
equally salient, wordplays.

MANFRED   What I have done is done; I bear within
A torture which could nothing gain from thine:
The mind which is immortal makes itself
Requital for its good or evil thoughts, –
Is its own origin of ill and end
And its own place and time – its innate sense,
When stripp'd of this mortality, derives
No colour from the fleeting things without,
But is absorb'd in sufferance or in joy,
Born from the knowledge of its own desert.
Thou didst not tempt me, and thou couldst not tempt me;
I have not been thy dupe nor am thy prey –
But was my own destroyer, and will be
My own hereafter. –

                                                    (III. 4. 127–140)

The pentameter line has, as throughout *Manfred*, an iambic base, and in this passage we see that all the lines are quite regular until we come to the initial foot of "Born from the knowledge of its own desert." The line opens with an inversion but then quickly resumes its iambic regularity. When we reach the final foot of the line, we would have another clear inversion *if* the word were spelled "desart," as it was spelled twice before. But here it is spelled "desert" and the difference exposes a wordplay that Byron achieves through prosodic ambiguity. If the accent is left to fall on the word's first syllable, then the line echoes the idea (and the word) of "In the desert a fountain is springing." But if it is left to fall on the second syllable, filling out the iambic rhythm, then the word means something else. It means "dessert," and we hear in the line a vulgate echo of Manfred coming at last to his just desserts.

Is Byron also playing with the phrase "Born from"? It is hard to think otherwise. And if we look closely at the next four lines, in particular the parallel syntax in the statement "I have been … my own destroyer and will be my own hereafter," more games with language are in play. "Hereafter" is primarily an adverb and here, at first encounter so to speak, that is how we read it. But because the parallelism encourages one to read it simultaneously as a noun, the line is made to carry a virtually Nietzchean meaning. Note how the word "own," under these pressures, also slightly shifts its meaning the second time we get around on it.

Or what about the comment Nemesis makes after "The Phantom of Astarte" leaves: "She's gone, and will not be recall'd" (II. 4. 180). Actually, Astarte will never *not* be "recall'd" (remembered) exactly because she is, like Manfred himself at the play's conclusion, "gone" forever. As such, she has become what the dead Leila is to the Giaour, "The Morning-star of Memory" (1130). This kind of Byronic loss is operating according to the argument we saw laid down in "Beneath a Picture." "Memory [grows] immortal" when loss is so absolute that one becomes "reconcile[d] with Despair."

These are some of the language games that play about *Manfred*, but there are others, and doubtless some have escaped my attention. In that connection, it is useful to recall that *Manfred*'s poetics depends in great measure on a handful of recurrent keywords that operate like musical motifs: fear [9], mind [11], hour [12], star [14], voice [15], soul [18], come [31], power [39], earth [46]. "Gone," though less frequently repeated, is yet another since it is invoked at three of *Manfred*'s most significant moments. First, when The Phantom of Astarte disappears:

NEMESIS   She's gone, and will not be recall'd.

(II. 4. 155)

Next, when the sun sets at the end of Manfred's invocation:

He is gone.
I follow.

(III. 2. 29–30)

And finally, in the poem's closing lines (III. 4. 152–153).

And of course "spirits" are everywhere. They are all transformations of what Manfred calls "the inborn spirit" (III. 2. 22), a humanist locution that draws a distinction with the spirit or soul of men created by God. Such words form a constellation of echoing motifs that recall the pervading presence of Manfred's epipsyche, Astarte, whose being and absent presence is specifically linked to music (see I. 1. 175–179 and II. 4. 134–135), as is Manfred's:

MANFRED   Oh, that I were
The viewless spirit of a lovely sound,
A living voice, a breathing harmony,
A bodiless enjoyment – born and dying
With the blest tone which made me!

(I. 2. 52–55)

These features of *Manfred*'s language put significant demands on a reader's attention. They underscore the aggressive strangeness of one particular passage that we want to look at carefully. Coming after Manfred turns off the Witch of the Alps and her offer to help him gain what he "wishes" (II. 2. 157), the passage is a kind of gloss on two enigmatic but crucial lines in the "Incantation": "Though thy death shall still seem near/ To thy wish, but as a fear" (I. 1. 256–257).

MANFRED   I have one resource
Still in my science – I can call the dead,
And ask them what it is we dread to be:
The sternest answer can but be the Grave,
And that is nothing – if they answer not –
The buried Prophet answered to the Hag
Of Endor; and the Spartan Monarch drew
From the Byzantine maid's unsleeping spirit
An answer and his destiny – he slew
That which he loved, unknowing what he slew,
And died unpardon'd – though he call'd in aid
The Phyxian Jove, and in Phigalia roused
The Arcadian Evocators to compel
The indignant shadow to depose her wrath,
Or fix her term of vengeance – she replied
In words of dubious import, but fulfill'd.

(II. 2. 178–192)

No one, I submit, can follow that passage and claim to understand what it is saying while it is being read. It is one of Byron's most astonishing acts of perversification. Even when we excavate its allusions it resists. Part of the difficulty is its odd juxtaposition of a famous but deeply mysterious biblical event with a recondite episode from Greek history. Perhaps even more obdurate are its rich and cryptic linguistic particulars. Consider as well how the fall of that arresting language follows upon a phrase – "if they answer not" – that floats in an ambiguous syntactic space. It comes at first as a hanging after-thought but then shifts to the opening of a sentence that completes its syntax but not its thought, the words dissolving into the dark exempla of two men who (vainly) sought helpful knowledge from the dead.

As if anticipating a reader's puzzlement, Byron added an explanatory note to clarify the second of those exempla:

The story of Pausanias, king of Sparta, (who commanded the Greeks at the battle of Platea, and afterwards perished for an attempt to betray the Lacedemonians) and Cleonice, is told in Plutarch's life of Cimon; and in the Laconics of Pausanias the Sophist, in his description of Greece.

(*CPW* IV. 473)

Such a note only doubles down on the obscure verse. It has all the perversity, though none of the slapstick, of those wonderfully preposterous notes Byron attached to *The Giaour*. Reading this note, one wants to reprise what Byron wrote in *Don Juan* of Coleridge's obscure "metaphysics": "Explaining his poetics to the nation,/ We wish he'd annotate his annotation."

And we *could* annotate Byron's annotation, as various editors have. But if we did, the original textual problems would scarcely be removed. All the words in the passage still preserve – indeed, they positively "fulfill" – their "dubious import." Certainly, we recognize that Pausanias and Cleonice are being offered as types to Manfred's and Astarte's antitypes, but after we make that equation our reflections on the ancient historical episode that Byron elliptically lays out simply run free. "Dubious import"? I *guess* so! The two sources Byron cites, Plutarch and Pausanias the Sophist, tell very different versions of the story. As we pause over a glorious phrase like "Arcadian Evocators," we might well think – or hear – the passage itself as *evocative*.

Verse and note are alike seriously *pro*vocative, inviting us to search out the relevance of Byron's recollected tale. But the language of the passage is such that it erects a kind of maze from its flagrant language. Where to begin researching those particulars? Suppose we bracket out everything but the central event, the murder of Cleonice, what do we get? This is what Byron's archival records – not Byron's note – tell us. Pausanias has taken Cleonice, a princess of Bithynia, for his mistress. When she comes at night to his chamber, she accidentally overturns the lamp burning at his bedside. In the darkness, he awakes startled and, thinking she is an enemy, kills her with his sword, "unknowing what he slew" (II. 2. 186). Although the scene might recall Astarte's death, the connection is blunted because Manfred did not actually murder her (II. 2. 119–123).[4] In the tale, it is the bedside lamp – unmentioned in Byron's verse or prose note – that leaps to attention, taking one back to the very opening line of *Manfred*: "The lamp must be replenish'd"! In the obscurely open text of *Manfred*, it is perhaps the poem's most arresting private enigma.

To register that odd nexus, to make the connection that is at once hidden and invited, produces a seriously uncanny effect. Were the deaths of Cleonice and Astarte in some unrecognized sense Manfred's fatality, the condition holding him – before the play or even his life began – to his "enduring" vigil? *Manfred* seems a play of language in which secrets lie about everywhere, awaiting – seeking – discovery. This passage fairly defines how *Manfred* repeatedly "send[s] us prying into the abyss" of its seductive intimations (*Childe Harold's Pilgrimage* IV. 166).

The first person to annotate Byron's annotation was Goethe, who was interested because he knew *Manfred* had been composed with his own *Faust* (Part I) in mind. Goethe's commentary illuminates why Byron found *Faust I* the perfect vehicle for roughing up the Western myth of Faust.

Goethe begins with fulsome praise for what he calls the "wonderful phenomenon" of *Manfred*, "Byron's tragedy":

This singular intellectual poet has taken my Faustus to himself, and extracted from it the strangest nourishment for his hypochondriac humour. He has made use of the impelling principles in his own way, for his own purposes, so that no one of them remains the same; and it is particularly on this account that I cannot enough admire his genius.[5]

Searching through "the alterations [Byron] has made" to his poem, Goethe recognizes in *Manfred* "the quintessence of the most astonishing talent born to be its own tormenter." Seeing that, admiring it, he then confesses his "dissatisfaction" with *Manfred*, judging "that the gloomy heat of an unbounded and exuberant despair becomes at last oppressive to us."

Peter Manning has wittily pointed out that Goethe's view is based on a comically mistaken piece of gossip about Byron's personal sin and guilt. Completely absorbed in Byronic mythology, Goethe writes:

When a bold and enterprising young man, he won the affections of a Florentine lady. Her husband discovered the amour, and murdered his wife; but the murderer was the same night found dead in the street, and there was no one on whom any suspicion could be attached. Lord Byron removed from Florence, and these spirits haunted him all his life after.[6]

Guess what? That would be a mash-up of the stories of *The Giaour*, *The Corsair*, and *Lara* set in Italy! Believing the Florentine tale to be true, Goethe goes on to argue that the Pausanias and Cleonice passage reflects Byron "select[ing] a scene from antiquity, appropriat[ing] it to himself, and burden[ing] his tragic image with it." Byron was much amused when he learned of Goethe's fantasy.

Yet, in one obvious sense, Goethe is correct. Byron did select and burden his poem and his hero with that tale from antiquity. But

Goethe's reading misfires not so much because it is so badly misinformed about Byron's actual life. It misses its mark because *Manfred* is about as far from what Goethe repeatedly calls it, a "tragedy," as that famous "Greatest Story Ever Told" hovering in *Manfred*'s background. Although guilt and suffering are the pivot points of both stories – Jesus is crucified and Manfred, like Ahab, has "a crucifixion in his face" – their finales are in the strictest sense comic.

Many have understandably glossed *Manfred*'s climactic scene with the closing lines of his poem "Prometheus," Byron's pastiche of a chorus from Aeschylus's lost play *Prometheus Unbound*: "Triumphant where it dares defy/ And making death a victory" (58–59). But *Manfred* does not actually conclude in a posture of triumphant defiance. That moment comes in the poem's penultimate scene, when the demons are dismissed. The finale comes afterward and centers in Manfred's famous, even complacent, last words: "Old man! 'Tis not so difficult to die." After the fitful fevers of his life, Manfred expects to sleep well.

Most telling, Manfred's last words echo St. Paul's gloss on the meaning of the life of Jesus, a tale whose argument is "that ye put off ... the old man ... and put on the new man" (Ephesians 4:22–24). Christian theology regards the life, death, and resurrection of Jesus as a fundamentally comic action, a view gloriously represented in Dante's *Divina Commedia*. *Manfred* is a comic action as well, but, being a kind of parody of the Christian story, it also involves a series of comical texts that help to build up the insidious, truly Nietzschean, joke on which *Manfred* concludes. The last state of Manfred is far different from the first.

Manfred, Goethe said, "closely touched me," and it is easy to see that *Faust* Part II marshals an argument against the "unbounded and exuberant despair" that he found in *Manfred* and thought so "oppressive." We know that in

December 1816 Goethe had sketched out a plan for Part II, but that plan did not indicate exactly how Part II would end. It seems that reading *Manfred* in 1817, which Goethe did, set him on his course to bring Faust to the redemption he receives in Part II Act V when angels "bear Faust's immortal essence" into heaven. The redeemed Faust is exalted because his struggles have purified him:

FAUST   Pure spirits' peer, from evil coil
He was vouchsafed exemption;
"Whoever strives in ceaseless toil,
Him we may grant redemption."

And when on high, transfigured love
Has added intercession,
The blessed will throng to him above
With welcoming compassion.

(II. 1934–1941)

As Goethe told Eckermann in 1831, he wanted Part II to move beyond the tragic action of Part I – he saw Part I as a tragedy – to install a poetic conception that "harmonizes perfectly with our religious views; according to which we can obtain heavenly bliss, not through our strength alone, but with the assistance of divine grace."[7]

I bring up Goethe and Part II of *Faust* in order to spell out the sharp differences between Byron's and Goethe's respective complacencies. In a late letter Goethe said that Part II was organized around a set of "very seriously intended jests (*Scherzen*)."[8] These enable the work's economy of grace and the redemption of Faust. But the finale of *Manfred* is different – indeed, it is deeply irreverent. Manfred has no interest in either atonement or redemption ("What I have done is done"). He rejects both as clearly as had Byron throughout his life.

What has happened in Byron's poem that has brought Manfred to his peaceful death? Consider again the Pausanias and Cleonice passage, in this case the opening lines:

MANFRED   I have one resource
Still in my science – I can call the dead,
And ask them what it is we dread to be:
The sternest answer can but be the Grave,
And that is nothing.

Though Manfred indeed has "no natural fear" (I. 1. 25), though he is proud and defiant in face of all circumstance, he is nonetheless – until his death – acquainted with grief and something "we dread to be." Indeed, he sees his life's purpose not to overcome but exactly to "champion human fears" (II. 1. 205).

So, what *is* it "that we dread to be," that Manfred dreads to be, and that he means to champion? He calls the dead, Astarte, to find out. The consequence of their interview at the end of Act II, and of Manfred's fearfully tormented prayer to her, is the entirely untormented Act III. The psychic change in Manfred is dramatic. We know, we can see, what has happened: in the end, Manfred has no fears at all, natural or unnatural. We want to know why. What is it that we are *not* seeing?

It helps to recall that Astarte declares "Manfred" the "one word for mercy." Byron is torqueing the syntax of Astarte's answer to Manfred's plea. "Manfred" is here, in this context, the one word that counts in this work's quest for a sign of merciful judgment. But it is in fact only "One word for mercy." Anyone's name would be a word for mercy since mercy is not an idea, an abstraction, but an action, given or received, in a merciful human world. In that world of action, every name is what Blake called "The Divine Image," and every name is the name of God:

> To Mercy, Pity, Peace, and Love
> All pray in their distress;
> And to these virtues of delight
> Return their thankfulness.
>
> For Mercy, Pity, Peace, and Love
> Is God, our father dear,
> And Mercy, Pity, Peace, and Love
> Is Man, his child and care.
>
> For Mercy has a human heart,
> Pity a human face,
> And Love, the human form divine,
> And Peace, the human dress.
>
> Then every man, of every clime,
> That prays in his distress,
> Prays to the human form divine,
> Love, Mercy, Pity, Peace.
>
> And all must love the human form,
> In heathen, Turk, or Jew;
> Where Mercy, Love, and Pity dwell
> There God is dwelling too.

It also helps to parse the cunning wordplays in "what it is we dread to be ... that is nothing." One can scarcely not think of Hamlet's famous soliloquy and the "consummation devoutly to be wished" that Hamlet could not, however, commit to. Before his interview with Astarte, Manfred dreads to be mortal and therefore finally "nothing." Manfred's is the Faustian fear *to be* mortal, simply to be Manfred: unpurified, unatoned, unredeemed, and – finally – "gone": "of the earth, earthy," and then at last – to appropriate and shift the Abbot's final word – "earthless."

A letter Byron wrote in 1819 to Richard Hoppner helps gloss the meaning of the Byronic "mercy" exposed in *Manfred*. Visiting Bologna, he stopped at the Certosa Cemetery and was deeply moved by the epitaphs engraved on the tombs of Martini Luigi and Lucrezia Pinini: "*implora pace,*" "*implora eterna quiete.*" "It appears to me," he wrote, "that these two and three words comprize and compress all that can be said on the subject – and then in Italian they are absolute Music" (*BLJ* 6. 147). That would be the absolute music of, say, *Don Giovanni*, not the Music of the Spheres, and the absolute music of *Manfred* and *Don Juan* where those two absolutist European myths are replayed.

Like *Faust II*, *Manfred* works a comic adaptation on the Faust myth, but, unlike Goethe, Byron frames it in classical, not Christian, terms. The work set the agenda for the soon-to-be-written *Beppo* and *Don Juan*. One thinks of Byron's cheeky reply to John Murray's request in 1819 to give up *Don Juan* and write "a great work," something serious – an "Epic"!

I'll try no such thing – I hate tasks – and then "seven or eight years!" God send us all well this day three months – let alone years ... You have so many "*divine*" poems, is it nothing to have written a *Human* one? without any of your worn out machinery?

(*BLJ* 6. 105)

Like *Don Juan*, *Manfred* has a lot of worn-out poetical – and religious – machinery, a lot of Cant, in fact.[9] It was Byron's first work to immortalize that machinery by giving it a final *quietus*. "Implora eterne quiete," plainly *Manfred*'s final prayer, can also be heard throughout the slowly accumulating sorrows of *Don Juan*. It feels a sincere prayer exactly because it pleads for something that only the void of death can give. But then it also feels a hopeless prayer not so much because it is prayed to a void, but because of the mortal rule that governs all of Byron's work: "quiet to quick bosoms is a hell" (*Childe Harold* III. 42).

That rule explains why *Manfred* operates in its darkly comic mode. Reading the prayer on the tombs in Bologna is one thing; praying for your own death is something else again. Manfred is by turns pitiful, brave, and ridiculous in his blundering yet persistent journey to "Oblivion," and never more so than in his final encounter with the Phantom of Astarte ("I know not what I ask, nor what I seek"). So does *Manfred* climax the history of the Byronic hero's conflicted and contradictory longing for "rest, but not to feel 'tis rest" (*The Giaour* 995). That is an impossible and a ludicrous thing to say. It is also entirely understandable, even human.

Reading *Manfred* in 1817, Murray and his editorial committee were uneasy, and especially uneasy with the outrageous comedy of the original third act where the Abbot is manhandled by Astarte's dark double, Ashtaroth, who carries him off singing a profane jingle.

> A prodigal son – and a maid undone –
> And a widow re-wedded within the year –
> And a worldly Monk – and a pregnant Nun –
> Are things which every day appear.

> (*CPW* 4. 469)

They begged him to rewrite the act and he did. But by 1819 he was no longer open to such pleas, having seen the first two cantos of *Don Juan* expurgated without his knowledge or permission.

And yet perhaps *Manfred* was improved by taking out those Monty Python hijinks. The work's generous if impious argument loses none of its force, or its comic charm, for being a little better mannered.

4

Byron and the "Wrong Revolutionary Poetical System"

> Only one thing remained reachable, close and secure amid all losses: language. Yes, language. In spite of everything, it remained secure against loss. But it had to go through its own lack of answers, through terrifying silence, through the thousand darknesses of murderous speech. It went through.
>
> (Paul Celan)

Byron began a new life on April 25, 1816, the day he left England. First with *Manfred* and *Beppo* and finally with *Don Juan* and *Cain*, the literary changes in particular were remarkable – a series of works every bit as spectacular as – if far less popular than – the poems that established his fame.

We rightly take *Don Juan* as the touchstone for this literary *vita nuova*, but, as the medley style of *Manfred* suggests, Byron's masterpiece wears a coat of many colors. Its satire ranges from genial to vicious, its moods and tones shift from the light fantastic to darknesses that are grim and even tragic. Besides, the work clearly changed in the writing of it. When he completed the first two cantos in 1819, its spirit was very close to *Beppo*: a narrative romp with his language that was "never intended to be serious," a verse free-for-all written merely "to giggle and make giggle" (to Murray, August 12,

1819: *BLJ* 6. 208). At that point, when Byron's publisher asked him if he had a plan for the work, his reply was casual and flippant: "I have no plan – I had no plan; but I had or have materials." By early 1821, however, he had quite definite plans.

> The 5th is so far from being the last of D. J. that it is hardly the beginning. – I meant to take him the tour of Europe – with a proper mixture of siege – battle – and adventure – and to make him finish as *Anacharsis Cloots* – in the French revolution. – To how many cantos this may extend – I know not – nor whether (even if I live) I shall complete it – but this is my notion.
> (To Murray, February 16, 1821: *BLJ* 8. 78)[1]

More wrangling with Murray over where *Don Juan* was going resulted in Byron's break with his publisher. When John Hunt finally brought out the much-delayed *Cantos VI–VIII* (1823), Byron prefaced them with a slash-and-burn attack on reactionary England and Europe ("the degraded and hypocritical mass which leavens the present English generation"; "the surviving Sejani of Europe"; "the impious alliance which insults the world with the name of 'Holy'"). *Also sprach* Byron in his letter to Moore commenting on his new cantos:

> With these things and these fellows, it is necessary, in the present clash of philosophy and tyranny, to throw away the scabbard. I know it is against fearful odds; but the battle must be fought; and it will be eventually for the good of mankind, whatever it may be for the individual who risks himself.
> (August 8, 1822: *BLJ* 9. 191)

The rhetoric of Byron's brief for *Don Juan* is now high, profligate, impressive.

> The hackneyed and lavished title of Blasphemer – which, with Radical, Liberal, Jacobin, Reformer, etc., are the changes which the hirelings are daily ringing in the ears of those who will listen – should be welcome to all who recollect on *whom* it was originally bestowed. Socrates and Jesus were put to death publicly as *blasphemers*.

So does Byron now foreground the moral and political issues of his poem. But in that very respect the work remains focused on the question of language: "the *cant* which is the crying sin of this double-dealing and false-speaking time of selfish spoilers" (or, earlier, "the nauseous and atrocious cant of a degraded crew of conspirators against all that is sincere and honourable"). Byron devotes more than half of his mid-poem's "Preface" to an unapologetic invective again the dead Castlereagh, "a *minister* (at least) who could not speak English, and that Parliament permitted itself to be dictated to in the language of Mrs. Malaprop."[2]

That kind of confident defiance was not Byron's frame of mind in the months after he left England. Like the prisoner of Chillon, if he only "regain'd [his] freedom" from his former life "with a sigh" ("The Prisoner of Chillon," 394), he had a newly clarified view of what it had entailed: "vacancy absorbing space,/ And fixedness without a place" (243–244). As the verse – indeed, all the writings – of May to August 1816 show, Byron was angry and uncertain. But he was far from despondent and, most decisive of all, he began to reflect on language and poetics in a general way and on his own poetry in particular. So, in August 1816, he struck out in a new direction. First of all came *Manfred*, which he took nearly a year to complete, then came *Beppo*, which was "written in two nights" (*CPW* 4. 483). Radically different as they are, those two poems announce the Second Coming of Byron's poetical life.

When he sent the original version of *Manfred*'s third act to John Murray on March 9, 1817, Byron wrote that "I have really & truly no notion whether [*Manfred*] is good or bad – & as this was not the case with the principal of my former publications – I am inclined to rank it but humbly" (*BLJ* 5. 183).

Manfred's drastic medley style was the problem, and Byron felt this in two ways. He first warned Murray not to be misled by the poem's outward form. *Manfred* was not a play, or what he called a "representation." For that, he wrote, "I have an invincible repugnance." He had composed *Manfred* as "A Dramatic Poem" to see if the form would focus the reader's attention on *Manfred*'s language and poetry. As we've seen, this was the chief object of his poetry from 1809 to 1816 and he confessed that he thought "the principal of my former publications" had been largely successful in that respect. But he worried that the conventions of drama and theatre would tempt readers to expect a realist representation.

It's worth recalling briefly that, when Byron turned to playwriting with *Marino Faliero* (1821), he was experimenting with dramatic conventions to create a "Mental theatre" – poetic drama – "addressed to the understanding," the aspiration of all his work.[3] In that effort he had two notable successes, *Cain* and *Sardanapalus*, and, had he lived to finish *The Deformed Transformed*, he may have left us with his most important venture in that form. Goethe, who more than anyone at the time ought to know, was greatly impressed.

But *Manfred* also troubled Byron because, despite its outward form, it clearly worked in the Gothic manner of his "former publications." "It is too much in my old style," he grumbled – "too much" signaling his awareness that the poem's ironic and burlesque features, like Manfred's complacent last words, had not swerved sharply enough from his grim tales of disaster – or, in this instance, Manfred's quest for "Oblivion, self-oblivion" (I. 1. 144). He closed his letter with a significant final comment: "I certainly am a devil of a mannerist – & must leave off – but what could I do? without exertion of some kind – I should have sunk under my imagination and reality" (*BLJ* 5. 185).

Byron would completely "leave off" in early October 1817 when he began *Beppo*, the conscious parody of the dark tales that established his fame. Inspired by Berni, he wrote it as a language "experiment" to exorcise his "mannerist" deviltries ("the style is not English, it is Italian"). "It will show," he told Murray, "that

I can write cheerfully, and repel the charge of monotony and mannerism."[4]

"Mannerist" and "mannerism." With good reason, scholars regularly translate those striking terms "Romantic" and "Romanticism." But the synonymy is not exact because Byron's terms have sharper edges, as becomes clear when we recall their source. He lifted them from a review Thomas Moore had written in 1813 about the disputes provoked in England by the "literary revolution" – as Moore called it – that we now call Romanticism. Moore's word for its "rising novelties" was "mannerism."[5] Though he refers to the poetic "revolutionaries" as "a cabal," he doesn't name names. His term is a portmanteau for the diversified upheaval that began with the ballad revival and that caught up such diverse figures and forms as William Jones, Burns, the Della Cruscans, Darwin, Gothic verse and plays, Wordsworth and the Lake School, Scott, Moore, and finally Byron.[6]

Poised to begin his anti-mannerist *Beppo*, Byron picked up on Moore's review in one of his most famous letters:

> With regard to poetry in general I am convinced the more I think of it that [Moore] and all of us – Scott – Southey – Wordsworth – Moore – Campbell – I – are all in the wrong – one as much as another – that we are upon a wrong revolutionary poetical system – or systems ... and that the present & next generations will finally be of this opinion. – I am the more confirmed in this – by having lately gone over some of our classics – particularly Pope – whom I tried in this way – I took Moore's poems & my own & some others – & went over them side by side with Pope's – and I was really astonished (I ought not to have been so) and mortified – at the ineffable distance in point of sense – harmony – effect – and even Imagination Passion – & Invention – between the little Queen Anne's man – & us of the Lower Empire.
>
> (*BLJ* 5. 265 – to John Murray, September 15, 1817)[7]

When Murray showed Byron's letter to Moore, he demurred that Byron used his critical review to launch such a wholesale attack.

Having seen by accident the passage in one of his letters to Mr. Murray, in which he denounces, as false and worthless, the poetical system on which the greater number of his contemporaries, as well as himself, founded their reputation, I took an opportunity ... of jesting a little on this opinion and his motives for it. It was, no doubt (I ventured to say), excellent policy in him, who had made sure of his own immortality in this style of writing, thus to throw overboard all us, poor devils, who were embarked with him.[8]

Since Byron had only recently finished *The Lament of Tasso* – an exceptionally "mannerist" work[9] – Moore's "jesting" demurral forced him to reconsider his sweeping comments. So, while he maintained that "all of 'us youth' were on a wrong tack," he added "I never said that we did not sail well" and significantly, "When I say *our*, I mean *all* (Lakers included), except the postscript of the Augustans." But the expressive freedoms licensed by the new "system – or systems" would set a dangerous example for "The next generation (from the quantity and facility of imitation)." Switching to an equestrian metaphor, Byron argued that "we keep the *saddle*, because we broke the rascal and can ride. But though easy to mount, he is the devil to guide; and the next fellows must go back to the riding school and the manège" (February 2, 1818: *BLJ* 6. 10).

Byron offered "the postscript of Augustans" – he had cited Rogers and Crabbe – as a better example for the future of poetry. That judgment proved spectacularly mistaken. But hindsight also reveals where his comments struck home. His take on the eclectic Spirit of his Age ("system – or systems") was as acute as Hazlitt's. But while Hazlitt mapped the many-sided Spirit in cultural/conceptual terms, Byron's focus was on language and, more particularly, on poetic practice. His approach was philological, not intellectual or philosophical. Contemporary verse seemed to him so various stylistically that only a Lovejoyan discrimination of Romanticisms could hope to describe what followed upon the opening of the field that was forecast by Macpherson's Ossian and Percy's *Reliques*.[10]

More pertinently, Byron's reference to "system – or systems" signals his refusal to ground poetic norms in systematic philosophy. His philosophic orientation was the humanist tradition's commitment to "the practice of free judgment" – Socrates, Cicero, Seneca, Montaigne.[11] That allegiance was never more explicitly declared than in this passage from *Childe Harold* Canto IV. His subject is "Reason," his orientation is moral, and his method of arguing is strictly poetic and rhetorical:

> Yet let us ponder boldly – 'tis a base
> Abandonment of reason to resign
> Our right of thought – our last and only place
> Of refuge; this, at least, shall still be mine:
> Though from our birth the faculty divine
> Is chain'd and tortured – cabin'd, cribb'd, confined,
> And bred in darkness, lest the truth should shine
> Too brightly on the unprepared mind,
> The beam pours in, for time and skill will couch the blind.

(stanza 127)

"Time and skill will couch the blind": how carefully chosen were each of those four keywords. Though technically a metaphor, "blind" here is virtually literal because it rhymes with "mind" (it is linguistically closer to proverbial expressions – dead metaphors! – like "the mind's eye" and "cast a blind eye"). Then Byron doesn't write "cure" or "heal" but "couch" because cataracts, like sin and error, can never be removed for good. So "reason" here is framed by the relative context of "time" and by a virtue – human "skill" – that has to be kept up.

The stanza is a moment – really an act – of "waking reason" (stanza 7) performed by someone conscious that he lives inside the nightmare of Western history, the central focus of *Childe Harold*

Canto IV. Like Walter Benjamin more than one hundred years later, Byron regarded the nightmare as a fatal human condition, the consequence of what he presented in *Childe Harold* Canto IV as "Man's worst – his second fall" (stanza 97). Benjamin's remarkable vision of the Angel of History, *Angelus Novus*, rhymes with Byron's dreadful vision of human "progress":

His face is turned toward the past. Where we perceive a chain of events, he sees one single catastrophe which keeps piling wreckage upon wreckage and hurls it in front of his feet. The angel would like to stay, awaken the dead, and make whole what has been smashed. But a storm is blowing from Paradise; it has got caught in his wings with such violence that the angel can no longer close them. The storm irresistibly propels him into the future to which his back his turned, while the pile of debris before him grows skyward. The storm is what we call progress.[12]

For Benjamin, the angel is beautiful and ineffectual because "the enemy has not ceased to be victorious." For Byron, *Angelus Novus* was battered once more by the French Revolution's merciless illusion of progress and social redemption. One recalls his stern comment to Moore: "What is Hope? nothing but the paint on the face of Existence; the least touch of truth rubs it off, and then we see what a hollow-cheeked harlot we have got hold of" (October 28, 1815: *BLJ* 4. 323). What both men took hold of was a commitment to "Work without Hope."[13] Thinking of Karl Kraus, Benjamin wrote in 1931 that "humanity proves itself by the destruction" that individual human beings suffer and resist.[14] For Byron as well, freedom is not a reward for a steadfast "endurance and repulse" of cant and illusion; it is the existential condition of an individual's "fate and force" ("Prometheus" 41, 46).

Byron added a telling footnote to stanza 127 – a quotation from the second-generation Scottish philosopher Sir William Drummond (1770–1828), whose *Academical Questions* (1805) he and Shelley greatly admired. Drummond exemplified "The free and philosophic spirit" of inquiry as the only "way to defend the cause of truth." Byron closed his note with a celebrated passage from Drummond's "Preface": "Philosophy, wisdom, and liberty support each other: he, who will not reason, is a bigot; he, who cannot, is a fool; and he, who dares not, is a slave." Later, when he recommended that the Countess of Blessington read the *Academical Questions*, he underscored the source of his admiration: that Drummond was a great philosopher because he was "an admirable writer," that famous sentence being "one of the best in our language":

He has all the wit of Voltaire, with a profundity that seldom appertains to wit, and writes so forcibly, and with such elegance and purity of style, that his works possess a peculiar charm.[15]

All that is the larger "philosophical" context of Byron's comments on the "literary revolution" Moore named in his review. The poetical revolutionaries were not, or not necessarily, "wrong" in practice, but the work went seriously wrong in theory – more specifically, *as* theory. He was arguing that poetry took a wrong "tack" when it made an idea of itself its chief subject, as he judged Wordsworth had done in the *Lyrical Ballads* and as he knew Coleridge and others were making the purport of their cultural polemics.

In Byron's perspective, poetic norms were best established by example and in practice, not by precept or in theory. Philosophy achieved true distinction in its acts of distinguished expression, its bequests of great speaking and writing. So, in the case of the acts of poets, Pope's *Essay on Man* and *Essay on Criticism* were impressive less for what they said than for how they said what they said: briefly, "What oft was thought but ne'er so well expressed."

Recall how Byron argues this view in his letter to Murray. He became "more confirmed" in his critical view of contemporary poetry by testing his judgment through a set of empirical comparisons ("in point of sense – harmony – effect – and even Imagination Passion – & Invention"). Though he does not cite chapter and verse, his approach begins and ends as an act of what I. A. Richards would later name "Practical Criticism." His conclusion is simple: considered in terms of traditional categories Pope writes better poetry than "us of the Lower Empire" ("The Age of Bronze").

Moore's pushback clarified for Byron what would count as a right revolutionary approach to poetry. It would not come as a postscript of Augustans but as a truculent proposal addressed to the contemporary poets he had the sharpest disagreements with. Though "shabby fellows," the Lakers were yet "duly seated on the immortal hill" of poetic aspiration ("Dedication" 6). Let a thousand flowers bloom:

> The field is universal, and allows
>   Scope to all such as feel the inherent glow –
> Scott, Rogers, Campbell, Moore and Crabbe, will try
> 'Gainst you the question with posterity.
>
> ("Dedication" 6, 7)

Compared with Suckling's and Rochester's "Session of the Poets," Byron's abuse is positively well-intentioned, if not always good-natured. He is writing to reimagine the "wrong revolutionary poetical system – or systems" as a "mixed company" invited to "try ... the question" of their skills not only with "posterity" but right now:

> And, recollect, a poet nothing loses
>   In giving to his brethren their full meed
> Of merit.
>
> ("Dedication" 8)

Besides, "Dedication's" closing eight stanzas show that Byron's serious fire wasn't directed at these poets at all, however much he enjoyed railing them. Invoking Milton "fallen on evil days, on evil tongues" (10), Byron was implicitly asking, or wondering, whether his rivals were prepared to cultivate a poetics or a "politics … all to educate" (17) about the social condition of England and Europe.

Because Byron was persuaded not to publish his free-wheeling "Dedication," readers would have to wait a few years before *Don Juan*'s music rose to its more caustic diapasons. Put right up front of his new poem, few would have been prepared to register what makes this verse so impressive: the voicing, how it says what it's saying. Such an effortless display of regulated hatred is not easy to manage. No one since Pope had delivered that kind of "honest, simple verse" (17), and we wouldn't hear such music again for more than fifty years (in Swinburne). Although it was a key element in the catholic poetic persuasion of his *ottava rima*, Byron kept it pretty much in check for five cantos. But he explained from time to time the essential requirement for a candid poetics in a mixed company: if you mean to be serious, even savage, and ask to be taken seriously, don't make what you are doing personal:

> You know, or don't know, that great Bacon saith,
>   'Fling up a straw, 't will show the way the wind blows;'
> And such a straw, borne on by human breath,
>   Is Poesy, according as the mind glows;
> A paper kite, which flies 'twixt life and death,
>   A shadow which the onward Soul behind throws:
> And mine's a bubble, not blown up for praise,
> But just to play with, as an infant plays.
>
> (XIV. 8)

So, as he began his new poetic adventure, he took a different line with his competitors:

> Prose poets like blank-verse, I'm fond of rhyme,
> Good workmen never quarrel with their tools.
>
> (I. 201)

In context, that couplet had Wordsworth as much in mind as Milton, and it made a fair *amende honorable* to a great poet he took great linguistic pleasure in traducing ("Wordswords" and "Turdsworth" were impossible to resist).[16] If he laid down poetical commandments ("Thou shalt believe in Milton, Dryden, Pope;/ Thou shalt not set up Wordsworth, Coleridge, Southey" I. 205), he was in fact making fun of the very idea of invariable principles and permitted practice. While he thought it a mistake for a poet to cultivate a myth of the language of "low and rustic life" (as did Coleridge), he was aware what could be achieved by playing with such language "as an infant plays." Which doesn't mean he could always recognize when that had been well done. Byron ridiculed "The Idiot Boy" in *English Bards*, but it seems clear to me – I'm hardly alone – that it is one of the three most impressive poems in *Lyrical Ballads*. Indeed, Wordsworth would never again manage such a self-effacing comic tone or mix it so deftly with his distinctively Wordsworthian "feeling."

Moore also drove Byron to think past his antipathy to systematic thought and consider the legacy of a contemporary poetic scene distinguished by its array of vital poetic practice. The variety of poetic experience in the Augustan scene was nothing like the idiomatic poetic forms that multiplied between 1786 (the emergence of Burns) and 1824 (the death of Byron). Implicit in the actual practice of Byron and his contemporaries was a far more stern message than Wordsworth delivered "for the sake/ Of youthful Poets, who among these hills/ Will be my second self when I am gone" ("Michael" 37–39). Byron's message was this: because you will now be working from an array of exemplary practices rather than recognized normative models, if you mean to write poetry of any worth in the future, you will have to start from a ground zero all your own.

Byron could thrill to the "liberty" such an approach held out for poetry: "Why Man," he wrote Murray of *Don Juan*, "the Soul of such writing is it's licence; at least the *liberty* of that *licence* if one likes – not that one should abuse it" (August 12, 1819: *BLJ* 6. 208). But where to draw the line between use and abuse? Southey was not wrong to call *Don Juan* an act of treason on the English language. (His remark was as precise an act of language – and as prejudiced – as Byron's when he called the School of 1798–1804 "shabby fellows"). But if *Don Juan* was treasonous, why wasn't *Childe Harold*, or *The Giaour*, or *Manfred*? (Many thought they were.) If Byron laughed at the idea of "every Poet his *own* Aristotle" (I. 204) – Aristotle meant "system" – he laughed with the idea of a poetry that licensed itself. But his laughter was compromised. He knew that to sail "in the Wind's eye" (*Don Juan* X. 3) was perilous. He had been doing just that since 1809, but from 1816 forward he chose to do it "henceforth" (*Childe Harold* IV. 106) and with complete deliberateness.

Byron's example left poets and poetry to face a permanent state of crisis and radical change. Neither a system nor a program, however, his verse was a portentous testimony because it was delivered from an inner – and necessarily an uncertain – standing point. It was a broken mirror held up to an actual world, a shattered, barely illuminating lamp to lighten it ("a lume spento," as Ezra Pound would say), and finally a "mental net" to snare and catch out hypocrite poets and their readers. Of such verse Hopkins might well ask: "Comforter, where is thy comforting" ("No worst, there is none" 3). It worked "According to the Mighty Working" that Thomas Hardy would register as trenchantly as anyone:[17]

I

When moiling seems at cease
In the vague void of night-time,
    And heaven's wide roomage stormless
    Between the dusk and light-time,
    And fear at last is formless,
We call the allurement Peace.

II

Peace, this hid riot, Change,
　　　This revel of quick-cued mumming,
　　　This never truly being,
　　　This evermore becoming,
　　　This spinner's wheel onfleeing
　　Outside perception's range.

[1917]

Like Byron in Canto IV of *Childe Harold's Pilgrimage*, Hardy mapped his poetry and poetics to a dark view of society and politics, as these famous verses, written in the thick of World War I, show. Yet if one stepped away from that ethical frame of reference to consider "literary history" per se, the more than two hundred years of social crisis that began in 1789 would foster a remarkable yield of poetic work, innovative as well as traditional. But at its very best, when it might seem most certain and even most sublime, it was actually performing on the brink. Wordsworth's climactic hymn of praise to the Romantic imagination as delivering "something evermore about to be" (*The Prelude* VI. 542) would be translated to Hardy's "never truly being ... Outside perception's range." A few years later (1923), Robert Frost would write a specific and devastating annotation on that sinking word "something" in his free irregular sonnet "For Once Then, Something."

Byron's example raised a question that many writers later, not least T. S. Eliot, would raise even more emphatically: what was the price to pay for the "dissociation of sensibility" predicated by a poetics of radical subjectivity? For an art and a poetry conceived to be autonomous, "not among the ideologies"?[18] For a poetry that "makes nothing happen," either for social "progress" or for maintained order? Tennyson, Byron's first inheritor of consequence, launched his career (1832) by posing exactly such questions in "The Lady of Shallot." Pope, Byron's master, closed his career by worrying it in his revised and expanded *Dunciad* (1743).

And then there's Byron, *in medias res* of a social and poetical history he may have realized more fully than anyone. Well launched into *Don Juan*, Byron is sure there's much yet to learn from "sharp Adversity" (IV. 2). Indeed, "the sad Truth" pervading the verse of 1812–1816 still "hovers o'er [his] desk." Don't be deceived if it "Turns what was once romantic to burlesque" (IV. 3). The perspective has shifted slightly but the condition is the same:

> And if I laugh at any mortal thing,
> 'Tis that I may not weep; and if I weep
> 'Tis that our nature cannot always bring
> Itself to apathy.
>
> (IV. 4)

Peter Cochran shrewdly annotated those lines with this passage from *The Corsair*:

> Strange though it seem – yet with extremest grief
> Is linked a mirth – it doth not bring relief –
> That playfulness of Sorrow ne'er beguiles,
> And smiles in bitterness – but still it smiles;
> And sometimes with the wisest and the best,
> Till even the scaffold echoes with their jest!
> It may deceive all hearts, save that within.
>
> (II. 13)[19]

In *Don Juan*, we are still immersed in the "waste and icy clime[s]" of 1812–1817 – so much so, in fact, that it is remarkable how easily we forget what *Don Juan* clearly is: a tale of the Byronic Hero brought home from the Middle East to where those tales always belonged, in savage Europe, the haunted and main region of Byron's songs. He was explicit about his plan to fashion a meticulously detailed story of Juan's five-year passage from his home in Spain to his death in 1794 in France on the guillotine ("to make him finish as Anarcharsis Cloots – in the French Revolution"). *Don Juan* is nothing more or less than a Byronic tale unfolding in catastrophic slow motion. The Clootz comparison, and the whole tone of this account, suggests that Byron may have been already imagining Juan's death as a bleakly burlesque event, like the finale of *The Life of Brian*. But perhaps he could have managed something for Juan like *Manfred*'s Nietzschean grave dance. In any event, the sentimental close of *A Tale of Two Cities* was not in Byron's tarot cards for his last disastered hero.

5

Byron, Blake, and the Adversity of Poetics

"I forgive you, Sir Knight," said Rowena, "as a Christian."
"That means," said Wamba, "that she does not forgive him at all."
                                        Walter Scott, *Ivanhoe*

[T]he Moral of a whole Poem as with the Moral Goodness of its parts ... belong to Philosophy & not to Poetry ... the Ancients calld it eating of the tree of good & evil.
                                        William Blake, *On Homers Poetry*

We locate the connection between Blake and Byron in *The Ghost of Abel* (1822), Blake's commentary on Byron's *Cain: A Mystery* (1821). But their relation actually goes out much further and in much deeper. Though Blake was hardly known in his time and Byron was a public byword, both covet a bold, candid, and often fierce address on cultural and political issues. Oddly but, as we shall see, truly, while each worked from a different English lexicon – Blake's religious and even theological, Byron's secular and Enlightened – they shared certain important ideas that skewed them from what their age demanded. (So there was "mad" Blake and also the "mad, bad, and dangerous" Lord Byron.) Beyond that and even more important, the decisive characters of their writing styles, especially their poetry and poetics, have notable affinities. David Erdman did well to call Blake a "Prophet against Empire," but, as it happened, that is how Blake presented Byron in his poetical commentary on *Cain*.[1]

Addressed specifically "To Lord Byron in the Wilderness," *The Ghost of Abel* names Byron a cultural force as consequential as "the Public," "the Jews," "the Deists," and "the Christians" who are directly addressed in the four chapters of *Jerusalem*. Byron appears to Blake's vision as the prophet Elijah *redivivus* in the age of the restoration of the thrones of Europe and the Congress of Verona.[2] No contemporary was so singled out by Blake or hailed with that kind of exalted rhetoric.

What led Blake to do that? It is a useful question to ask – though it cannot really have an "answer" – because posing it helps clarify two more imposing and equally unanswerable questions: the question of Romanticism and the question of the claims of reason and imagination, or philosophy and poetry. Because both men were, as we have already seen and as is well known, decidedly critical of both secular and Romantic Enlightenment, a history of their ideas is less consequential for understanding their work than an account of their actual practice. But a history of their ideas can't be altogether dispensed with because it was the context that propelled them to overturn ideas on the adverse wheels of poetic expression.

I

Scholars sometimes question whether Blake even read *Cain* in toto, much less the whole of the volume, which included *Sardanapalus* and *The Two Foscari*. The cost (15 shillings) would have been prohibitive for Blake.[3] But consider that the only verbal echoes of Byron in *The Ghost of Abel* are not to *Cain* but to *Don Juan* (Canto I) and *The Two Foscari*.[4] The *Don Juan* echo is significant for what it implies about Blake's reading before the scandal of

Cain. Besides, the quotation lifted from *The Two Foscari* shows that Blake probably read the whole of Byron's volume, which would have interested him as a critical reflection on cycles of historical violence. When Blake's Jehovah asks the Ghost of Abel "What Vengeance dost thou require?" the wraith replies, "Life for Life! Life for Life!" His answer echoes Loredano's appeal – against the authority of Jesus (Matthew 5: 38–39) and St. Paul (Romans 12: 17) – to Leviticus 24: 17–21: "life for life, the rule/Denounced for retribution from all time" (*The Two Foscari*, IV. 1. 22–23).

Consider as well that Byron's three plays in the *Cain* volume schematize a universal history of violence – psychic, social, and imperial – that echoes the tormented history Blake imagined in similarly epochal terms in *The Four Zoas* and further codified in *Milton* and *Jerusalem*.[5] With *Cain* and its unfinished sequel *Heaven and Earth* (1823), Byron would follow Blake in tracking the Western progress of that history to primitive biblical sources. Byron read those sources, like Blake, against their orthodox interpretive grain.[6] In the epoch of the French Revolution and its reactionary aftermath, Blake's antinomian religion and Byron's Enlightenment skepticism often spoke a common tongue.

Parsing where and how Blake's and Byron's works converge (and diverge) helps clarify their imaginative use of key articles of Christian faith – the myth of the fall, vicarious atonement, sin and forgiveness, death and resurrection. Every one of those ideas was as important for the agnostic Byron as they were for the Christian Blake. The convergence will also shed light on regulative Blakean terms like "Nature," "the human form divine," "Last Judgment," "Eternal Life," and "Eternal Death." But most important – this will be my final subject – it will expose how each wrote under the rule of what Blake called "minute particulars" or – Byronically – "every poet his own Aristotle" (*Don Juan* I. 204).

I start from one of those normative Romantic terms, Nature. A. O. Lovejoy pointed out long ago that the keywords of Romantic scholarship – imagination, nature, and myth, for example – are conceptual abstractions that can seriously distort the actual practice of different writers and artists if they are not used with care.[7] Blake, Wordsworth, and Byron imagine Nature in very different ways. Wordsworth's benevolent reading of natural process is neatly expressed in his formula "Nature never did betray/ The heart that loved her." But for Blake, the very *nature* of Nature was to deceive and betray.[8] For his part, Byron does not view Nature in sentimental or pantheist terms, as both Blake (negatively) and Wordsworth (positively) do.[9] *Manfred* and *Cain* demonstrate an assumption pervading Byron's work: that Nature is indifferent to human enterprise.[10] Consequently, in the Byronic relation between Man and Nature, all love and care must come, if it comes at all, from the human side, for it is Man who, "enamour'd of distress/ Would mar it [Nature] into wilderness" (*The Giaour* 50–51).

Blake's natural world is a wilderness created by a human imagination that has shrunk in fear from primal existence where "Death was not, but Eternal life sprung" (*The First Book of Urizen* plate 3). He deplored Wordsworth's celebration of Nature's benevolence and all related forms of "Natural Religion," including "Natural Supernaturalism." By contrast, Byronic Nature is inhuman and amoral but, exactly on that account, spiritually useful. Byron regularly turns the power and indifference of Nature to an objective standard for judgment and self-judgment. In its signature forms, Byronic Nature is the imagination of a wanderer in the traditional wilderness of spiritual trial, Hegel's "highway of despair" and negative Enlightenment.[11] So the characteristic posture of Byron and his desperate heroes:

> Then let the winds howl on, their harmony
> Shall henceforth be my music.
>
> (*Childe Harold's Pilgrimage* IV. 106)

is repeatedly echoed in Blake's Gothic scenes: "Rintrah roars and shakes his fires in the burdend air"; "the just man rages in the wilds/ Where lions roam" (*The Marriage of Heaven and Hell* plate 2). For Blake, tormented landscapes – Legion in every sense throughout his work – are territories where spiritual commitments are engaged.

Given the sharp things Blake wrote against "unbelief" and the critical spirit of Enlightenment science and philosophy, we might wonder how he made common cause with the infidel Byron. But Blake would have recognized the special quality of Byron's skepticism, which called doubt itself to judgment.[12] In that perspective, Byron's Enlightenment allegiances were for Blake, like the writings of Voltaire and Thomas Paine, the voice of one crying in a spiritual wilderness created by empirical science on the one hand and ecclesiastical orthodoxy on the other. Reporting his visionary conversations with Voltaire, Blake spoke of the corrupt "natural Sense" of the Bible that

Voltaire was commissioned by God to expose ... "I have had ... much intercourse with Voltaire – And he said to me 'I blasphemed the Son of Man And it shall be forgiven me – but they [the enemies of Voltaire] blasphemed the Holy Ghost in me, and it shall not be forgiven to them.'"[13]

Both Blake and Byron endorsed and practiced Kant's Enlightenment injunction, *sapere aude*, each daring to think critically about knowledge and the pretensions of education, both secular and religious.[14] Manfred begins his career as a chastened and desperate *philosophe*, confessing that "The tree of knowledge is not that of life" (*Manfred* I. 1.12). Blake took the same point of biblical reference when he told Crabb Robinson that "education ... is the great Sin. It is eating of the tree of the Knowledge of Good and Evil" (Robinson 696). Would Blake not have seen that the plot of *Manfred* follows the track of a Faustian fool persisting in his folly until he became wise enough to see and say, "Old Man, 'tis not so difficult to die" (III. 4. 451)? Could he have failed to register Manfred's final telling allusion to St. Paul, or to recognize its imaginative significance? Byron's poetic drama is a version of the story Blake himself had told in *Milton*, of a Modern prophetic hero passing through what Blake called "A Last Judgment" on himself: "I in my Selfhood am that Satan ... To claim the Hells, my Furnaces, I go to Eternal Death" (*Milton* 14/ 15: 30, 32)? What is remarkable is that while Manfred's death is essentially pagan and the death of Blake's Milton is essentially Christian, both are presented as non-transcendental events.

Paradoxically, certain foundational aspects of Blake's theology give a special insight into the depth of Blake's interest in Byron. An Arianist Christian, Blake thought Jesus was not only human but a sinner – or, more precisely, a lawbreaker, a "transgressor" (for Byron, a "blasphemer"). Founded on Blake's severe, Pauline view of "the Wastes of Moral Law" (*Jerusalem* 24: 24), no Blake conviction is more firmly held than his hatred of "righteousness" and judgment. "What are called the Vices in the natural world, are the highest sublimities in the spiritual world" (Robinson, 700). He asserted this view as early as *The Marriage of Heaven and Hell*, although its startling declarations on plates 23 and 24 are sometimes read as hyperbolic satire. But they were religious convictions Blake held to the end of his life, as is apparent from the late Notebook fragments he wrote for "The Everlasting Gospel."

His remarks to Crabb Robinson in 1825 and 1826 about Jesus, the angels, and God Himself ("the Supreme Being") reveal the literality of his signature formula "human form divine." "Jesus Christ," he told Robinson, "is the only God" – but then he added – "And so am I and so are you" (Robinson 696). He "spoke of error as being in heaven" and "extend[ed] this liability to error to the Supreme Being" (Robinson 696), adding that "he did not believe in the Omnipotence of God" (Robinson 700), nor in the purity of angels or men ("Is there any purity in God's eyes?" he asked, and answered "No": Robinson 696). "There is suffering in Heaven," he told Robinson, "for where there is the capacity of enjoyment, there is the capacity of pain" (Robinson 698). Though Jesus was the very model of divine humanity for Blake, he often spoke of "the errors of Jesus": "turning the money changers out of the Temple," for example, which "he had no right to do" (Robinson 705). Most remarkable of all, he said that Jesus "ought not to have suffered himself to be crucified" (Robinson 696). Indeed, that mistake might have been for Blake Jesus's "worst" error since it helped license the law of vicarious atonement, "a horrible doctrine" according to Blake (Robinson 705).[15]

He could not have known that Byron dismissed the doctrine of vicarious atonement with similar contempt, though Byron expressed himself in the idiom of Enlightenment rationalism.[16] Both judged that vicarious atonement shifted the responsibility for human error, transgression, and guilt to a transpersonal order of normative law. For Blake, the doctrine codified a cruel system of unpayable indebtedness initially proclaimed, Blake thought, in the tale of Genesis, which opened a gulf, rather than a sympathetic relation, between Time and Eternity, God and Man.[17] Blake went on to explain that sinlessness – more precisely for Blake, faultless-ness – is an error of a human imagination that has turned away from the sympathetic "Mercy Seat" to ascend a throne of self-righteous judgment.[18]

Even for such a deeply committed Christian as Blake, these are not religious views that carried much public approval. They are Blake's "Visions of Judgment" – judgments passed on judgment. Like Byron, he has an ever-ready critical perspective that multiplies his work's severe tensions and contradictions. Irresolution is a pervasive quality of both their poetic styles because, for both, "Energy is the only life" of their artistic practices. If "Reason is the bound and outward circumference of Energy," it is a bound that energy is bound to break (*The Marriage of Heaven and Hell* plate 4). "Jesus was all virtue," Blake declared, because he "acted from impulse: not from rules" (*The Marriage of Heaven and Hell*, plates 23–24).

So while each made a virtue of exposing the limits of their own art, their characteristic form of action was to negate negation, turning a poetic wheel (Blake) against the wheels of the canting world (Byron). Byron doesn't make a virtue of his poetic and moral limitations in *English Bards and Scotch Reviewers* (93–102); he lets them take the measure of all poetic action and critical/moral judgment. Virtually Byron's last word on his masterwork *Don Juan* was "I leave the thing a problem, like all things" (*Don Juan* XVII. 13). Virtually Blake's first move in his masterwork *Jerusalem* was to deface his text. Blake so severely gouged what he had engraved on plate 3, its opening text page, that the sense of the passage is abrupted. That action on what most consider his master-work is perhaps its most dramatic event.

Operating within the limits of the human lifeworld, neither Blake nor Byron coveted an art of finished appearances. Formal irregularities and aesthetic irresolution – the distinguishing feature of what Blake called "living form" (*On Virgil*) – signaled the presence of spirited poetic action. That conviction led him to tell Crabb Robinson that aesthetic method was the one field where education was imperative.[19] Byron's poetics too, like his politics, were "all to educate" both himself and his readers. But it was a special kind of anti-education devoted to opening doors of per-ception that were firmly closed. A "Proverb of Hell" announced their new dispensations: "The tygers of wrath are wiser than the horses of instruction."

Keeping faith with an Enlightenment Reason chastened by reflection on the French Revolution and its reactionary aftermath, Byron undertook in his last eight years a broad critical analysis of the Western history of political and social ideas and the realities they fostered. Those works run an uncanny parallel with Blake's

To the Public

After my three years slumber on the banks of the Ocean, I again display my Giant Forms to the Public. My former Giants & Fairies having recievd the highest reward possible: the [love] and [friendship] of those with whom to be connected, is to be [blessed]: I cannot doubt that this more consolidated & extended Work, will be as kindly recieved ——— The Enthusiasm of the following Poem, the Author hopes ———

——— [I] also hope the Reader will be with me, wholly One in Jesus our Lord, who is the God [of Fire] and Lord [of Love] to whom the Ancients look'd and saw his day afar off, with trembling & amazement.

The Spirit of Jesus is continual forgiveness of Sin: he who waits to be righteous before he enters into the Saviours kingdom, the Divine Body: will never enter there. I am perhaps the most sinful of men. I pretend not to holiness! yet I pretend to love, to see, to converse with daily, as man with man, & the more to have an interest in the Friend of Sinners. Therefore [Dear] Reader, [forgive] what you do not approve, & [love] me for this energetic exertion of my talent.

Reader! [of] books! [of] heaven,
And of that God from whom [all books are given,]
Who in mysterious Sinais awful cave
To Man the wondrous art of writing gave,
Again he speaks in thunder and in fire!
Thunder of Thought, & flames of fierce desire:
Even from the depths of Hell his voice I hear,
Within the unfathomd caverns of my Ear.
Therefore I print; nor vain my types shall be:
Heaven, Earth & Hell, henceforth shall live in harmony

Of the Measure, in which
the following Poem is written

We who dwell on Earth can do nothing of ourselves, every thing is conducted by Spirits, no less than Digestion or Sleep. ———

[When] this Verse was first dictated to me I consider'd a Monotonous Cadence like that used by Milton & Shakspeare & all writers of English Blank Verse, derived from the modern bondage of Rhyming; to be a necessary and indispensible part of Verse. But I soon found that in the mouth of a true Orator such monotony was not only awkward, but as much a bondage as rhyme itself. I therefore have produced a variety in every line, both of cadences & number of syllables. Every word and every letter is studied and put into its fit place: the terrific numbers are reserved for the terrific parts ——— the mild & gentle, for the mild & gentle parts, and the prosaic, for inferior parts: all are necessary to [each] other. Poetry Fetter'd, Fetters the Human Race! Nations are Destroy'd, or Flourish, in proportion as Their Poetry Painting and Music, are Destroy'd or Flourish! The Primeval State of Man, was Wisdom, Art, and Science.

Figure 3 Image of *Jerusalem*, plate 3, Copy 1. Reproduced with the permission of the William Blake Archive

similarly ambitious imaginative studies of Western history and culture. In each case, their work was precipitated by a personal crisis that forced Blake and Byron to reimagine their vocational inventions in light of their failures as poets and cultural prophets. (Human) self-betrayal and (human) self-diremption – not redemption – are the subjects of those two "extended crisis lyrics," Blake's *Milton* (1803–1804) and Byron's *Manfred*.[20]

Blake's sojourn at Felpham (1800–1803) turned into a spiritual trial that would shape all of his later work, as his letters from 1802–1804 show. Briefly, he rededicated himself to his "primitive and original ways" of monumental historical art that focused "on the Spiritual & not on the Natural World" (Erdman 724). Ironically, Blake was moved to this determination because of his well-meaning patron, William Hayley, who had brought him to Felpham but who disparaged Blake's visionary work and pressed him toward more financially advantageous labors. As his letters to his brother James and to Thomas Butts show, Blake grew to see Hayley as "the Enemy of my Spiritual Life" (Erdman 728) and determined to leave Felpham. His feelings of "shame & confusion" (Erdman 725) are explicit in his letter to Butts of January 10, 1803, where he compares his betrayal of his prophetic vocation to Judas's betrayal of Jesus.

He saw his mission as an assault on what he called "the detestable gods of Priam" (*Milton* 14/15: 15) – that is, the thrones, principalities, powers, and dominions committed to war, violence, and empire in the contemporary world.[21] But this was to be a spiritual and imaginative, not a political and worldly, engagement, according to the explicit formula: "travellers from Eternity. pass outward to Satans seat,/ But travellers to Eternity. pass inward to Golgonooza" (*Milton* 15/17: 29–30).[22] Blake's commitment was fortified when, late in his Felpham stay, he was brought to trial on a Crown charge of sedition. He was eventually acquitted but the incident reinforced his retreat from the satanic world to the city of art. Attacks on money changers (like Jesus) or on Crown officers (like Blake) were not acts of "Mental Fight" against Mammon, War, and Empire. They were, for him, "errors" of imagination.

So Blake began composing what he judged "the Grandest Poem that This World Contains" (Erdman 730), *Milton*, and wrote with enthusiasm even to "the Enemy of my Spiritual Life" (i.e., William Hayley) that his trials at Felpham were a kind of redemption: "O lovely Felpham, parent of Immortal Friendship, to thee I am eternally indebted for my three years' rest from perturbation and the strength I now enjoy" (Erdman 756). The poem would reflect more deeply on the interpretation of *Paradise Lost* Blake had set down ten years earlier in *The Marriage of Heaven and Hell*. The Satan of *Milton* is the creature named in the *Marriage* (plate 5) "Milton's Messiah" – that is, "The Accuser Who Is The God of This World" (Erdman 269) and the promoter of the system of vicarious atonement. *Milton* tells the story of Milton's realization that he had himself become the spokesman for the satanic Accuser (see *Paradise Lost* 3: 209–212) and that from his work "a black cloud [of moral righteousness] redounding spread over Europe" (15/17: 50). Milton's "precipitate descent" (20/22: 26) from heaven to earth represents his conscious choice to join "the Devils party" of the *Marriage*, a decision that involves "Self annihilation" and "go[ing] to Eternal Death."

That move is the central event in both *Milton* and *Jerusalem*. It signifies the judgment of sin turning back on itself, "as cogs are form'd in a wheel to turn the cogs of the adverse wheel" (*Milton* 27: 9 and *Jerusalem* 13: 14). Blake's figure explains the doubled valence of his key term "Eternal Death": in one perspective, it is "the Abomination of Desolation"; in another, it is the transformational death and resurrection Blake described when he signed himself "Born 28 Nove[mbe]r 1757 in London & has died several times since" (Erdman 698). Blake's story of Milton's spiritual death and rebirth is the tale of Blake's own imaginative death and rebirth at Felpham (*Milton* 36/40: 21–27).

And then there is *Manfred*, which, like *Milton*, gives an inverted reading of the "great argument" of *Paradise Lost* (I. 24). Both aim to justify the ways of man to God by adversely reflecting on Milton's orthodox views of sin, mercy, and forgiveness. When Byron again addressed these topics in the fourth canto of *Childe Harold* (1818), he shifted the focus so that *Manfred*'s psychic space was folded into the "base pageant" (st. 97) of guilt and violence in society and history. The move brought the critical spirit of Enlightenment, "waking Reason" (st. 7), to a more extensive critical accounting. Even more important, it led Byron to the notorious Forgiveness Curse stanzas (sts. 130–137), one of the most extraordinary passages in his work and of special importance when we try to assess the Blake/Byron relation and how to read *The Ghost of Abel* in particular.[23]

The argument of *Childe Harold* Canto IV delivers an exemplary history of violence (Rome's history), the claims of Reason, and Byron's personal reflections on his marriage. It is a manifesto for the practice of art at a time he would soon name *The Age of Bronze* (1823). The poem constructs what amounts to a Cainite interpretation of history, or what Byron names "man's worst – his second fall" (st. 97). For Byron (as for Blake), the expulsion from Eden is an existential condition; the murder of Abel is a horror. The first fall is not subject to redemption. It is, rather, the very condition of human life, which Byron presents as a trial of human endurance for those "wanderers o'er Eternity/ Whose bark drives on and on, and anchored ne'er shall be" (*Childe Harold* III. st. 70; see also Canto IV sts. 104–106).[24] The result is one of Byron's signature poetic styles, Byronic gloom and glory: "There is a very life in our despair"; "Roll on, thou deep and dark blue Ocean – roll!"; "Then let the winds howl on! Their harmony/ Shall henceforth be my music." That is human life lived under the sign of the (first) fall.

The second fall is different, doubled, duplicitous. Unlike the first fall, which is a Fate, the second is a human contrivance – what Byron, reflecting on himself in 1816, called being "cunning in mine over-throw/ The careful pilot of my proper woe" ("Epistle to Augusta" 23–24). While "The Incantation" in *Manfred* is its conspectus, Canto IV of *Childe Harold* exposes its machinery in a sequence of lyric meditations that extend from Byron's entrance into Rome in stanza 78 to the end of the canto. Rome labors in "The double night of ages, and of her,/ Night's daughter, Ignorance" (st. 81). In the condition of the second fall, people and even nations appear "doubly curst" (st. 124): ruins among ruins (st. 25), slaves of slaves (st. 89), tyrants of tyrants (st. 96). "The yoke that is upon us doubly bowed" (st. 95) is this second fall, whose curse is not simply that it will "recur, ere long" (st. 125). The deepest truth is that while the brutal recurrence is "allowed/ Averr'd and known" (st. 95), human beings continue to repeat it, well knowing that they "plod in sluggish misery" and "Bequeath ... their hereditary rage" generation by generation (st. 94). For Byron (as for Blake), the "progress" of history is dismal.

Byron's response to the second fall is a countermove of repeated resistance. These unfold as the series of lyric reflections that organize all four cantos of *Childe Harold's Pilgrimage*. Recall the important reflection on art and imagination at Canto IV stanzas 115–127, where he studies a mind diseased of its own beauty and power. The passage is written to deconstruct the supreme illusion at work within our supreme fictions. Fantastic desires people the heavens with gods and unseen seraphs (st. 121). Faithful though martyred to that "desiring phantasy," the mind then "fevers" into the imagination's secondary acts of "false creation" (st. 122) – "false" because while true as art, they are untrue, unreal, unrealiz*able* as life ("Can Nature show so fair?"). Even a lifetime of recognized error and folly "allowed/ Averr'd and known" will prove no defense against the "phantom" of a trans-mortal condition.

That admission gives remarkable force and pathos to Byron's final pledge of allegiance to "waking Reason" (st. 7):

> Yet let us ponder boldly – 'tis a base
> Abandonment of reason to resign
> Our right of thought – our last and only place
> Of refuge.

(stanza 127)

"The truth" that will dawn on the intrepid and errant mind, if it persists in its quest for truth, is that the "faculty divine" (st. 127) is a human faculty, according to the Blakean proverb "Attempting to be more than Man We become less" (*The Four Zoas* Night the Ninth: Erdman 403). This mind is "chain'd and tortured – cabin'd, cribb'd, confined/ And bred in darkness" (st. 127). Imagining itself otherwise, the mind keeps slipping into various "overweening phantasies" such as the fantasy of triumph that Lucifer offers Cain in his last speech. When these are shaped as a paradisal politics – Byron's judgment on the French Revolution – they become "fatal ... to Freedom's cause" (st. 97).

But not fatal always and everywhere, Byron argues. The "base pageant" of the second fall need not be "the pretext for [an] eternal thrall" (st. 97). Recurrent as it is – "The Triumph of Life," as Shelley called it – the pageant also moves within a history of resistant currents.[25] An "Abandonment of reason" is explicitly a base echo of the base pageant (st. 127). So Byron's version of Blake's adverse wheel counters apocalypse with a machinery drawn from cyclic seasonal change: "So shall a better spring less bitter fruit bring forth" (st. 98). The comment echoes Byron's reflection in Canto III on what counts as an adequate response to the afflicted histories studied in *Childe Harold*.[26] Given the choice "to punish or forgive," Byron says that "in *one* [i.e., in the impulse to punish] we shall be slower" (III. st. 84). Judgment itself becomes afflicted when guilt and innocence, right and wrong, are pervasive and ambiguous.

11

Byron's personal life becomes seriously pertinent in that context. Reflections on venerable histories – the Bible, ancient Rome – trade on a license of critical distance. Contemporary histories – the wars with France – shrink that privilege of enlightened removal. It is erased altogether when personal history is folded into, even identified with, "objective" histories, which is the project of all the cantos of *Childe Harold*. Reflection then works at the uncertain inner standing point where judgment cannot separate itself from the process of judgment it is itself driving.

Working at that inner standing point, in 1816, Byron returned to the position he had staked out but only briefly defended in 1809: "To learn to think, and sternly speak the truth." The masquerades of *Manfred* and later *Cain* recovered and built up that redoubt by an objective linguistic address – their "mental theatre" – just as, earlier, the dark satanic tales and the fiction of Harold had worked up tale-telling as a "mental net." But the venture of *Childe Harold's Pilgrimage* had raised the stakes by exposing the subjective element involved in learning to think and deciding to speak. *English Bards* was seriously personal and, despite its nominal hero, *Childe Harold* was even more so. Remarkably, by 1816, the awkward mask of Harold would help show Byron that, to "speak the truth," he needed an unspeakable poetics. In his sweeping passage from England thence on to Italy – Cantos III and IV of *Childe Harold* – Byron found his verse being weighed in the balance – and found wanting – by his own exorbitant fears and feelings on the one hand and his artful stylistic ways on the other. This two-year-long trial by poetics would climax in the notorious Forgiveness Curse stanzas of Canto IV (sts. 130–137) where Byron's style reached an "extreme verge" (*Don Juan* IV. 106) of lyrical expression.

Don Juan is where we are pleased to track his free poetic flights. But Byron had to pay a stiff price to access that *aurora borealis* of language. Blake called it "the Price of Experience" costing "all that a man hath" (*The Four Zoas* "Night the Second") – in Rousseauist terms, Byron's *amour de soi*. The price to pay was to become what he beheld: to know himself a full citizen of a world he judged a "peopled desert" and a "waste and icy clime." And not just to become that, but to know himself as such and, more painful yet, to find a way to declare it and so escape the dissimulating fictions of any poetic address that would remove itself to some safe "nook" apart (*Don Juan* XV. 3), paring its sharp fingernails.

How fiercely he resisted paying that price is perhaps the central story being told in the last two cantos of *Childe Harold*, which begins with Byron "Awaking with a start" from a happy dream of his daughter. His quest to remake himself declared (1–6), he summons the mask of Harold, specifically echoing a Socratic *nosce teipsum*: "he knew himself the most unfit/ Of men to herd with Man, with whom he held/ Little in common" (*Childe Harold* III. 12). But *Caveat lector*: "unfit" is a perfect instance of the language – sometimes even the "defensive paradox" – that pervades the early Byronic tales. Byron is not just coolly reflecting on his Harold mask, though we are invited and expected to read it that way. The invitation is a second-order illusion meant to underscore the presence of an adverse artifice. The cunning repetition releases the self-centered irony that would become a signature Byronic device – the unbearable but certain sign of the *poète maudit*. This is poetry that is knowingly compromised, addressed to the unfit few who are still alive to the culture and language of Cant.

That cursed poetics is deployed all over Canto III as a series of wildly veering moods and feelings that come slowly or suddenly and then abruptly cease or gradually recede. Because there is no order to or rest from the poem's turns toward and then away from what it encounters, it breathes a contagious agitation (43–44) that finally breaks out clearly as the storm over the Jura (III. 92–97). The poetic action maps a crisis of language for which Rousseau's "burning page" is the agent of "the thrilled spirit's love-devouring heat" (sts. 78–79), perversely consuming and self-consuming.

The canto dramatizes the encounter of a "Soul" bent on aspirations "Beyond the fitting medium of desire" (st. 42).

> Their breath is agitation, and their life
> A storm whereon they ride, to sink at last,
> And yet so nurs'd and bigotted to strife,
> That should their days, surviving perils past,
> Melt to calm twilight, they feel overcast
> With sorrow and supineness, and so die;
> Even as a flame unfed, which runs to waste
> With its own flickering, or a sword laid by
> Which eats into itself, and rusts ingloriously.
>
> (st. 44)

Is there any medium, any means, or any measure able to carry the thrilled spirit's passage that doesn't at the same time torment the medium and thwart the desire? The stanza – the entire canto – suggests not. But the experience of debility and failure is so extreme that it provokes a vital action in the very "gaps where desolation work'd" (st. 45). Because disaster and loss never end, "There is a very life in our despair" (st. 34).

> Could I embody and unbosom now
> That which is most within me, – could I wreak
> My thoughts upon expression, and thus throw
> Soul, heart, mind, passions, feelings, strong or weak,
> All that I would have sought, and all I seek,
> Bear, know, feel, and yet breathe – into one word,
> And that one word were Lightning, I would speak;
> But as it is, I live and die unheard,
> With a most voiceless thought, sheathing it as a sword.
>
> (st. 97)

The canto's relentless rhythm embodies and unbosoms itself here, wreaking its clashing thoughts and feelings into a dissonant music that the Spenserian stanza had never known before Byron. From that fitful poetic fever burst this canto's many convulsive, and often grammatically unnatural, chords and expressions. Here they pivot around a particularly striking one: "most voiceless." In one sense a simple poetic ellipsis, it comes here as a thought being wrecked on its own violent will to expression, emerging like a fragment torn from a language "beyond the fitting medium of desire."

The canto plunges recurrently through a world of Byronic perversifications that startle because they come so unexpectedly, as here:

> I have not loved the world, nor the world me;
> I have not flattered it's its rank breath, nor bow'd
> To it's its idolatries a patient knee, –
> Nor coin'd my cheek to smiles, – nor cried aloud
> In worship of an echo; in the crowd
> They could not deem me one of such; I stood
> Among them, but not of them; in a shroud
> Of thoughts which were not their thoughts, and still could,
> Had I not filed my mind, which thus itself subdued.

> (113)

"And still could"? What does that mean? The grammar seems to be saying that, while Byron moved among "the crowd," he kept himself apart and aloof, like Lara. But then why would Byron even consider living that way again, especially given the final line here? He might have continued moving like "a stranger in [the] breathing world" (*Lara* I. 315) of Regency Cant had he not "filed [his] mind." In a note, Byron instructs us to read "filed" as meaning "defiled," taking Shakespeare as his authority. But if he kept himself to himself, his thoughts inviolate, how did he "defile" his mind?

Such perversification sends us "pry[ing] into the abyss" of the questions and problems the verse provokes. If we return to or recall stanzas 7–12, we will be inclined to take "filed" as a wordplay, meaning simultaneously "defiled" and "filed down/smoothed out." Doing that, we may also glimpse an import that has been a pressing concern for Byron since 1809: the commitment to full ("stern") self-disclosure. While the betrayal of that imperative is confessed here, the confession is no less compromised than it was at the outset of the canto. Emily Dickinson would make intense poetry by telling truth at strange diagonals and in slanted ways. Byron's obliquities are different, enacting instead a tormented abandonment to voiceless thought. At the same time – absurdly yet exactly – they would also free him to reimagine new possibilities of poetic expression.

While *Don Juan* is the great exponent of Byron's quest for poetic freedom, the Forgiveness Curse stanzas in *Childe Harold* IV are even more revealing because their contradictions are so defiantly embraced. To begin engaging those contradictions, consider how the passage makes a conscious reprise of the poetry of 1816. First of all, it recalls the pastiche of the lost chorus from *Prometheus Unbound* that Byron had fashioned in his "Prometheus" lyric. But where the latter climaxes as a celebration of victorious if untriumphant courage, here Byron fashions a pastiche harangue of Prometheus with hard "iron in [his] soul" (131).[27]

Byron begins by addressing "Time" with "offerings" of his past life, both its "Ruins" and the "Good" he enjoyed in his recent Years of Fame (131). Then – thinking of Aeschylus ("Hear me, my mother Earth! behold it, Heaven!" 135) – he calls "Great Nemesis" to "Awake!" and "hear my heart." The Capitoline ruins exposed such a lavish history of "human wrong" (132) that they seemed to dwarf Byron's "petty griefs" lamented just a few stanzas earlier (106). But now his abrupt about-face indexes a change of mind and, crucially, a change of voice from elegy to a high rhetoric of ultimately prophetic indignation. When he writes "I sleep, but thou shalt yet awake" (133), his sleep is far from the sleep of dreams that played throughout Canto III.

Though his language here is classical and pagan, Byron was
never closer to the Blake who declared that his poetry was "dictated from Eternity."

> And if my voice break forth, 'tis not that now
> I shrink from what is suffered: let him speak
> Who hath beheld decline upon my brow,
> Or seen my mind's convulsion leave it weak;
> But in this page a record will I seek.
> Not in the air shall these my words disperse,
> Though I be ashes; a far hour shall wreak
> The deep prophetic fulness of this verse,
> And pile on human heads the mountain of my curse!
>
> (134)

"If my voice break forth"; "my minds convulsion"; and, decisively,
"wreak": the stanza is explicitly reaching back to Canto III, especially stanza III. 97, where his effort to "wreak/ My thoughts upon
expression" ended in convulsed frustration. But while the "speech-
less obloquy" (136) of Byron's detractors echoes his earlier "voiceless thought," the symmetry is an illusion called out here that it
might be recognized.

That move locates a key feature of Byron's poetic practice: his
allegiance to "Reason," or what he made the watchword for
Childe Harold Canto IV: "waking Reason" (7). For Byron the
poet, Kant's *sapere aude* meant little unless it took the specific
and active form of *loquere aude*. Canto IV's first ten stanzas say
farewell to "the strange constellations," "fantastic sky," and "wild
universe" of a Romantic address that "came like Truth – and
disappeared like dreams" (6–7). At the outset of Canto IV, Byron
declared himself not just awaking from sleep but "waking [to]
Reason" and its stern rejection of "phantasies unsound." To
write, as he did in 1816, that "I have been cunning in mine
overthrow/ The careful pilot of my proper woe" is a request for
Augusta's – for a reader's – sympathy. It is to be asleep at the wheel

of adversity. Canto IV is after something beyond "The soothing thoughts that spring/ Out of human suffering":

> Meantime I seek no sympathies, nor need;
> The thorns which I have reaped are of the tree
> I planted, – they have torn me, – and I bleed:
> I should have known what fruit would spring from such a seed.

(10)

In 1816, he should have but he didn't and – given his commitment to direct poetic address and its correspondent breeze, living *in medias res* of the world's waste and icy clime – he couldn't. Nor could he, given that poetic posture, deploy a poetry of sentimental reflection like *The Prelude*. The "record [that] he seek[s]" is a direct but impersonal first-person address with no poetic guardrails:

> That curse shall be Forgiveness. – Have I not –
> Hear me, my mother Earth! behold it, Heaven! –
> Have I not had to wrestle with my lot ?
> Have I not suffered things to be forgiven?
> Have I not had my brain seared, my heart riven,
> Hopes sapp'd, name blighted, Life's life lied away?
> And only not to desperation driven,
> Because not altogether of such clay
> As rots into the souls of those whom I survey.

(135)

This Forgiveness Curse is shocking because its candor makes no ordinary sense in any sense. It is a fearful curse as well as a prayer for love and forgiveness. It is all-embracing, the expression itself – Byron's act – being completely swept up in (swept away by?) its painful judgment and behindhand, equivocal forgiveness. It is a knowing and daring poetic show-and-tell where Byron's "thoughts of worst or best" (*Don Juan* XV. 3) have been told but have not been torn or told apart. This is Language being exposed at its worst and best by Byron's act of speaking what Language can only deliver as expressive contradictions, the language of punishment confounding the language of forgiveness, blessing with cursing. Reading it one scarcely knows what to think or say. And so you leave it wondering: after such revelation, what forgiveness – or what judgment?

These contradictions cannot be resolved in language; they can only be enacted and, in that event, escape the threat of what Byron deplored in *Don Juan* as poetry's evasive "dissimulation[s]" (XV. 3). His most aggressive demonstration of that view in the Forgiveness Curse passage comes in the stanza that made a candid display of the unresolvable contradiction pervading even the great Christian injunction to forgive one's enemies. This was exactly the stanza that his monitors back in London, his publisher and his friends, told him he had to remove.[28]

> If to forgive be "heaping coals of fire"
> As God hath spoken – on the heads of foes
> Mine should be a Volcano – and rise higher
> Than o'er the Titans crushed Olympus rose
> Than Athos soars, or blazing Aetna glows:
> True – they who stung were creeping things – but what
> Than serpent's teeth infects with deadlier throes.
> The Lion may be goaded by the gnat –
> Who sucks the slumberer's blood – the Eagle? no, the Bat.

(135a)

No longer silent or slumbering, Byron quotes that inconvenient New Testament passage (Romans 12: 20) to drag his Christian judges before the bar. And he is going beyond the cautionary thought of Matthew 7: 1–2 ("Judge not, that ye be not judged. For with what judgment ye judge, ye shall be judged: and with what measure ye mete, it shall be measured to you again"). He is arguing that their accusations are so righteous and hypocritical as to require positive chastisement.

Christian forgiveness "does not forgive at all," as the fool
Wamba points out in *Ivanhoe*, when it assumes the authority of
the knowledge of good and evil. But as Byron calls the "dread
Power" of Nemesis to show that the Christian scale of Justice is
fatally "unbalanced," the language of his own indictment, extrava-
gantly unbalanced, turns fatefully around. "Doomed to inflict or
bear" (*Childe Harold* III. 71) does not give a nearly adequate
account of the dialectic of righteous judgment. The Forgiveness
Curse stanzas rewrite judgment as "doomed to inflict *and* bear."
Wrapping his cursed prayer in the language of cruelty and sorrow,
Byron shows that the armor of righteousness is a shirt of Nessus, as
Blake too insisted:

> [M]y Clothing shall be Cruelty
> And I will put on Holiness as a breast & as a helmet
> And all my ornaments shall be of the gold of broken hearts
> And the precious stones of anxiety & care & desperation & death
> And repentance for sin & sorrow & punishment & fear
> (*Milton* 18/20: 20–24)

Because Byron's verse is always more personal than Blake's,
even when he is working a high style, it often forces itself to an
unsettling limit of expression. The culminating stanza of the
Forgiveness Curse passage is a notable instance.

> But I have lived, and have not lived in vain:
> My mind may lose its force, my blood its fire,
> And my frame perish even in conquering pain,
> But there is that within me which shall tire
> Torture and Time, and breathe when I expire;
> Something unearthly, which they deem not of,
> Like the remembered tone of a mute lyre,
> Shall on their softened spirits sink, and move
> In hearts all rocky now the late remorse of love.

(137)

Echoing the mood of the "Stanzas to Augusta," the first five lines
mark a precipitous descent from the tone of self-lacerating right-
eousness that Byron sustained through three climactic stanzas
(135, 135a, 136). The semicolon at the end of the fifth line of
stanza 137 half closes that syntactic unit, but only "half" because
"Something unearthly, which they deem not of" is being torqued
into two syntaxes: in apposition to "there is that within me" and as
the subject of "shall . . . sink." The former is the Promethean "fire"
that, even low burning, can "tire/ Torture and Time"; the latter is
"Something unearthly" and identified only by a cunning simile:
"like the remembered tone of a mute lyre."

The lines promise that this remembered music will move hard
hearts to "the late remorse of love." How and why that will happen
is difficult to understand because the pivotal phrase – "mute lyre" – is
an impossible to miss wordplay that replays the ancient paradox of
the lying Cretan. Certainly it stands in the sharpest contrast to the
uncurbed address now being shut down. The Byronic Hero's mute
lying differs from "learning to lie with silence" only because it makes
no effort to "*seem* true." As "defensive paradox," it is not false; it is
self-lacerating. Here and now, in any case, its "tone" is just a memory
since the Forgiveness Curse practices candid speech. *Don Juan* will
hold nothing back ("I *don't hint*, but *speak out*" *Don Juan* XI. 88):
no hinting even when he's hinting. Everything gets outspoken.

In that context, what can this insinuating music signify? How
will the recollection of Byron's self-strangled speech soften hard
hearts, moving them "to the late remorse of love"? The passage
closes on a note of expressive darkness most visible in that final
ambiguous phrase "remorse of love." Is it love or the loss of love
that is belatedly regretted? One thinks of *Don Juan*'s unnerving
proverb that, "soon or late, Love is his own avenger" (IV. 73).
Here is Byron once again foreseeing a visionary company of The
Less Deceived – pessimistic and thoughtful, cynical and
sympathetic.

III

The blowup precipitated by *Cain* in 1822 has had a long cultural afterlife, including the Mental Fight among scholars, still engaged, about Blake's representation of Byron in *The Ghost of Abel* and, as we'll see, in his last engraved work, the *Laocoön*. The controversy hangs on what Blake meant by identifying Byron with the prophet Elijah. Most scholars have read it as an endorsement of Byron's controversial life and work, and in particular of *Cain*.[29] But two prominent Blake scholars, Leslie Tannenbaum and W. H. Stevenson, have demurred.[30]

The action of *The Ghost of Abel* follows upon the question that introduces the action: "Can a Poet doubt the Visions of Jehovah?" Tannenbaum/Stevenson assume that the answer to this rhetorical question has to be no because, in their reading, *The Ghost of Abel* promotes a New Testament vision of absolute faith based on "forgiveness and reconciliation" (Stevenson 860). *The Ghost of Abel*'s climactic Chorus of Angels, Tannenbaum writes, maps "a progressive movement from the primitive concept of propitiatory atonement in *Genesis* 4 to the prophetic attack on false atone-ment – Elijah-Byron's iconoclastic reinterpretation of the Genesis story – to Blake's announcement of the true atonement represented by Christ" (Tannenbaum 364). In this view, Byron's *Cain* has not escaped the "alien and inhospitable universe" (Tannenbaum 364) of the Old Testament. Raging in the wilderness of the restored thrones of Europe, Byron wrote a play that "doubt[ed] the Visions of Jehovah."

If we enlarge the context of the Blake/Byron nexus, we get a different view of this controversy. Like Elijah in King Ahab's Israel, Blake's Byron is indeed plunged into the "alien and inhos-pitable universe" of the England and Europe of 1821–1822. That is the universe addressed by and depicted in *The Ghost of Abel*, which consists of a play, a counter-play (a vision within the play), a choral finale, and then a final illustration glossing the whole work with a revelation of the world in which it lives and moves and has its resistant being.

The initial action is utterly desolate, "A rocky Country" cursed with a covenant founded in death and judgment. When Eve correctly cries out against it as "all a vain delusion/ This Death & this Life & this Jehovah!" the visionary play within the play opens with "A Voice ... heard coming on." It is the Voice of the Ghost of Abel crying out for vengeance in words that echo both *The Two Foscari* and *Leviticus*: "Life for Life! Life for Life!"

Tannenbaum and Stevenson read the visionary action that follows this event as a redemptive promise grounded in "the Forgiveness of Sins" and attested by an angelic chorus singing of "Peace Brotherhood and Love." And while that is a truthful and accurate reading, it is far from the whole story Blake is retelling. The "Revelation ... Seen by William Blake" in these "Visions of Jehovah" – the work's subtitle – is more demanding.

Look closely at the central action as Satan "arises" from Abel's grave "*Armed in glittering scales with a Crown & a Spear*":

Satan – I will have Human Blood & not the blood of Bulls or Goats
And no Atonement O Jehovah the Elohim live on Sacrifice
Of Men: hence I am God of Men: Thou Human O Jehovah.
By the Rock & Oak of the Druid creeping Mistletoe & Thorn
Cains City built with Human Blood, not Blood of Bulls & Goats
Thou shalt Thyself be Sacrificed to Me thy God on Calvary
Jehovah – Such is My Will. *Thunders*
                         that Thou Thyself go to Eternal Death
In Self Annihilation even till Satan Self-subdud Put off Satan
Into the Bottomless Abyss whose torment arises for ever & ever.
           On each side a Chorus of Angels entering Sing the following
The Elohim of the Heathen Swore Vengeance for Sin! Then Thou stoodst
Forth O Elohim Jehovah! in the midst of the darkness of the Oath! All
   Clothed

In Thy Covenant of the Forgiveness of Sins: Death O Holy!
  Is this Brotherhood
The Elohim saw their Oath Eternal Fire; they rolled apart
  trembling over The
Mercy Seat: each in his station fixt in the Firmament
  by Peace Brotherhood and

Love.
The Curtain falls –

Though the "Chorus of Angels" hymns "Thy Covenant of the Forgiveness of Sins," Blake's regulative formula of redemption, here Blake presents it as a covenant of judgment. The doubled identity of a "Heathen" Jehovah – explicitly "Elohim Jehovah" – is forecast when the "will" of Satan – "I will have Human Blood" – is echoed and endorsed by Jehovah: "Such is My Will."

The paradox is extreme but precise. Opposed to "Atonement," Satan desires an eternity of vengeance for sin and evil. So when he prophecies (truthfully) that "thou Human" Jehovah "shalt Thyself be Sacrificed to Me thy God on Calvary," Satan knows that he is the God of the Jehovah of an atonement by stipulated human sacrifice, in this case the crucifixion of Jesus. Unlike what happens in Blake's *Milton*, in *The Ghost of Abel* neither Satan nor Jehovah choose to "go to Eternal Death." Rather, entering Satan's will to judgment, neither Jehovah nor Satan choose "Self Annihilation," though Jehovah decrees it for Satan. So are judgment and right-eousness perpetuated in Jehovah's last judgment (and fearful vision): Satan being cast "Into the Bottomless Abyss whose torment arises for ever & ever."

The "Curtain falls" on a chorus of angels hymning the holiness and "Brotherhood" of this "Bottomless Abyss" of human sacrifice. That Brotherhood and that Abyss are then represented by the illustration at the foot of the plate. It reaches back to the play's opening: the Byronic "Wilderness" scene (seen) as "A rocky Country" with "Eve fainted over the dead body of Abel."

Figure 4 Image of *The Ghost of Abel*, plate 2, Copy A. Reproduced with the permission of the William Blake Archive

Reading the action of the play, one may recall either Blake's remark to Henry Crabb Robinson (Jesus "ought not to have suffered himself to be crucified"), or perhaps the closing verses of the late engraving "To The Accuser Who Is The God of This World":

> Tho thou art Worshipd by the Names Divine
> Of Jesus & Jehovah thou art still
> The Son of Morn in weary Nights decline
> The lost Travellers Dream under the Hill.

The Ghost of Abel ends with an illustration of its world gripped in the tormenting Wastes of Moral Law. It is a critical wheel turned against the angelic hymn: a vision of the finger of God writing *De profundis clamavi* with the finger of the tormented ghost of Abel pointing to "The Voice of Abels Blood" swirling above the corpse of the world.

Not much had changed in English or European society since Blake had written the portentous "Argument" for *The Marriage of Heaven and Hell* some thirty years before. That's why Byron/Elijah is still in the wilderness and why a poet – Byron as well as Blake – can doubt the visions of Jehovah even though the vision of mutual forgiveness might be judged a great, visionary truth: the knowledge of the Tree of Life, even a truth that could set you free (John 8:32). That's why, for Blake, "Imagination is Eternity," not moral ideas or judgments.[31] Without imagination's point of view, one might actually believe that the wilderness cry of Byron's *Cain* was untruth, its moral detractors in the English press the Children of Light, and even that Blake's *Jerusalem* had built Jerusalem in the waste and icy climes of 1820s England and Europe.

When Blake defaced the first page of the text of *Jerusalem*, he was letting his readers see that no one should have any illusions about what art can and can't do. A vision of the world from the point of view of Eternity is not likely to be a pretty picture. Here is one of Blake's – a vision of salvation, of going to Eternal Death – that he dared to frame as a bacchic ceremony of Eucharistic feast and sexual crucifixion:

> But in the Wine-presses the Human grapes sing not, nor dance
> They howl & writhe in shoals of torment; in fierce flames consuming,
> In chains of iron & in dungeons circled with ceaseless fires.
> In pits & dens & shades of death: in shapes of torment & woe.
> The plates & screws & wracks & saws & cords & fires & cisterns
> The cruel joys of Luvahs Daughters lacerating with knives
> And whips their Victims & the deadly sport of Luvahs Sons.
> They dance around the dying, & they drink the howl & groan
> They catch the shrieks in cups of gold, they hand them to one another:
> These are the sports of love, & these the sweet delights of amorous play
> Tears of the grape, the death sweat of the cluster the last sigh
> Of the mild youth who listens to the lureing songs of Luvah.
>
>   (*Milton* 27/29: 30–41)

III

Like Julia Wright, most readers of Blake's *Laocoön* situate it in the context of the art-historical controversy the statue provoked.[32] So far as I'm aware, no scholar has thought to connect Blake's last engraved work with Byron's celebrated stanza 160 in *Childe Harold* Canto IV, the ekphrasis of the Vatican *Laocoön*. Making that connection, however, underscores a clear symmetry between Blake's long-standing attack on neoclassical ideas and ideals and Byron's afflicted poetics, especially as they played out in his Italian tour of Western art, for which that stanza is a virtual epitome. *Childe Harold* IV's map of the dark backward and abysm of historical passage makes a dour rhyme with Blake's vision of the struggle of "Empire against Art" – a heritage of violence that Blake inscribed in all the void regions of his engraving: of "Greece & Rome," of "War & Misery & Heroism," of "Morality" and "NATURAL MAN" and "Money" and "Antichrist Science" and "tax" and "the Two Impossibilities Chastity & Abstinence the Gods of the Heathen."

Figure 5 Image of *Laocoön*, plate 1, Copy B. Reproduced with the permission of the William Blake Archive

Had Byron's notorious libertine life become one of Blake's touchstones for those two impossibilities? Certainly he could have been drawn back to Byron in 1825, to complete the work he had begun on the *Laocoön* ten years before, if he had read Byron's latest attack on money and empire in *The Age of Bronze* (1823).[33]

Wright argues that Blake's last engraving gave a brilliant *coup de gras* to the neoclassical ideal of "the orderly structure of verbal media" (Wright 113). "A multi-media refutation of contemporary art theory and the cultural values it supported" (Wright 121), the engraving's interstices are filled with verbal tags designedly transformed from aphoristic truths to texts caught up, like the represented figures, in a disordered clash of struggling ideas. The result is a vision of an art whose "design shatters sequence as well as completion" (Wright 114).

That view makes the engraving a performative proof of the argument advanced about art and poetry in *On Homers Poetry* and *On Virgil* (1822): that it ought to have nothing to do with either "unity" or "morality" ("Unity & Morality, are secondary considerations & belong to Philosophy & not to Poetry" Erdman 270). On this face of the matter, Blake seems far removed from the Byron who praised Pope and the Augustans, defended "waking Reason" as "our last and only place of refuge," spent his life ruminating on the art and history of the ancient world, and even proclaimed – irreverently – the "regularity of [*Don Juan*'s] design" and its moral purpose (*Don Juan* I. 7). But, in all those respects, Byron's face was wearing a mask of truths that were quite congruent with Blake's judgments – a mask worn according to the formula later made explicit by Oscar Wilde: "Give [a man] a mask and he will tell you the truth."[34] *The Ghost of Abel* tells us how well Blake read the truths of Byron's poetic masquerades. But it also shows that he saw Byron, like Elijah, in a wilderness flight and in need of the "still, small voice" (1 Kings 19: 12–15) of a "Revelation" like *The Ghost of Abel*.

To Blake's imagination, the ancient pagan artist of *Laocoön* and the modern infidel poet are both struggling within their own cultural traditions, which, in Blake's reading, at once drive and frustrate the desire to get "Naked Beauty displayed."[35] So does Blake's engraving bring a notable commentary to Byron's ekphrastic response to the Vatican *Laocoön*.

> Or, turning to the Vatican, go see
> Laocoön's torture dignifying pain, –
> A father's love and mortal's agony
> With an immortal's patience blending: vain
> The struggle; vain, against the coiling strain
> And gripe, and deepening of the dragon's grasp,
> The old man's clench; the long envenomed chain
> Rivets the living links, – the enormous asp
> Enforces pang on pang, and stifles gasp on gasp.

(stanza 160)

Those broken lines show how artfully Byron could wield the Spenserian stanza, which he received as a complex and dignified form, but – as here – delivered over to the expression of torment and trial. Like Manfred, Byron learned to make the "torture" of his writing life "tributary to his [poetic] will" (*Manfred* II. 4. 185). Even Tennyson – in *Maud* – would run a cold reprise on this sort of spasmodic verse, and, from *Sordello* forward, Browning made careful studies of Byron's diremptive song.

Blake's prophetic works run a similarly disturbed and energetic prosody that reaches its spectacular finale in the *Laocoön* engraving. He is a seer of spiritual extremity and the *Laocoön* is as much an act of aesthetic self-reflection as a commentary on Byron-as-Laocoön. In Blake's prophetic books, the lark-and-flower hymns – "Vision[s] of the lamentation of Beulah over Ololon" (*Milton* plate 31/34) – stand out because they are rare events in his calamitous tales of creation and redemption. If we think Blake's ideology of "mutual forgiveness of sins" casts a soothing spell of comfort, we surely falsify his works' aggressive and bedeviled qualities: what he himself gloried to call his "Gothic" style. "Going to Eternal Death" is no walk in the park. On the contrary, it is still the strait gate.

But one does register a significant difference between the "Torments of Love and Jealousy" that both men's work track so closely. The comic pathos of *Don Juan* – Byron's insolent response to God's laughter in *Paradise Lost* – is not a style in Blake's repertoire. Blake cultivates a far more direct address because his works and his words are normally, as he often declared, "dictated from Eternity." Byron's come straight from the "unfathomed gulfs of guile" of a heart he knows too well – a heart whose "imagination," as the demonic God of the Old Testament understood, "is evil continually" (Genesis 8: 21). For all the similar revelations each bring to their benighted worlds, Byron's accounts nearly always *feel* more painful because, unlike Blake, he is still in love with all the ruinous productions of the West and their still living Muses: all "the lady Carolines and Franceses" (*Don Juan* IX. 80). But, to Blake, the contemporary cultural remains of ancient Greece and Rome are in a fundamental sense contemptible. Indeed, he can't even look at the Vatican's *Laocoön* without telling us it is a miserable copy of a work of "HEBREW ART" and that its proper title is יְהֹוָה [Yod] *& his two Sons Satan & Adam*.

Or rather showing and telling us. *Laocoön* is an argument by practical performance, the last of his three great works executed in that mode: *The Marriage of Heaven and Hell, Milton: A Poem in Two Books*, and finally יְהֹוָה [Yod] *& his two Sons Satan & Adam*. In that respect, it mirrors Byron's methodical verse: arguments driven by practical example, not by expository precept. For both men, the office of poetry was not the pursuit – vain in both senses – of "the Knowledge of Good & Evil," but the representation of human life struggling to persist in a dissimulate world where "few men dare show their thoughts of worst or best." Life goes on in a world of Good and Evil.

Look at the text curving around the right hand of Laocoön. The gesture signals an arm raised up against an inevitable defeat. And it is glossed with these words: "Without Unceasing Practise nothing can be done Practise is Art If you leave off you are Lost." Blake wasn't the first or the last person to salute the "baffled energy" of Byron's art or to recognize that its relentlessness was carried far less by his ideas than by his artfulness: verse of sharp and practiced perversities, the embattled prophet Byron in the Wilderness of the Age of Cant.

6

The Stubborn Foe
Bad Verse and the Poetry of Action

Son siècle épouvanté de n'avoir pas connu
Que la mort triomphait dans cette voix étrange!
  (Stéphane Mallarmé, "Le Tombeau d' Edgar Poe")

[S]tyle is the difference,
a way of doing,
a way of being done.

(Charles Bukowski, "Style")

Many are as certain that Mallarmé, the most cultivated of poets, did not write bad verse as they are that Poe and Bukowski did – Poe in disturbingly cold designs, Bukowski in coarse and ugly registers. So we are arrested when Bukowski brazenly reads us a poetic lecture on style and scandalized when we watch Mallarmé, like Baudelaire before and Valéry after, tell a nervously cultured world that Poe was its alien angel. In each case, fairly settled norms and expectations about poetry and poetics are being fairly unsettled.

Behind both of those moves and all three men stands the disruption of Byron and his work's gravity field of contradictions. Though he was hardly the first to write bad verse, no English poet before Byron made the question of bad poetry such an urgent cultural problem, not even Pope. This happened because Byron's work undermined a broad range of judgments about cultural mores, poetry, and poetics – most especially about whether the criteria for making judgments about bad poetry should be broadly ethical or more strictly poetic.

Francis Jeffrey's long 1822 review essay of Byron's work – the publication of *Cain* was its immediate occasion – illuminates some of the basic difficulties, what Jeffrey called the "paradox" of Byron's poetry (458).[1] On the one hand, his "genius" – his eminence and perhaps even his preeminence – was, for Jeffrey, beyond question, and granted even by some of his fiercest detractors; on the other hand, Jeffrey agreed with most recognized custodians of culture who found "the tendency of his writings to be [so] immoral" as to threaten the very foundations of social order by "destroy[ing] all belief in the reality of virtue" (448).

Because Byron's sharpest critics judged that he had purposely devoted his talents to wickedness, he seemed to many the demonic leader of what Southey called the Satanic School of poetry. Sympathizing with Southey's cultural fears, Jeffrey registered but couldn't resolve his Byronic paradox. This happened because his response to what Walter Scott called Byron's "inexhaustible resources" was as complete and wholehearted as his response to Southey's moral charges.

We have not been detractors from Lord Byron's fame, nor the friends of his detractors ... we are ... most sincere admirers of Lord Byron's genius – and have always felt a pride and an interest in his fame [since] his poems abound with sentiments of great dignity and tenderness, as well as passages of infinite sublimity and beauty. But their general tendency we believe to be in the highest degree pernicious; and we even think that it is chiefly by means of the fine and lofty sentiments they contain, that they acquire their most fatal power of corruption.

(457)

But if Jeffrey didn't think – as he added – "that Lord B. had any mischievous intention" for his scandalous works, what did he think Byron was trying to do? Forty pages of generous quotation and close commentary can't say.

In this context – the moral character of Byron and his poetry – Shelley's views are important. While he judged Byron the supreme poet of the period in England, his letter to Thomas Love Peacock on the fourth canto of *Childe Harold* shows how his civilized ideals put him at odds with Byron and some of Byron's most important works. No critic ever wrote more sharply against Byron than this.

> The spirit in which it is written is, if insane, the most wicked & mischievous insanity that ever was given forth. It is a kind of obstinate & selfwilled folly in which he hardens himself. I remonstrated with him in vain on the tone of mind from which such a view of things alone arises. For its real root is very different from its apparent one, & nothing can be less sublime than the true source of these expressions of contempt & desperation. The fact is, that first, the Italian women are perhaps the most contemptible of all who exist under the moon; the most ignorant, the most disgusting, the most bigotted, the most filthy. Countesses smell so of garlick that an ordinary Englishman cannot approach them. Well, L[ord] B[yron] is familiar with the lowest sort of these women, the people his *gondolieri* pick up in the streets. He allows fathers & mothers to bargain with him for their daughters, & though this is common enough in Italy, yet for an Englishman to encourage such sickening vice is a melancholy thing. He associates with wretches who seem almost to have lost the gait & phisiognomy of man, & who do not scruple to avow practices which are not only not named but I believe seldom even conceived in England.[2]

That is more than a judgment on *Childe Harold*. Giving a firsthand report of Byron's life in Italy, he goes on to fashion a biographical gloss on Byron's other recent publication, *Beppo*, Byron's act of homage to his beloved Venice. Though "the seat of all dissoluteness" to the fastidious English specifically addressed by the poem, Byron's "fairy city of the heart" (*Childe Harold* IV. 18) uprises in *Beppo* as "a pleasant place" (41), at once earthy and magical.[3]

As "an Englishman," Shelley recoils from the "sickening vice[s]" of Byron's Italy and "practices which are not only not named but I believe seldom even conceived in England." These remarks, as we shall shortly see, are deeply pertinent for understanding the sources of Byron's bad poetry. For now, it's enough to register the irony that while Shelley shrank from the dissoluteness celebrated in *Beppo*, three years later, he would judge that *Don Juan*, forecast by *Beppo*, had for him "the stamp of immortality ... It fulfils ... what I have long preached of producing – something wholly new and relative to the age, and yet surpassingly beautiful."[4]

Unlike Jeffrey, Shelley did not see "paradox" in Byron's contradictions. Rather, they were the natural outcome of the disappointed hopes in revolutionary political reform experienced by "generous and amiable natures" (ix) like Byron's.[5] This is the explicit argument of the "Preface" to *The Revolt of Islam* (1818).

Thus many of the most ardent and tender-hearted of the worshippers of public good have been morally ruined by what a partial glimpse of the events they deplored, appeared to show as the melancholy desolation of all their cherished hopes. Hence gloom and misanthropy have become the characteristics of the age in which we live, the solace of a disappointment that unconsciously finds relief only in the wilful exaggeration of its own despair.

(xi)

The comments reflect Shelley's Enlightenment conviction that the failure of the Revolution was "produced by a defect of correspondence between the knowledge existing in society and the improvement or gradual abolition of political institutions" (ix). Byron's "gloom and misanthropy" represented "a wilful exaggeration of ... despair" before that utopian prospect. But, adapting a more strictly materialist line of Enlightenment thought, Byron judged human vice and virtue in far more primitive and physical terms than Shelley. "France got drunk with blood to vomit crime"; "Rotting from sire to son, from age to age": the shocking language of Canto IV abandons abstract Enlightenment explanations like Shelley's. It issues a set of relentless prophetic warnings, alternately brutal and lamenting, against the perils of transhuman fantasies. Blake's humanist formula – "Attempting to become more than man we become less" (*The Four Zoas*, "Night the Ninth" 709) – is written across the whole of Byron's work. In this case, the course of the French Revolution – the story of the second fall – is simply – dismally – presented as a familiar, a continuing, and a never-ending story – "Averr'd and known – and daily, hourly seen" (*Childe Harold* IV. 95).

Echoing the most conservative voices of his age, Shelley called Byronic malaise a "wilful exaggeration of despair." But of those three keywords, only "wilful" is precise (an *exaggeration* of despair?). Byron's verse is rather a willful and repeated engagement with morally equivocal conditions that are desperate because unrecognized. As Jeffrey regretted to observe, "Our notions of right and wrong are ... confounded [and] our confidence in virtue shaken to the foundations" (449) by Byron's poetic address, and virtually all quarters of English society except the radical press agreed. But Byron seriously questioned those foundations on the grounds – very solid religious grounds – that individuals ought to prosecute their notions of right and wrong in fear and trembling.

Jeffrey's critical reflections on Julia in the first canto of *Don Juan* are instructive. Judging her a "shameless and abandoned woman," he was dumbfounded that she could end by writing "an epistle breathing the very spirit of warm, devoted, pure and unalterable love" (450). But if we try to read the poem in the same spirit in which the author had written it, it's clear Jeffrey has it all pretty much exactly backward. Touching and comical in her naiveté, Julia is mercilessly delivered to a story Byron fashions to celebrate her natural feelings and to deplore the social conditions that could judge her "a shameless and abandoned woman." Besides, if her love for Juan is faithful to the end, as it is, the letter she writes is far more insidious than Jeffrey realizes. It implicitly passes a calamitous judgment on the conventional ideologies of "warm, devoted, pure and unalterable love" in which Juan is himself beginning his own gradual, calamitous course of instruction.

Byron's verse has succeeded in confounding Jeffrey's conventional views, but it has not moved him to rethink them. Yet Jeffrey's confounded reading of *Don Juan* takes the measure of such verse because it is a negative reflection of Byron's own judgment on contemporary poetry and poetics, whose desperate condition he saw reflected in himself and his own self-deceptions, not least his tormented and failed pursuit of "warm, devoted, pure and unalterable love."

Henry Brougham exposed the dishonesty that pervaded *Hours of Idleness*, and Byron began to take that lesson to heart in *English Bards and Scotch Reviewers*. But that he was prepared for Brougham's severe truth-telling is clear from the truest poem in the deplorable *Hours of Idleness*, "Damaetas." Byron launched it in masquerade.

> In law an infant, and in years a boy,
> In mind a slave to every vicious joy,
> From every sense of shame and virtue wean'd;
> In lies an adept, in deceit a fiend;
> Versed in hypocrisy, while yet a child;
> Fickle as wind, of inclinations wild;
> Woman his dupe, his heedless friend a tool;
> Old in the world, though scarcely broke from school;
> Damaetas ran through all the maze of sin,
> And found the goal when others just begin:
> Even still conflicting passions shake his soul,
> And bid him drain the dregs of pleasure's bowl;
> But, pall'd with vice, he breaks his former chain,
> And what was once his bliss appears his bane.

(*CPW* I. 51–52)

The poem involves multiple deceptions, the most pertinent concealed in its deceptive title. In the single surviving (partial) manuscript, the copy made in 1821 by Byron's lover Teresa Guiçcioli (who was learning English by transcribing some of Byron's early poems), the title is "My Character." But, writing in 1807, Byron was more circumspect. "Damaetas" is a name he lifted from Theocritus's "Idyll 6," which is a homosexual singing contest between Damoetas [*sic*] and Daphnis that they play out as a dispute about heterosexual wooing.[6] So the poem anticipates the strategy of *Childe Harold's Pilgrimage: A Romaunt* and, even more, the future perfect masterpiece in *Manfred*, "The Incantation." As always with Byron's masquerades, the disguise is revealing. Here the concealment shows that Byron didn't need Brougham to tell him about the "character" he began to make public in *English Bards and Scotch Reviewers* – the man and poet "Just skill'd to know the right and chuse the wrong."

A comparison with Wordsworth is instructive. While *Lyrical Ballads* and its "Preface" launched an attack on the debilities of contemporary poetry and culture, Wordsworth justified his work by identifying with what he represented as an uncorrupted social order of "rural life." Shaped by those virtuous conditions, Wordsworth's thoughts, feelings, and language pass into such verse "that the understanding of the being ... address[ed] ..., if he be in a healthful state of association, must necessarily be in some degree enlightened, and his affections ameliorated" (292). As for the poems and the poet, the relation is complementary: "Poems to which any value can be attached, were never produced on any variety of subjects but by a man, who being possessed of more than usual organic sensibility, had also thought long and deeply" (291).

Poetry installs what Wordsworth called a "contract" drawn up between poet and reader. Its terms were established, as we might say, "from time immemorial" because they reflect the "Effort, and expectation, and desire" (*Prelude* VI. 607–608) of all communicative exchange. But poetry has the special office to reveal "what oft was thought but ne'er so well expressed": in Romantic terms (Wordsworth's formulation), "The soothing thoughts that spring/ Out of human suffering" ("Intimations Ode" 188–189), or (Byron's) the "sluggish misery" that is everywhere "Averr'd and known – and daily, hourly seen." For Wordsworth, his soothing thought is "Not without hope we suffer and we mourn"); for Byron, it's that "no home nor hope nor life" of consequence is possible without first committing to the "hopeless flight" (*Childe Harold's Pilgrimage* III. 70) that he judges the more primal "endurance, and repulse/ Of [an] impenetrable Spirit" ("Prometheus" 41–42).

Byron's contract entails the possibility – perhaps even the necessity – of bad poetry because it assumes that both parties, with and sometimes without knowing it, act from a fatal inheritance of bad faith indexed by the many confounded moral judgments Byron's work provoked. Crucially, he warrants his disastrous music by holding himself out not simply as the poetic mirror of that bad faith but its living exemplar, the hypocrite reader's secret sharer, the *poète maudit*.

Acute to see the danger in Byron's program – the serious cultural problems it raised – Wordsworth thought the case against him should not be made in moral but in artistic terms. After declaring "Fare Thee Well!" "disgusting in sentiment, and in execution contemptible," he went on to argue that Byron's poetic "power," all but universally acknowledged, should be the focus of every attack.

The true way of dealing with these men is to show that they want genuine power. That talents they have, but that these talents are of a *mean* order; and that their productions have no solid basis to rest upon. Allow them to be men of high genius, and they have gained their point and will go on triumphing in their iniquity; demonstrate them to be what in truth they are, in all essentials, Dunces, and I will not say that you will reform them; but by abating their pride you will strip their wickedness of the principal charm in their own eyes.[7]

Coleridge would echo that view in his *Table Talk*: "It seems, to my ear, that there is a sad want of harmony in Lord Byron's verses. Is it not unnatural to be always connecting very great intellectual power with utter depravity?"[8]

Over the next hundred years and more, the case against Byron would shift from charges against his morals to a judgment upon his art. As we've seen, the move was first clearly made when Matthew Arnold used Goethe to argue that Byron had an undistinguished mind. But because Arnold strongly endorsed the "imperishable ... sincerity and strength" of Byron's verse, Wordsworth's line of attack – that his verse was of a "mean" order – would not be fully developed until Eliot went after Byron's "defective sensibility." Being an arresting conversationalist and raconteur, Byron could turn out driving tales that discovered a kind of perfection in the dazzling spectacle of *Don Juan* for which, as Byron said at its start, he "had no plan" at all. But, for Eliot, this casual approach to language and poetry – "Carelessly I sing" – meant that his work was susceptible to all kinds of vulgarities, not least of all in his late masterwork. As a poet, Eliot's Byron was the epitome of Arnold's "Barbarian," a patrician slumming among the nightingales.

Like Arnold, Eliot's essay resolves Jeffrey's paradox by bracketing out the relevance of ethical questions. Nor does Eliot judge, in his essay's most judgmental moment, that Byron's "fake" poetry is dishonest. He doesn't put Byron's sincerity into question at all; he keeps his focus on language and literature. You need a virtuous sensibility – not a virtuous soul – to know the difference between good and bad verse and then act on what you know. In the case of the passage he specifically deplored, Eliot argued that the language got away from Byron, that the closing stanza of Canto 15 was slipshod. Had Eliot considered the stanza's transitional place in the English Cantos narrative, however, he might have wondered why Byron might have wanted to finish the canto on a stanza of limp, commonplace figures.[9] While he could be "careless" to a fault about his writing, as he once told his publisher, he stressed that he worked hard and deliberately ("whatever faults [my verse has] must spring from carelessness and not from labour" (to John Murray, June 6, 1822: *BLJ* 9. 168). *Don Juan*'s "careless" graces and disturbing perversifications were cultivated.

Eliot's was a shrewd move because it exploited Byron's own dismissive comments about poetry and poets. Shrewd but also misleading, as becomes clear when you look closely at the famous passage from Byron's *Journal* (November 24, 1813) where he suggested that literary and intellectual work often exhibited mere "debility of . . . mind" (*BLJ* 3. 219). Notably, he sees no place for himself in the *Gradus ad Parnassum* he sketches, which he even discounts with a critically pertinent note: "I have ranked the names upon my triangle more upon what I believe popular opinion, than any decided opinion of my own" (*BLJ* 3. 220). Besides, in ranking these currently celebrated men, Byron's only unequivocal praise is for Lady Melbourne's prose:

To Lady Melbourne I write with most pleasure – and her answers, so sensible, so *tactique* – I never met with half her talent. If she had been a few years younger, what a fool she would have made of me, had she thought it worth her while, – and I should have lost a valuable and most agreeable *friend*.

(*BLJ* 3. 219)

Recalling his exchanges with the talented Lady Melbourne nourished his scorn for the "importance [of] authorship," provoking him to lay out the special character of his poetic aspirations, which stand sharply opposed to the current "preference of *writers* to *agents* – the mighty stir made about scribbling and scribes."

Who would write, who had any thing better to do? "Action – action – action" – said Demosthenes: "Actions – actions," I say, and not writing, – least of all, rhyme. Look at the querulous and monotonous lives of the "genus;" – except Cervantes, Tasso, Dante, Ariosto, Kleist (who were brave and active citizens), Æschylus, Sophocles, and some other of the antiques also – what a worthless, idle brood it is!

(*BLJ* 3. 220)

This is as pivotal a text for understanding Byron's work as his attack on the language of Cant. He is arguing that unless writing, and especially poetic writing, registers as an action in the actual world, it is just "scribbling." A "debility ... of mind" is Byron's description of defective sensibility.

Twelve days before this *Journal* entry, he sent a letter to William Gifford explaining that *The Bride of Abydos*, which Gifford had just read for John Murray and was then going through the press, was written "to apply my mind to something – any thing but reality" (*BLJ* 3. 161).[10] When he added that it was "the work of a week, and scribbled *stans pede in uno*," we have long learned to underread the remark as a brazen expression of his unseriousness as a poet, as we've also underread his later comment about the composition of *Lara*: that he wrote it "while undressing after coming home from balls-and-masquerades in the year of revelry 1814" (to John Murray, June 6, 1822). Though rarely noted, both comments mark the relation between Byron's writing and his actual life and physical experience. This relation is commonly reduced to a "biographical reading" of the verse, an understandable move that has the often unfortunate result of reducing the poetic action to a matter of moral or psychological interpretation.

The more salient point is what these texts reveal about Byron's quest for a "Poetry of Action." Byron's verse – the verse he sought to practice – is not a message delivery system but a massive *exemplum* of his acts of "Mind" executed as embodied performances. What he wrote to John Hunt in 1823 about his poetry could hardly be more explicit: "I continue to compose for the same reason that I ride, or read, or bathe, or travel – it is a habit" (*BLJ* 10. 123) like other habits, a function of long-lived and desired experience. You read that and can hardly not recall Blake's famous aphorism: "Energy is the only life and is from the Body and Reason is the bound and outward circumference of Energy" (*The Marriage of Heaven and Hell* plate 4). Byron's verse is not just physically grounded in the actual world; it is (literally) a way of living literally that holds out the practice of language as an ideal model for all human intercourse.

His outrageous account of the sources and virtues of *Don Juan* is nothing less than an *ars poetica* for an age that had, as Blake also thought, confused "Morality" and "Poetry."

As to "Don Juan" – confess – confess – you dog – and be candid – that it is the sublime of *that there* sort of writing – it may be bawdy – but is it not good English? It may be profligate – but is it not *life*, is it not *the thing*? – Could any man have written it – who has not lived in the world? – and tooled in a post-chaise? in a hackney coach? in a gondola? against a wall? in a court carriage? in a vis a vis? – on a table? – and under it?

(to Douglas Kinnaird, October 26, 1819: *BLJ* 6. 232)

Is that act of expressive freedom shameful or shameless? Because the brilliant prose raises the question and prevents us from answering it with certainty, a spectacular act of style leaves us abandoned to the precarity of our moral convictions.

II

The passage exposes one of the most difficult and most important issues about poetry and Byron's poetry in particular. It was an issue that forcibly struck him when he was rereading Burns in November and December 1813. Burns's greatness was so apparent that it forced Byron to a critical self-reflection about the influence of class and his Scottish heritage on his work: "What would he have been, if a patrician? We should have had more polish – less force – just as much verse, but no immortality" (*BLJ* 3. 207). Burns's "force" made Byron uncertain about the value of his own "polish."

In Scott's view, however, the class issue was not relevant to assessing the work of his two compatriots. "Rank in life was nothing to either" so far as their poetry was concerned. Not only were they "both great Poets,"

Burns and Byron [were] the most genuine poetical geniuses of my time and half a century before me. We have however many men of high poetical talent, but none of that ever-gushing, and perennial fountain of natural water.[11]

Reading more of Burns a month later – "a quantity of his unpublished, and never-to-be published" prose and verse – Byron found his example even more pressing and provocative:

They are full of oaths and obscene songs. What an antithetical mind! – tenderness, roughness – delicacy, coarseness – sentiment, sensuality – soaring and grovelling, dirt and deity – all mixed up in that one compound of inspired clay!

(*BLJ* 3. 239)

At that point, Byron's published *Journal* was expurgated by Thomas Moore, its first editor, and since the manuscript was subsequently lost (and probably, like Byron's *Memoirs*, destroyed), we don't know what Moore censored. But we do know what Byron was reading: the radical prose and "obscene" verse that Burns's editors were keeping out of circulation. Moore erased the next section of the *Journal*, which, when it resumed, shows Byron must have been citing verse like this:

Ken Ye Na Our Lass, Bess?[12]

O ken ye na oor lass, Bess?
An ' ken ye na our lass, Bess?
Between her lily white thies
She 's biggit a magpie 's nest.

An ' ken ye na our lad, Tam?
An ' ken ye na our lad, Tam?
He 's on o ' a three-fitted stool,
An ' up to the nest he clamb.

An ' what did he there, think ye?
An ' what did he there, think ye?
He brak a ' the eggs o ' the nest,
An ' the white 's ran down her thie.

"Inspired clay" indeed, and the devil's own work to do it justice. "Tenderness, roughness – delicacy, coarseness – sentiment, sensuality soaring and grovelling": Byron almost matches the poem's deeply touching effect by laying out his groping effort to explain what can't be explained but only registered as the "immortality" of such deeply mortal verse. Set it beside the nest-stealing episode in Wordsworth's *Prelude* (I. 326–339) to see Burns's Romantic Profound take the measure of Wordsworth's Romantic Sublime. But, to do Wordsworth justice, he found his way to Burns in "The Idiot Boy," where he could bracket out the profound but for him untouchable subject of erotic desire. You need a strong sense of humor to dare making calls on the Laughing Goddess.

Expurgating Byron is always a bad move – a sign of a defective sensibility even. One can glimpse how splendid this entire passage on Burns must have been from Byron's final comment on what he was reading:

It seems strange; a true voluptuary will never abandon his mind to the grossness of reality. It is by exalting the earthly, the material, the *physique* of our pleasures, by veiling these ideas, by forgetting them altogether, or, at least, never naming them hardly to one's self, that we alone can prevent them from disgusting.

(*BLJ* 3. 239)

Byron is unsettled by the difference he sees between Burns's "force" and his own "patrician" tendency to "exalt" and "veil" "the earthly, the material, the physique of our pleasures." It's apparent that he judges Burns's more direct treatment not just better than his own obliquities, but more strikingly delicate and pure, the very opposite of the "disgusting" effect that a polished style goes in fear of. Indeed, Byron here is inquiring into the issues that were central to Wordsworth's *Lyrical Ballads* experiment with poetic style. But while Byron is venturing out much further and in much deeper than Wordsworth would ever be prepared to go, Burns's achievement would remain "something longed for, never seen" in Byron's lifetime, or by anyone else for many decades to come.

But if – before *Don Juan* – Byron's poetry strangled in the taboo of erotic desire and expression, he understood its linguistic and cultural relevance for those two very different "thing[s] of words": poetry and its insidious (or ludicrous) double, cant. While Henry Brougham made fun of Byron's canting first book of verse, Byron took it all seriously because he knew ("Damaetas") that Brougham told the truth. The event set the watchword for all of his subsequent things of words: canting could not be countered or escaped, and poetrying could not be practiced unless he let his language betray what he kept trying and failing to say. So, when he tells us that his story of Juan's life in England will be forthright – "Ne'er doubt/ *This* – when I speak, I *don't hint*, but *speak out*" (*Don Juan* XI. 88) – well, the poem leaves no doubt that his promise won't, can't, be kept. Byron is always faithful to his language, as the song says, "in my fashion."

But his fidelity was hard won, as we see in the blundering poetic adventure that made him famous, *Childe Harold's Pilgrimage: A Romaunt*. It's amazing that anything eventful should have come from a poem that starts like this:

> Whilome in Albion's isle there dwelt a youth,
> Who ne in virtue's ways did take delight;
> But spent his days in riot most uncouth,
> And vex'd with mirth the drowsy ear of Night.
> Ah, me! in sooth he was a shameless wight,

> Sore given to revel and ungodly glee;
> Few earthly things found favour in his sight
> Save concubines and carnal companie,
> And flaunting wassailers of high and low degree.
>
> (stanza 1)

That's not simply doggerel. It's doggerel practiced by a refractory ("defective") sensibility on an audience whose moral and aesthetic judgment it doesn't trust or take seriously. A similar mistrust motivates Wordsworth's *Lyrical Ballads* project. But Byron's is different and more disturbing because it doesn't invite his audience to sympathize with what is either being written or being said because, while it flaunts its deliberate action, its sole care is for the perverse candor it prosecutes end to end. It is poetry written at zero degree, impressive because so unseemly and shameless.

Nor is Byron just fooling around. He goes on with this for twelve more dismal stanzas, like this:

> Childe Harold was he hight: – but whence his name
> And lineage long, it suits me not to say;
> Suffice it, that perchance they were of fame,
> And had been glorious in another day:
> But one sad losel soils a name for aye,
> However mighty in the olden time;
> Nor all that heralds rake from coffin'd clay,
> Nor florid prose, nor honeyed lies of rhyme,
> Can blazon evil deeds, or consecrate a crime.
>
> (stanza 3)

that culminate in a lyric effusion, Childe Harold's "Good Night," with nine stanzas like this:

> "Come hither, hither, my little page!
> Why dost thou weep and wail?
> Or dost thou dread the billows' rage,
> Or tremble at the gale?

> But dash the tear-drop from thine eye;
>   Our ship is swift and strong:
> Our fleetest falcon scarce can fly
>   More merrily along."

(lines 134–141)

All that is bad poetry with a vengeance because it takes Pope's ironic parody of Longinus, the *Peri Bathous* (1728), to an even deeper dive. Pope's second chapter opens with the thought "That the Bathos, or Profund, is the natural Taste of Man, and in particular, of the present Age."[13] Pope lets us know that, while he recognizes that natural state, he can hold it in critical check. But in *his* "present Age," Byron deliberately moves *in medias res*, writing at what D. G. Rossetti explicitly solicited: "an inner standing point" on his subjects.[14]

Unlike the parodies of Butler, Prior, Swift, or Gay, Byron's verse is disturbing because it leaves us no room to draw a clear distinction between itself and its ostensible subjects: not just Childe Harold but, more importantly, its own linguistic and literary address.

> Oh! many a time and oft had Harold lov'd,
> Or dream'd he lov'd, since Rapture is a dream;
> But now his wayward bosom was unmov'd,
> For not yet had he drunk of Lethe's stream;
> And lately had he learn'd with truth to deem
> Love has no gift so grateful as his wings:
> How fair, how young, how soft soe'er he seem,
> Full from the fount of joy's delicious springs
> Some bitter o'er the flowers its bubbling venom flings.

(I. 82)

It's not simply that Byron is, so to say, sympathetic with Harold; it's that he makes his own verse the index of the Childe's pervading malaise. Nor is any of this an accident. Many a time and oft, as in this stanza, he lets his reader know that his poem's vengeance is self-directed and self-inflicted, what he would later describe as wreaking his thought on his own expression (*Childe Harold* III. 97). So, in the dead language of what Byron wanted to imagine might have been a better world than "the present Age," Byron footnotes this stanza, glossing it as the *fons et origo* of a spoiler's art.

> Medio de fonte leporum
> Surgit amari aliquid quot in insis floribus angat. LUC.
> [from the fountain's central delights upsurges something
>   bitter that chokes its flowers: Lucretius, *De rerum natura* 4.
>   1133–1134]

To later audiences – like ourselves – it can seem inexplicable that such verse, prosecuted for hundreds of stanzas, should have taken its world by storm, as it did. It's true that this dreary verse pilgrimage is punctuated now and then by an arresting passage, like this energetic reflection on the Peninsular War:

> Such be the sons of Spain, and strange her fate!
> They fight for freedom, who were never free,
> A Kingless people for a nerveless state;
> Her vassals combat when their chieftains flee,
> True to the veriest slaves of Treachery:
> Fond of a land which gave them nought but life,
> Pride points the path that leads to liberty;
> Back to the struggle, baffled in the strife,
> War, war is still the cry, "War even to the knife!"

(I. 86)

Or the address to Parnassus that vaults the poem out of its sorry reflections into an experience – also *in medias res* – that is at once immediate and inspiring.

> O, thou Parnassus! whom I now survey,
> Not in the phrenzy of a dreamer's eye,
> Not in the fabled landscape of a lay,
> But soaring snow-clad through thy native sky,
> In the wild pomp of mountain majesty!

(I. 60)

While that moment is fleeting (I. 60–64), it forecasts the poem's most consequential – strictly poetic – event. A chance encounter in mid-November 1809 delivered Byron to an experience that would break – once again briefly but this time in an even more dramatic and personal way – the poem's enervated spells. Passing through the Ambracian Gulf in northwestern Greece, Byron's party stopped for a week near Lutraki to explore the nearby region, homeland of the fiercely independent Suliotes. The evening feast and night "revelrie" that caught Byron's admiring attention – "Their barbarous, yet their not indecent, glee" – drove his verse into a completely different key:

> And, as the flames along their faces gleam'd,
> Their gestures nimble, dark eyes flashing free,
> The long wild locks that to their girdles stream'd,
> While thus in concert they this lay half sang, half scream'd:

> I
> Tambourg! Tambourgi! thy 'larum afar
> Gives hope to the valiant, and promise of war;
> All the sons of the mountains arise at the note,
> Chimariot, Illyrian, and dark Suliote!

> (II. 72; 643–662)

We are not in Kansas anymore – or Southwell, or Nottingham, or London. From the "half sung, half screamed" ballad comes a storm of music that untunes the poem's insipid "Good Night" lyric, and, instead of the sentimental Inez invoked in Cadiz (I. 84–85), a different muse presides:

> 7
> I love the fair face of the maid in her youth,
> Her caresses shall lull me, her music shall soothe;
> Let her bring from the chamber her many-ton'd lyre,
> And sing us a song on the fall of her sire.

8

> Remember the moment when Previsa fell,
> The shrieks of the conquer'd, the conquerors' yell;
> The roofs that we fir'd, and the plunder we shar'd,
> The wealthy we slaughter'd, the lovely we spar'd.
>
> (673–680)

Caught up, like Rimbaud and Hart Crane, in the call of a wild as unsentimental as the world of Achilles, Byron's civilized doors of perception fling open to an archaic world that he enters by composing a pastiche modern Greek ballad. The action uplifts the verse into a muscular transformation of Spenserian prosody that English literature had never heard before, and that Byron would explore and elaborate in *Childe Harold*'s two later cantos.

> Fair Greece! sad relic of departed worth!
> Immortal, though no more! though fallen, great!
> Who now shall lead thy scatter'd children forth,
> And long accustom'd bondage uncreate?
> Not such thy sons who whilome did await,
> The hopeless warriors of a willing doom,
> In bleak Thermopylae's sepulchral strait –
> Oh! who that gallant spirit shall resume,
> Leap from Eurotas' banks, and call thee from the tomb?
>
> (693–701)

The passage (II. 73–76) is a performance of artistic freedom carried out according to his own express precept and call to action: "Who would be free themselves must strike the blow" (721). "Scattered children" is self-consciously global, though the biblical event is also being recalled, "whilome" echoes but dismisses the shameless parody Byron flaunted at the start of Canto I, and "bleak Thermopylae's sepulchral strait" is the first time Byron's verse strikes his signature Promethean gesture of "making Death a Victory" ("Prometheus" 59). Most telling of all is the elliptical syntax of "Not such thy sons" that makes the last five lines so unnerving and provocative. Their import (cultural as well as political) is different, if equally dire, if the sons of this imagination of Greece are the living or the dead, or for that matter – like Byron – citizens of the world or merely poets.

That point – whether the stanza's subject is primarily political or poetic freedom – is held in an uncertain balance. The political valence is carried by the poem's travel itinerary and the elaborate prose notes, where Byron reflects sharply on the imperial policies of England, France, Russia, and Turkey and the ineffectual resistance of the Greeks. But the poetic subject pervades the poem's politics because the journey is first to last a *pilgrimage* to the mythic source of European art and culture. Because that mythic focus is intensified by the poem's regular and self-conscious acts of prosodic attention, the balance always leans to the poetic side. But the bleak account of contemporary societies and politics keeps raising an inconvenient question for the poem and contemporary poetry: Are you of any real consequence? Do you make anything happen, even in the tight little island of literature?

The music of this breakout experience gradually slips and fails, finally overwhelmed by the disheartening prospect of a return to England ("Soon shall thy voice be lost amid the throng/ Of louder minstrels in these later days" II. 94) and the deaths of "The parent, friend, and now the more than friend" II. 96). As an event of poetic style, the final stanzas of Canto II circle back through a Levantine party at Constantinople (II. 78–81) to passages that echo the opening of Canto I. But it is a return with a difference. The enervated ironies that distinguish so much of the poem have mutated to a despair that "leaves the flagging spirit doubly weak" (II. 97). With the Suliote "revelrie" still fresh in the poem's memory, now Byron hears the call of a very different "Revel" – unlike the dissonant song of Suli, a civilized and canting music "vainly loud" and "false to the heart." Drawing attention to that sharp contrast, Byron is recalling the stylistic discovery of November 1809: that his muses live in wild places. The language of their rhapsodes, like Homer – as shocking as their savage songs, gods, and heroes – has deep relevance for contemporary culture. Byron's heart, like Burns's, is in the highlands. From 1812 forward, that music will have no ending for Byron's language and poetry, bearing it "in [his] heart/ Long after it was heard no more."

It took wildly different forms – *The Giaour* and *Manfred*, *Childe Harold*, *Don Juan*, *Cain* – but, in all cases, it involved an exploration of language being tracked "beyond the fitting medium of desire." We hear it in sinister lyrics like "Fare Thee Well!" and "The Incantation" and in forbidden ones like "Stanzas for Music" ("I speak not – I trace not – I breathe not thy name"), each sent into the world wearing camouflage. Eventually, cultivated and even friendly readers would be sorely troubled by a career that moved increasingly out of bounds. William Gifford's disgusted recoil from two of the most extraordinary passages in *The Siege of Corinth* forecasts reactions that grew more insistent with *Manfred*, *Don Juan*, and *Cain*.

It's difficult to feel comfortable or certain about anything Byron wrote. His "defective sensibility" was the mirror in which his readers might find ways to glimpse our "debility … of mind." Moving steadily across that unstable ground, Byron found what he needed in the historiated English language, imperial as it had become. But it wasn't all he needed. Equally important was a commitment to poetic address, the staging area for making "raid[s] on the inarticulate." While Eliot thought the problem lay with the "shabby equipment" of his language, Byron thought that "Good workmen never quarrel with their tools." The equipment would serve. The question was: if you use it, are you prepared to let it take your measure?

Here is a test case – one of the most celebrated lyrics Byron ever published, "She Walks in Beauty," the verses that open his *Hebrew Melodies* collection.

> She walks in beauty, like the night
>   Of cloudless climes and starry skies;
> And all that's best of dark and bright
>   Meet in her aspect and her eyes:
> Thus mellow'd to that tender light
>   Which heaven to gaudy day denies.
>
> One shade the more, one ray the less,
>   Had half impair'd the nameless grace
> Which waves in every raven tress,
>   Or softly lightens o'er her face;
> Where thoughts serenely sweet express,
>   How pure, how dear their dwelling-place.
>
> And on that cheek, and o'er that brow,
>   So soft, so calm, yet eloquent,
> The smiles that win, the tints that glow,
>   But tell of days in goodness spent,
> A mind at peace with all below,
>   A heart whose love is innocent!

If you follow the poem's train of thought, what justifies the conclusions it draws about this woman's mind and heart? That she walks in those things of words – the commonplace expressions – that the verse unwinds? Not that the poem at any point treats those expressions ironically. There is no canting in this melody, but there is also nothing certain. It operates under this fundamental Byronic thought:

> Nothing more true than *not* to trust your senses,
> And yet, what are your other evidences?
>
> (*Don Juan* 14. 2)

Of course we do have other evidences – frail reason, dangerous desire, defenseless imagination – and while each has its humanities, all have only their humanities. Here the evidence of the senses leads the verse and the reader through a series of "desiring fantas[ies]" that the poem's rhetoric – its direct reader address – puts into a grammar of assent. But if we watch Byron yielding to the spell of this creature – Byron's muse come in yet another form – what we see is not her but the enspelled Byron. All the readers I have ever known agree to trust the sense and sensibility Byron lays out. But what he does here is no more or less than what Keats did when he began *Endymion* with a series of brave and unbelievable declarations about poetry as "a thing of beauty" being an imperishable "joy for ever."

And "nameless grace" signals more than an indefinable charm of her person. To this day no one knows who the woman was or if she was real. Consider the difference it would make if you decided the poem's subject was Annabella, or Augusta, or Mrs. Wilmot (a favorite speculation), or indeed someone else. "Nameless" is here as carefully chosen a word as is the "name" of Augusta that Byron carefully chose to leave without a trace in the "Stanzas for Music."

Read in isolation, as it nearly always is, "She Walks in Beauty" is an act of poetry as simple and poignant in its veiled ways, perhaps even as profound, as Burns's direct treatment of young erotic desire in "Ken ye na our Lass, Bess?" But Byron didn't publish it in isolation. He set it at the head of *Hebrew Melodies* (1815), the first of a series of poems in the collection that appear to have little relation to the work's explicit social and political focus. What is it doing there? To address the question, which is more pertinent than it might appear, it helps to retreat briefly from 1815 to look once more at the crisis year of 1813.

There's little question that, from 1809 forward, Byron was bent upon trying to change the world for the better. Scribbling and poetry? "Who would write, who had any thing better to do? 'Action – action – action.'" But by the time he wrote that – late 1813 – he saw how ill-fitted he was for a life of political action. His speechmaking in the House of Lords, if attractive in certain ways, was a clear failure because he could put no faith in political institutions or the men, even those he admired, who served them. The epigram he sent in September 1813 to Lady Melbourne was his farewell to all that:

I passed through Hatfield the night of your *ball* – suppose we had jostled at a turnpike!! – At Bugden I blundered on a Bishop – the Bishop put me in mind of ye Government – the Government of the Governed – & the governed of their *indifference* towards their governors which you must have remarked as to all *parties* – these reflections expectorated as follows – you know I *never* send you my scribblings & when you read these you will wish I never may. –

> Tis said – *Indifference* marks the present time,
> Then hear the reason – though 'tis told in rhyme –
> A King who *can't* – a Prince of Wales who *don't* –
> Patriots who *shan't* – Ministers who *won't* –
> What matters who are *in* or *out* of place
> The *Mad* – the *Bad* – the *Useless* – or the *Base*?
>
> (BLJ 3. 117)

"Though 'tis told in rhyme": Byron joins this grim company by spitting on his epigram in a sympathetic act of revulsion. The tortured couplets underscore how difficult he was finding it to believe that he could turn his literary work into a poetry of consequential action. But the move from scribbling to spitting was not unimportant because it showed Byron he would have to prove the problem on his own pulses. For the next four years, he would prosecute that difficulty as his great subject. It would be consequential because it staged a Byronic Drama whose theatrical action would put his readers to severe tests of their ideas and beliefs.

The severity is declared in the poem that is, from a strictly poetic point of view, the book's touchstone lyric and *ars poetica*, "Sun of the Sleepless!" Though an explicit address to Romantic Imagination, its difference from every other comparable Romantic poem is absolute.

Like Shelley's superb platonic epigram, Byron's poem addresses the "melancholy star" Venus/Hesperus. The comparison is useful because the poems are so different.

> Thou wert the morning star among the living,
> 'Ere thy fair light had fled;
> Now, having died, thou art as Hesperus, giving
> New splendor to the dead.[15]

No Shelleyan splendor comes to the dead from Byron's stern verses, only a fresh encounter with the cold and, in traditional terms, powerless clarities of the Byronic imagination.

> Sun of the sleepless! melancholy star!
> Whose tearful beam glows tremulously far,
> That show'st the darkness thou canst not dispel,
> How like art thou to joy remember'd well!
> So gleams the past, the light of other days,
> Which shines, but warms not with its powerless rays;
> A night-beam Sorrow watcheth to behold,
> Distinct, but distant – clear – but, oh how cold!

It took a clear and cold imagination to see, as Byron sees, that Agamemnon, Iphigenia, and the Trojan War are darkly mirrored in the story of "Jephtha's Daughter," or that the latter should be reprised in the decadent tale of the quisling Jew Herod and his murdered wife Mariamne. Perhaps even more insidious is that Byron's verse texts only refer to Jerusalem by its original Canaanite name, Salem, inevitably if obliquely recalling that the Jews were strangers in a strange land that their God sent them to possess and, if necessary, to hold by acts of exterminating violence. The Assyrians were not the only warriors to come down like a host of wolves on a sheepfold.

Perhaps most telling of all, the dominant Jewish figure in the strictly historical poems is not Moses or David but Saul, whom Byron presents as suffering under "supernatural" torments. In

Hebrew Melodies, he is ultimately as tragic as Agamemnon is in Aeschylus. The "Song of Saul before his Last Battle" replays the barbaric Greek war song "Tambourgi, Tambourgi!" that Byron composed to celebrate the Suliotes. As he told Isaac Nathan, who was shocked that Byron spoke well of Saul and his suicide on Mount Gilboa, Saul should "not to be utterly despised as a coward whom supernatural evils have worn down,"

> nor is it difficult to account for the subsequent weakness of Saul, who was once gloriously surrounded by strength, power, and the approbation of his God, when we perceive that he had sunk from this, to a reliance on his own exertions even for safety. The confidence he possesses; the power he beholds, was all blighted ere he sunk to pusillanimity; in spite of which, I cannot but uphold him originally a brave and estimable man. That he cherished the man fated to destroy him, was more his misfortune than his fault.
>
> (*Fugitive Pieces*, pp. 42–43)[16]

This interesting comment might and probably ought to remind us that Byron was neither proto-Zionist nor anti-Semitic, though it's not difficult to read both out of any number of his poems and letters.[17] To see Byron's position more clearly, it helps to start with what was one of the first poems he wrote for the series, "Magdalen." Although probably composed before any of the other poems that orbit in the unstable solar system of *Hebrew Melodies*, and months before Isaac Nathan approached Byron to write lyrics to the music he had in mind, the poem was never included in the series and even remained unpublished until 1887. In a canny move, Peter Cochran put it at the head of his online edition. In truth, it has the deepest relevance to the *Hebrew Melodies* project.

If you start with the title, you realize the poem is a dramatic monologue spoken at the foot of the cross by Mary Magdalen, the Jewish prostitute whose thousand sins were linked with one virtue, her love for the Jewish radical Jesus. The poem begins with a prophetic vision of a dreadful history of "bloody rites" that will be dated from his deathday. Recollecting the Mass ritual as an "unbloody sacrifice," Byron switches the perspective from liturgical to secular history.

Given the two millennia of disgraceful Christian anti-Semitism, it is important to see that the dramatic perspective, like the source texts, are Jewish. In the second stanza, drawn from Matthew 27, Magdalen sees "struggling crowds" consumed by an "idiotic hatred," stirred to an "eagerness of blood" by the Sanhedrin's and other Jewish leaders' hatred of Jesus. "Salem's giant sin" is not Jewish at all; it is older than the Jews, perhaps even aboriginal.

Remarkably, out of the contemptible charge that Christians cultivated for millennia against Jews – that they were the murderers of Jesus – Byron raises up the original race of Byronic Heroes: a dark company of cursing and accurst Jews, "Yet . . . still enduring all, and all in vain" (11–12).

> Scourged – scorned – unloved – a name for every race
> To spit upon – the chosen of disgrace;
> A people nationless, whom every land
> Receives to punish – and preserves to brand;
> Yet still enduring all, and all in vain,
> The doomed inheritors of scorn and pain,
> Untaught by sufferance, unreclaimed from ill –
> Hating and hated – stubborn Israel still!
>
> ("Magdalen" 19–26)

As Philip Roth might say, that's a Sabbath's Theatre, cruelly unsentimental and bleakly sympathetic. Like all of his tales from 1813 forward, "Magdalen" draws its savage action out of a history moralized by fear. It's one of his many acts of poetry – visions of judgment – that stand against acts of judgment, especially those that have, like Christian anti-Semitism, run for so long on such well-laid iron rails.

In such a world, who walks in beauty? Perhaps "She" isn't a woman at all but simply Byron's loving, figurative memory of the magical Levantine nights of "cloudless climes and starry skies" that haunted him all his life, and where he learned to take a walk on a wild side that could take him even further back, to Never Never Land.

NOTES

1. See Byron's *Letter to John Murray Esq. (1821): Lord Byron. The Complete Miscellaneous Prose*, ed. Andrew Nicholson (Oxford: Clarendon, 1991), 128.
2. *Reading Byron: Poems, Life, Politics* (Liverpool: Liverpool University Press, forthcoming); I quote from the typescript of the book.
3. For Goethe on Byron's poetry, see William Hale White ("Mark Rutherford"), "Byron, Goethe, and Mr. Matthew Arnold," *Contemporary Review* 40 (August 1881): 179–185. See also E. M. Butler's more general study *Byron and Goethe: Analysis of a Passion* (London: Bowes and Bowes, 1956) and G. Wilson Knight, *Poets of Action: Incorporating Essays From the Burning Oracle* (London: Methuen, 1967), chapters 5 and 6.
4. My quotations from Byron's verse are made to *Lord Byron: The Complete Poetical Works*, ed. Jerome McGann, 7 vols. (Oxford: Clarendon, 1983–1992); when necessary, cited here as *CPW*.
5. For an insightful commentary on the context that has shaped the academic misperception of Byron, see James Chandler, "I. A. Richards and Raymond Williams: Reading Poetry, Reading Society," *Critical Inquiry* 46 (2010): 325–352. Chandler argues that Williams's idea of a "structure of feeling" points to the Wordsworthian/Coleridgean norm for

responding to "Romantic feeling" as an ordered and "structured" condition. By contrast, Blake and Byron posit a Lucretian context that puts both poet and reader in a testing engagement with powerfully energetic disorder. Chandler has an interesting discussion of Williams's concern with "drama" that, in my reading of Williams, signals his awareness of the deep fault line running through the normative Romantic theory of sensibility and feeling (see Chapter 6).

6. For Wordsworth's comment, see Lord Houghton, *The Life and Letters of John Keats [1848]: A New Edition* (London: Edward Moxon & Company, 1867), 91. I steal the word "forlorn" from the final stanza of Keats's "Ode to a Nightingale," only one of his searching poetic inquiries into what Byron called "The unreach'd Paradise of our despair" (*Childe Harold* IV. 122).

7. As with so much in Byron scholarship, G. Wilson Knight was the first to reflect on "the evidence of the asterisks" in Byron's work, though in the case of his provocative book Knight focused on the expurgated prose: *Lord Byron's Marriage: The Evidence of the Asterisks* (London: Routledge and K. Paul, 1957).

1 DON JUAN AND THE ENGLISH LANGUAGE

1. *The Diary of Virginia Woolf, vol. 1, 1915–1919*, ed. Anne Olivier Bell, introduction by Quenten Bell (New York: Harcourt Brace Jovanovich, 1977), 180.

2. The scholarship I have found most useful for investigating Byron and Language is the following: Ronald Bottrall, "Byron and the Colloquial Tradition in English Poetry," *Criterion* 18 (1939): 204–224; Marius Bewley, "The Colloquial Mode of Byron," *Scrutiny* 16 (1949): 8–23; J. D. Jump, "*Byron's Don Juan:* Poem or Hold-All" (Thomas Lecture, University College, Swansea, 1968); A. B. England, *Byron's* Don Juan *and Eighteenth-Century Literature: A Study of Some Rhetorical Continuities and Discontinuities* (Lewisburg, PA: Bucknell University Press, 1975); E. Kegel-Brinkgreve, "Byron and Horace," *English Studies* 57.2 (1976): 128–138; Peter Manning, "*Don Juan* and Byron's Imperceptiveness to the English Word," *Studies in Romanticism*

18.2 (1979): 207–233; Edwin Morgan, "Voice, Tone, and Transition in *Don Juan*," *Byron: Wrath and Rhyme*, ed. Alan Bold (London: Vision and Barnes and Noble, 1983): 57–77; Peter Graham, *Don Juan and Regency England* (Charlottesville: University Press of Virginia, 1990); Bernard Beatty, "Continuities and Discontinuities of Language and Voice in Dryden, Pope, and Byron," *Byron: Augustan and Romantic*, ed. Andrew Rutherford (New York: St. Martin's Press, 1990), 117–135; Jane Stabler, "Introduction: Byron and the Poetics of Digression," *Byron, Poetics and History* (Cambridge: Cambridge University Press, 2002), 1–17; Gioia Angioletti, "'I Feel the Improvisatore': Byron, Improvisation, and Romantic Poetics," *British Romanticism and Italian Literature: Translating, Reviewing, Writing*, ed. Laura Bandiera and Diego Saglia (Amsterdam: Rodopi, 2005), 165–180; Richard Cronin, "Words and the Word: The Diction of *Don Juan*," *Romanticism and Religion from William Cowper to Wallace Stevens*, ed. Gavin Hopps and Jane Stabler (Aldershot: Ashgate, 2006), 137–153; Gavin Hopps, "Byron and Grammatical Freedom," *Liberty and Poetic License: New Essays on Byron*, ed. Bernard Beatty, Charles Robinson, and Tony Howe (Liverpool: Liverpool University Press, 2008), 165–180; Jim Cocola, "Renunciations of Rhyme in Byron's *Don Juan*," *Studies in English Literature* 49.4 (2009): 841–862.

3. Robert Southey, *The Life and Correspondence of Robert Southey*, ed. Charles Cuthbert Southey (New York: Harper, 1851), 384. "Treason" and "high treason" were clearly bugbears for Southey. He denounced "treason" twice and "high treason" five times (see 139, 146, 189, 242, 245, 473). Originally written in 1937, Eliot's essay "Byron" was collected in his *On Poetry and Poets* (London: Faber and Faber, 1957), 193–206.

4. In his otherwise dismissive essay, Eliot concluded with some pages of high praise for *Don Juan* (203–206).

5. Letter to John Murray, September 15, 1817, in *Byron's Letters and Journals*. 13 vols. Ed. Leslie A. Marchand (London: John Murray, 1973–1994), 5:265 (hereafter *BLJ*). See the discussions in what follows

of Byron's involvement in the Pope–Bowles controversy, where he confessed his ambivalence about his own "Romantic" writings. For a different take on Byron's remark, see Hermann Fischer, "Byron's 'Wrong Revolutionary Poetical System' and Romanticism," *Byron: Augustan and Romantic*, ed. Andrew Rutherford (New York: St. Martin's Press, 1990), 221–239.

6. Laura Riding Jackson, *The Telling* (New York: Harper and Row, 1973), 66.

7. Wordsworth, "Preface" to *Lyrical Ballads* (1802), in *Wordsworth & Coleridge: Lyrical Ballads*, ed. R. L. Brett and A. R. Jones (London: Methuen and Company, 1963), 244, 249. Hereafter cited parenthetically in the text.

8. I choose that year because of two events that date from 1760, one literary, one political. In 1760, George III ascended to the throne of England, and James Macpherson published his small but greatly influential pamphlet *Fragments of Ancient Poetry, collected in the Highlands of Scotland and translated from the Galic or Erse Language*.

9. See Manning, "*Don Juan* and Byron's Imperceptiveness to the English Word," n. ix.

10. Here and in what follows I quote from *The Poems of T. S. Eliot*. 2 vols. Ed. Christopher Ricks and Jim McCue (Baltimore, MD: Johns Hopkins University Press, 2013), 1:209.

11. This is the text from Byron's holograph manuscript, which differs from the first published version (*CPW* IV. 211).

12. See my essay "Romantic Subjects and Iambic Laws: Episodes in the Early History of Contract Negotiations," *New Literary History* 49.4 (2018): 597–615.

13. Discussing "The *Orlando Furioso* and English Literature," the distinguished Italianist Barbara Reynolds observed that "It was Byron who, above all, possessed an exceptional capacity for assimilating and recommunicating the spirit of Ariosto … his ability to pass from one thing to another with the greatest ease, to throw out reflections apparently casual but full of profundity. The light raillery, the good-natured fun, the tolerant cynicism, the philosophy of humour" (*Orlando Furioso (The Frenzy of Orlando): A Romantic*

Epic by Ludovico Ariosto. 2 vols. Translated with an introduction by Barbara Reynolds (London: Penguin, 1975), 1:83.

14. Byron's medley poetics actually began a bit earlier, in 1816, with *Manfred*. See my *Byron and Romanticism*, ed. James Soderholm (Cambridge: Cambridge University Press, 2002), 193–200. As to the Italian influence, especially Pulci and Casti, Peter Vassallo's *Byron: The Italian Literary Influence* (New York: Macmillan, 1984) remains, alas, the only major study.

15. I allude to Eugene Jolas's Modernist manifesto "Revolution of the Word" (published as a "Proclamation" in the June 1929 double issue of *transition*).

16. That is, the letter of September 15, 1817, cited in note 5.

17. For more complete discussions of what Byron had in mind when he objected to the contemporary "wrong revolutionary poetical system – or systems," see Chapter 4. I lift the phrase "the simple Wordsworth" from John F. Danby, *The Simple Wordsworth: Studies in the Poems 1797–1807* (New York: Barnes and Noble, 1961).

18. The phrase is from "The Recluse" fragment Wordsworth published with *The Excursion*. In his 1821 *Letter to John Murray Esq.*, Byron quoted it derisively (*Miscellaneous Prose*, 156).

19. Michael Scrivener has an incisive discussion of the Jacobin Enlightenment in his *Seditious Allegories: John Thelwall and Jacobin Writing* (University Park: Pennsylvania State University Press, 2001), 37–42: "[R]eligious dissidence ... radical parliamentary reform ... participatory democracy, an expanding public sphere, activism, internationalism, and a rationalistic rigor" (42). Byron's letters of September 15 and 17 and October 23, 1817, bookend the period when he was composing *Beppo*, reading *Biographia Literaria*, and consciously reassessing contemporary poetry – "my own and some others" – in relation to Pope (*BLJ* 5. 265).

20. Consisting only of stanzas 1–2, 4–8, 10–19, 17, the first draft was primarily an argument about poetry and poetics, not politics.

21. Byron replied to Bowles's *The Invariable Principles of Poetry* (1819) in a pair of "letters," only one of which was published at the time (in 1821). A good commentary on the dispute is James Chandler, "The Pope Controversy: Romantic Poetics and the English Canon,"

Critical Inquiry 10.3 (1984): 481–509. See also Peter Cochran's (online) essay and edition: https://petercochran.files.wordpress.com /2009/03/letter_to_john_murray.pdf and Tony Howe, "Uncircumscribing Poetry: Byron, Johnson, and the Bowles Controversy," *Liberty and Poetic License: New Essays on Byron*, ed. Bernard Beatty, Charles Robinson, and Tony Howe (Liverpool: Liverpool University Press, 2008), 206–218, especially 214–215, where he points out the signal difference between Byron's "flat" prose contributions and the comments in *Don Juan*'s "Dedication."

22. See *His Very Self and Voice: Collected Conversations of Lord* Byron, ed. Ernest J. Lovell (New York: Macmillan, 1954), 129.

23. For Blake, see *The Marriage of Heaven and Hell*, Plate 21. Byron's famous remark was made in a letter to Thomas Moore, June 1, 1818 (*BLJ* 6. 46). He repeated it in a slightly different form in his *Letter to John Murray Esq.* (*Miscellaneous Prose* 156).

24. For his critical view of his own involvement in an "erroneous system" of poetical work, see *Miscellaneous Prose* 107, 110, and especially 148–149. James Chandler rightly finds in Byron's prose writings an "awareness of the contradictions in his position" ("The Pope Controversy," 506).

25. *Biographia Literaria.* 2 vols. Ed. James Engell and W. Jackson Bate (Princeton, NJ: Princeton University Press, 1983), 2:73.

26. See *BLJ* 4. 321–324. Byron's enthusiasm for Coleridge's poems is especially clear in his letter to Moore of October 28, 1815.

27. *Christabel; Kubla Khan: A Vision; The Pains of Sleep* (London: John Murray, 1816).

28. Letter of September 17, 1800, in *The Collected Letters of Samuel Taylor Coleridge.* 6 vols. Ed. Earl Leslie Griggs (Oxford: Oxford University Press, 1956–1971), 1:623.

29. Dante, *Paradiso* 33. 145: "l'amor che move il sole e l'altre stele."

30. The most comprehensive treatment of this aspect of Romantic literature is Jeffrey Robinson, *Unfettering Poetry: The Fancy in British Romanticism* (New York: Palgrave Macmillan, 2006); see in particular 2–9.

31. See as well Byron's "[Epigram on Mr. Coke's Philogenitiveness]," *CPW* VII. 74 and 148n. He sent it to Leigh Hunt in a letter of January 1823, commenting "I trust that it is decent."

32. See J. G. Spurzheim's "Preface" to *The Physiognomical System of Drs. Gall and Spurzheim*, second edition (London: Baldwin, Cradock, and Joy, 1815), ix.

33. Rogerson had a notorious reputation for the severity of his remedies. After he became Catherine's private physician in 1776, he was specially charged with checking her lovers for venereal diseases. See Anthony Cross, "John Rogerson: Physician to Catherine the Great," *Canadian Slavic Studies* 4 (1970): 594–601; J. S. Jenkins, "Dr. John Rogerson: A Physician at the Court of Catherine the Great," *Journal of Medical Biography* 10 (2002): 189–193.

34. See Frank Stiling and Bruno Meinecke, "Byron, Don Juan X, xli," *Explicator* (March 1949): article 36.

35. See Hopps's superb essay on Byron's lapses and mistakes, deliberate and otherwise, in "Byron and Grammatical Freedom."

36. My stylistic approach to Byron's meaning to "escape from fiction" should be read in relation to Bernard Beatty's moving religious and philosophic approach in "Fiction's Limit and Eden's Door," *Byron and the Limits of Fiction*, ed. Bernard Beatty and Vincent Newey (Liverpool: Liverpool University Press, 1988), 1–38; see especially 33–34.

37. See also the pages for stanzas 15 and 129, which are similarly defaced.

38. Drummond Bone discusses this feature of *Beppo* in fine detail: see Drummond Bone, "Beppo: The Liberation of Fiction," *Byron and the Limits of Fiction*, ed. Bernard Beatty and Vincent Newey (Liverpool: Liverpool University Press, 1988), 97–125.

39. Byron regularly exploits the *ottava*'s closing couplet to effect different kinds of reversals: compare II. 139, III. 87, V. 3, XVI. 10.

40. Alfred Jarry, *Exploits and Opinions of Doctor Faustroll, 'Pataphysician*, trans. Simon Watson-Taylor with an introduction by Roger Shattuck (1907; Boston: Exact Change, 1996), Book II, Chapter 8.

41. She also forecasts Julia's even more capacious vernacular skills, both oral and literary (*Don Juan* 1. 146–157 and 192–197).

42. Byron's prose note to the penultimate line is about chemistry, not politics, which only reinforces the last line's bizarre, angry turnabout.

43. This general description of *Don Juan's* language might be applied almost exactly to Pulci's *Morgante Maggiore*. While I cannot here take up the subject of the influence of the *Morgante* on *Don Juan*, I hope to do so in a subsequent essay. It is worth pointing out that Byron's medley style also cultivated certain neoclassical features. See Beatty's essay on the influence of Dryden and Pope on Byron.

44. Byron was echoing Pope's "Epistle to Dr. Arbuthnot," 4–5.

45. Paul West, *Byron and the Spoiler's Art* (London: Chatto and Windus, 1960).

46. Eliot put the quotation from Heraclitus as the epigraph to *Four Quartets*.

2 BYRON AGONISTES, 1809–1816

1. See Emily Bernhard Jackson, "Manfred's Mental Theater and the Construction of Knowledge," *Studies in English Literature 1500–1900* 47.4 (2007): 799–824.

2. The literature on the eighteenth-century ballad revival, the rise of antiquarianism, and the turn to philology is massive. For some guides, see the following, and in particular their bibliographies: Nick Groom, *The Making of Percy's Relics* (Oxford: Clarendon, 1999); Martin Myrone and Lucy Peltz, eds., *Producing the Past: Aspects of Antiquarian Culture and Practice 1700–1850* (Oxford: Routledge, 2018, reprinting Ashgate 1999); Joanne Parker and Corinna Wagner, eds. *The Oxford Handbook of Victorian Medievalism* (Oxford: Oxford University Press, 2020); Rosemary Sweet, *Antiquaries: The Discovery of the Past in Eighteenth-Century Britain* (London: Hambledon and London, 2004). For Byron, in particular his interest in Oriental anthropology and history, see Naji Oueijan, *Lord Byron's Oriental World* (Piscataway, NJ: Gorgias Press, 2011).

3. Wordsworth's famous attack on poetic diction has fed a widespread misunderstanding of Pope's poetic language. While I cannot deal with the subject here, it is worth pointing out two things: first, Pope also wrote a famous attack on poetic diction (the *Peri Bathous*); second, his

vocable range – his diction and usage – is very large, much larger than Wordsworth's. While both put a high value on "correct" expression, Wordsworth proceeded by severely limiting his linguistic range. By contrast, Pope relied on his understanding of the rules of poetic decorum – what was appropriate under different expressive conditions. See the citation in Chapter 1, note 9, Geoffrey Tillotson's *Augustan Poetic Diction* (London: Athlone Press, 1964), and most recently, Nicholas Gayle, *Byron and the Best of Poets* (Cambridge: Cambridge Scholars, 2016). While Gayle's close analyses of Byron's verse are especially welcome, the range of Byron's work that he examines is much more limited than, in my view, it might and ought to have been. But his governing view for the book is, I believe, the right perspective to take: "Byron was a deep thinker whose movement of thought – were it to be expressed in musical terms – was contrapuntal in nature" (xv). But I would say with Goethe that a phrase like "deep thinker" can be greatly misleading if it is taken to suggest Byron's work is important for its ideas. See the discussions pp. 99, 109–118, 152–153.

4. *Alexander Pope: The Dunciad*, third edition, ed. James Sutherland (London: Methuen and Company, 1963): 307. I shall be citing Pope from the other volumes in the Twickenham edition.

5. See the antepenultimate poem (no. 48) in Baudelaire's *Petits poèmes en prose* (1869).

6. *The Complete Poetical Works of Sir Walter Scott*, the Cambridge edition, ed. Horace E. Scudder (Boston: Houghton Mifflin Company, 1900), 230.

7. See Johann Peter Eckermann, *Gespräche mit GoetheiIn den letzen Jahren des Lebens* (Leipzig: F. A. Brockhaus, 1868) *passim*; see especially 176 and 133.

8. When Coleridge discusses imagination, he is forced to introduce the concept of a poet's conscious "will." So in *Biographia Literaria*, chapter 14, he speaks of the imagination as "put in action by the will and understanding, and retained under their irremissive, though gentle and unnoticed, control." For an insightful account of the history of the idea of *inventio* into the Romantic period, see Rocío G. Sumillera, *Invention: The Language of English Renaissance Poetics* (Cambridge: Legenda, 2019).

9. The prefatory paragraphs are themselves delivered in different registers. Lines 68–102 differ notably from the rhetorical posture taken in the rest of the passage, and those other sections – lines 7–67 and 103–167 – exhibit sharp modulations. The first long verse paragraph (7–67) begins "Fair clime! Where every season smiles/ Benignant o'er these blessed isles" but ends "So soft the scene, so form'd for joy/ So curst the tyrants that destroy!"

10. In his letter of October 27, 1818, to Richard Woodhouse, Keats took Shakespeare to exemplify his famous phrase for "the poetical Character." Had Keats a less captious view of Pope he might have seen how much in common his idea of "negative capability" had with what Pope, following a long line of traditional commentary, had called Homer's supreme gift: "Invention." See in particular Pope's discussion of Homer's treatment of his characters and his distinction between Homer's "dramatic" narrative and Virgil's more subjective verse (*Alexander Pope: The Iliad of Homer*, ed. Maynard Mack et al. (London: Methuen and Company, 1967), I. 7–8.

11. *Rokeby* was published in January 1813, the first edition of *The Giaour* in early June. This passage was added in the second edition, which came out a month later.

12. Up to 1813, the word "numbers" appears in Byron's verse fourteen times; it specifically means "poetry" eleven times. This is the only instance when he exploits the ambiguity.

13. See the splendid recent essay by Aleksandra Wacławczyk and Adam Mickiewicz, "What Is Aphrodite Laughing At? An Attempt at Interpretation of the Epithet in the Archaic Greek poetry," *Święto – Zabawa – Uroczystość w świecie starożytnym*, ed. Lidia Ożarowska, Karolina Sekita, and Jesse Simo (Sub Lupa, 2011): 133–141. While Byron picks up that tone frequently in *Don Juan*, it is absent from the early tales. The Wacławczyk and Mickiewicz essay is available online: https://studenckakonferencjastarozytnicza.files.wordpress.com /2015/01/schole_06_2011_12_waclawczyk.pdf.

14. In one respect, Keats's ideal of "the Poetical Character" is close to certain key ideas of Byron's. Keatsian "Negative capability" and

Byronic "mobility" are close kin, and when Keats reflects on a poet's chameleonic identification with his creations, he might have cited Homer or, for that matter, *The Giaour*'s bard. Byron would have judged the enlightened "Speculation" that is the value of such poetry for Keats merely "a thing of words without the smallest influence on human actions."

15. My italics. See Partch's *Bitter Music: Collected Journals, Essays, Introductions, and Librettos*, ed. Thomas McGeary (Champaign-Urbana: University of Illinois Press, 2000), 13.

16. See *Edgar Allan Poe: Essays and Reviews*, ed. G. R. Thompson (New York: Library of America, 1984), 52–56. See also the discussion of the pointing of Byron's verse. For Poe's "Grammars," that would be the primary interpretive act.

17. Samuel Johnson, "Milton," *Lives of the English Poets: Waller Milton Cowley* (London: Cassell & Company, 1891), 133.

18. *The Poetry of Byron, Chosen and Arranged by Matthew Arnold* (London: Macmillan 1881), xv.

19. Canto I stanzas 17 – 19 in *Lara* reprise *The Corsair* Canto I stanzas 9–11.

20. In the introduction to his online edition of the two poems, he invokes *The Ivanhoe Game* as his authority for his comical travesty of *The Corsair* (www.newsteadabbeybyronsociety.org/works/downloads/turk_4.pdf). As a critical method, we invented the Ivanhoe Game – and named it such – as a critical rescue operation for a famous work that had for more than one hundred years fallen on evil days and evil tongues. For an introduction to the Ivanhoe Game, see the special issue of *Text Technology* 12.2 (2003) and my essay "Like Leaving the Nile: IVANHOE, a User's Manual" (www2.iath.virginia.edu/jjm2f/old/compass.pdf). Cochran's witty travesty was performed to confirm a judgment of Byron's poem that had grown an academic commonplace.

21. Throughout his learned commentaries on Byron's work, Cochran is committed to the idea of what he calls the "seamless" poem and its correspondent ideal poetics. Because he judges that Byron achieved this in his *ottava rima* work, he has trouble dealing with works like

these, which are anything but seamless. But to my mind, unseamlessness – what Dante judged the poet's "le man che trema" (*Paradiso* 13.78) – is the end-to-end quality, and the glory, of Byron's poetry. Byron told Murray that *Don Juan* was to be a "Human" not a "divine" work. *Childe Harold* and the early tales are every bit as "Human" – in certain respects, even more so.

22. The same note glossed one of *Lara*'s key characters, Ezzelin. Byron was inviting his readers to recall Ezzelino III da Romano (1194–1259), a byword of cruelty and the mortal enemy of the Este family, in particular Azzo VI and Azzo VII.

23. That is, at any rate, the focal point of Byron's entanglement in the forbidden. There were many other scandalous – even taboo – liaisons.

24. The speculation about Byron's personal connection to the first four tales (1813–1814) was rampant at the time.

25. *The Prisoner of Chillon*, 244.

26. This is Bernard Beatty's "general sense of the section": "that [Lara] was known to have had faults in the past but he is now older and changed so – in a series of 'mights' – it is possible that he may be reformed (though it is only a 'might'). He is still proud (where earlier 'haughty') but his brow speaks of past rather than present passions. So 'but his sins/ No more than pleasure from the stripling wins' must fit the general repeated pattern that he might now and in the immediate future no longer be as bad as he had been or, at any rate, in the way that he had been" (from an email correspondence).

27. Francis Jeffrey, "Unsigned review of *The Corsair* and The Bride of Abydos," *Edinburgh Review* 23 (July 1814): 198–229.

28. So the passage as it stands in the first edition – which I give here – does not need any of the emendations that editors have proposed, including the one I adopted in 1981 from the Moore/Wright edition of 1832. The latter has at least the minor merit of not creating more problems than it tries to solve. Byron's irregular grammatical adventures are finely treated by Gavin Hopps, "Byron and Grammatical Freedom," *Liberty and Poetic License: New Essays on Byron*, ed. Bernard Beatty, Tony Howe, and Charles E. Robinson (Liverpool: Liverpool University Press, 2008), 165–179.

29. The histories usually spell his name "Minotto." I have kept Byron's spelling.

30. See the commentary in *CPW* III. 477–481.

31. The work was originally published in 1701. For a good general account of Jones as an historian, see Henry Snyder, "David Jones, Augustan Historian and Pioneer English Annalist," *Huntington Library Quarterly* 44.1 (1980): 11–26. It is pertinent to know that Jones's history of the Turks borrows heavily from the work of other English historians (15). His account of Turkish history, and of the siege in particular, is thoroughly English and "European" in its presentation of the Ottoman Empire.

32. Byron uses this source text exactly – adversely – as he used Castelnau in recounting the Siege of Ishmael episode in *Don Juan* (Cantos VII–VIII). See *CPW* V. 717–735.

33. It is impossible not to think that in his Corinthian explosion Byron was recalling the Venetian attack on the Athenian acropolis in 1687 and Morosini's destructive bombardment of the Parthenon, which he (in)famously called "a 'lucky hit.'"

34. See the "Lines Associated with the Siege of Corinth," the first-person prelude that Byron wrote when he began the poem in 1812 but decided in the end not to include. Specifically dated to Byron's travels in the region in 1810 (1–5), the lines lament the lost comradeship of a company made up of "all tongues and creeds" (18).

35. Recapitulating the scholarship on *The Siege*, Robert MacColl focuses on the "structural opposition" that defines the poem – it is "awash with genuine oppositions" (235) – and works to show that the poem resists the "assimilations" that causal history promotes (245): "'Best Success were Sacrilege': Investigating Antitheses in *The Siege of Corinth*," *Byron and Orientalism*, ed. Peter Cochran (Cambridge: Cambridge Scholars, 2006), 232–245. (Unaccountably, MacColl dates the siege to 1710.) Gavin Hopps looks at the poem from a very different vantage but has interesting things to say about its "superstitious" anomalies: "Inhabiting a Place beyond 'To Be or Not to Be': The Playful Devotions of Byron and Coleridge," *Coleridge Bulletin*, new series 25 (2005): 15–39.

36. *CPW* III. 485, 487: Gifford called it "despicable stuff."

3 MANFRED: ONE WORD FOR MERCY

1. This chapter extends the discussion of the medley style of *Manfred* that I gave in *Byron and Wordsworth* (Nottingham: Byron Foundation, University of Nottingham, 1999); it is reprinted in *Byron and Romanticism*, ed. James Soderholm (Cambridge: Cambridge University Press, 2002).

2. It might be argued (by a certain kind of theologian – for example, by Goethe) that the demons are acting through the grace of God. But Manfred emphatically rejects such a view as an irritating irrelevance (for which the Abbot is the spokesperson).

3. Burns supplies good instances of the Scots usage – for instance, in "Tam O'Shanter," 141.

4. Although scholars and editors – myself included – have not interpreted it this way, the passage suggests that Astarte committed suicide after gazing on Manfred's heart.

5. Byron heard of Goethe's 1820 review of *Manfred* and asked Richard Belgrave Hoppner to make a translation of it for him. It is printed by Rowland E. Prothero in his edition of *The Works of Lord Byron: Letters and Journals* (London: John Murray, 1901) V. 506–507.

6. Peter Manning, "'My Pang Shall Find a Voice': *Manfred* and *The Sufferings of Young Werther*," *On the 200th Anniversary of Lord Byron's Manfred: Commemorative Essays.* Romantic Circles Praxis Series (June 2019): https://romantic-circles.org/praxis/manfred/praxis .2019.manfred.manning.html.

7. *Conversations of Goethe with Eckermann and Soret*, trans. John Oxenford (London: George Bell and Sons, 1875), 554.

8. The matter is discussed in Herman Meyer, "'These Very Serious Jests,'" reprinted in the first Norton Critical Edition of *Johann Wolfgang Von Goethe: Faust. A Tragedy*, ed. Cyrus Hamlin (New York: W. W. Norton, 1976), 603–615.

9. Tracking the linguistic confusions in *Manfred*, Philip W. Martin sees them as a map of miswriting: see *Byron: A Poet before His Public* (Cambridge: Cambridge University Press, 1982), chapter 5.

4 BYRON AND THE "WRONG REVOLUTIONARY POETICAL SYSTEM"

1. The rest of the account is also interesting: "I meant to have made him a Cavalier Servente in Italy and a cause for a divorce in England – and a Sentimental 'Werther-faced' man in Germany – so as to show the different ridicules of the society in each of these countries – and to have displayed him gradually gâté and blasé as he grew older – as is natural. – But I had not quite fixed whether to make him end in Hell, or in an unhappy marriage, – not knowing which would be the severest." The "gâté and blasé" comment suggests why the comparison to Anacharsis Clootz came to his mind. I refer to Juan's "five-year passage" because with the third installment of *Don Juan* (Cantos VI–VIII) Byron made clear he was dating Juan's career 1789–1794 (see *CPW* 5. xxiii–xxiv where I date it from the mid-1780s to 1792 or 1793; I now think the 1789–1794 dating – to coincide with the French Revolution – is more likely).

2. Castlereagh's language and politics were the chief object of attack when Byron began *Don Juan* (see the "Dedication" and the discussion below).

3. *BLJ* 8. 186–187: to John Murray, 23 August 1821. See Alan Richardson, *A Mental Theater: Romantic Drama and Consciousness in the Romantic Age* (University Park PA: Pennsylvania State University Press, 1988).

4. To John Murray, March 25, 1818 (*BLJ* 6. 25). On the composition date of Beppo, see *CPW* 4. 482–483.

5. "Mannerism" was the English translation of "la maniera," the complex sixteenth-century art historical turn against High Renaissance classical style. As the very term "la maniera" suggests, while the movement took many forms, they all exhibited a self-conscious and more or less spectacular virtuosity. Promoted by Vasari, later art historians – Bellori and Winckelmann, for example – took a more critical view, as did Moore (and Byron).

6. *Edinburgh Review* 22 (October 1813): 38–39.

7. As Hermann Fischer pointed out (in the only essay that tries to parse what Byron meant by his critique), Byron seriously qualified his

comments the following February in a letter to Thomas Moore (*BLJ* 6. 9–11: February 2, 1818). See *The Merry Muses of Caledonia*, ed. James Barke and Sydney Goodsir Smith (New York: G. P. Putnam Sons, 1964), 181.

8. Thomas Moore, *Letters and Journals of Lord Byron, with Notices of His Life* (London: John Murray, 1830), 2, 111n.

9. See Mirka Horova's fine essay "Byron's *The Lament of Tasso* and the Mannerism of Madness," in *Byron and Latin Culture. Selected Proceedings of the 37th International Byron Society Conference*, ed. Peter Cochran (Cambridge: Cambridge Scholars, 2013), 217–224.

10. A. O. Lovejoy, "On the Discrimination of Romanticisms," *PMLA* 39.2 (1924): 229–253.

11. Montaigne was particularly important for Byron because he was a post-classical philosopher who "moved from a conception of philosophy conceived of as theoretical science, to a philosophy conceived of as the practice of free judgment" ("Michel de Montaigne," *Stanford Encyclopedia of Philosophy*: https://plato.stanford.edu /entries/montaigne/#FreJud). Like other humanists, Byron included Jesus in this company.

12. Walter Benjamin, "These on the Philosophy of History," *Illuminations. Essays and Reflections*, trans. Harry Zohn, ed. Hannah Arendt, with a preface by Leon Wieseltier (New York: Shocken, 2007, 1968), 257–258.

13. Coleridge's poem of this title (1825) contrasts sharply with the "hopeless" stances taken by Byron and Benjamin. Whereas hopeless reflection conjures "spells that drowse my soul" (12) in Coleridge's poem, hopelessness in Byron and Benjamin is the condition that makes human freedom possible.

14. Walter Benjamin, "Karl Kraus," *The Work of Art in the Age of Technological Reproducibility and Other Writings on Media*, ed. Michael W. Jennings, Brigid Doherty, and Thomas Y. Levin (Cambridge, MA: Belknap Press of Harvard University Press, 2008), 387.

15. *Conversations of Lord Byron with the Countess of Blessington* (London: Henry Colburn, 1934), 238–239.

16. See *The Blues*, "Eclogue the First," 9; also Byron's 1821 epigram "Of Turdsworth the Great Metaquizzical Poet" (*BLJ* 8. 187, 191).

17. *Thomas Hardy: The Complete Poems. Variorum Edition*, ed. James Gibson (London: Macmillan, 1979), 571.

18. The phrase is Louis Althusser's (quoting Marx): see Jerome McGann, *The Romantic Ideology* (Chicago: University of Chicago Press, 1983), 66.

19. See Cochran's note to the line: https://petercochran.files.wordpress.com/2009/03/don_juan_canto_4.pdf.

5 BYRON, BLAKE, AND THE ADVERSITY OF POETICS

1. David Erdman, *Blake: Prophet against Empire* (New York: Doubleday, 1969).

2. For a good account of the hostility Byron's play provoked, see Robert Mortenson, *Byron's Waterloo: The Reception of Cain, A Mystery* (Seattle, WA: Iron Press, 2015).

3. William Blake, *Milton: A Poem and the Final Illuminated Works, The Ghost of Abel On Homers Poetry [and] On Virgil Laocoön*, ed. Robert N. Essick and Joseph Viscomi (Princeton, NJ: William Blake Trust and Princeton University Press: 1993), 224 n5. In referencing *The Ghost of Abel*, I cite this edition as *Ghost1993*.

4. See *Ghost1993*, 223, and Angus Whitehead, "A Quotation from Lord Byron's *The Two Foscari* in William Blake's *The Ghost of Abel*," *Notes and Queries* (September 2006), 325–326.

5. See the subtitle of Blake's epic account of universal psycho-political history, *The Four Zoas: The Torments of Love & Jealousy in the Death and Judgement of Albion the Ancient Man* (1797). The thrust of Green's essay (*op. cit.*) is to emphasize the general character of Byron's and Blake's attacks on state religion and social violence.

6. Byron set out to extend *Cain*'s critical commentary on the foundational Old Testament texts with his drama *Heaven and Earth: A Mystery* (1823), but he lived to complete and publish only Part I. Both Byron and Blake seem to have read the recently discovered and translated book of Enoch, which calls for the extermination of the line of Cain. See G. E. Bentley Jr., "A Jewel in an Ethiop's Ear," *Blake in*

His Time, ed. Robert N. Essick and Donald Pearce (Bloomington: University of Indiana Press, 1978), 213–240, and *CPW* 6. 682–683.

7. These are Rene Wellek 's influential descriptors of the Romantic ethos: "imagination for the view of poetry, nature for the view of the world, and symbol and myth for poetic style" ("The Concept of Romanticism in Literary Scholarship," *Concepts of Criticism* [New Haven, CT: Yale University Press, 1963], 161).

8. "Imagination is the real and eternal world of which this vegetable universe is but a faint shadow" (*Complete Poetry and Prose of William Blake*, newly revised edition, ed. David V. Erdman (New York: Doubleday, 1988), 231. For Blake's severe criticisms of Wordsworth, see his annotations to *The Excursion* (666–667), and, for his extensive comments to Crabb Robinson, see 700–703. Unless otherwise indicated, I cite this text as *Erdman*.

9. While the terms "sentimental and pantheist" often carry valuative inflections, I use them here simply as cultural descriptors.

10. See the representations of both the "Spirits of the unbounded Universe" in Act I scene 1 and the actions of the Destinies in Act II scenes 3 and 4. Equally notable is Manfred's rejection of the Witch of the Alps in Act II scene 2, Byron's lyric "Darkness," his comments on nature in the "Alpine Journal," and throughout cantos III and IV of *Childe Harold*, perhaps especially in the famous "Address to Ocean" that concludes the fourth canto. Cuvier's catastrophic paleontology is central to the presentation of nature in *Cain*. For the contemporary relevance of these approaches to nature, see Ricardo J. Quinones, *The Changes of Cain: Violence and the Lost Brother in Cain and Abel Literature* (Princeton, NJ: Princeton University Press, 1991), 100–104.

11. See Hegel's *Phenomenology of Spirit*, "Introduction," paragraph 78.

12. "I deny nothing, but doubt everything" (*BLJ* 2. 136). The religious face of Byron's skepticism has recently been brought back to scholarly attention in interesting ways. It has a distinguished earlier history: see especially Elizabeth Atkins, "Points of Contact between Socrates and Byron," *PMLA* 41. 2 (1926): 402–423 and A. J. Marjarum, *Byron as Skeptic and Believer* (Princeton, NJ: Princeton University Press,

1938), and compare Gavin Hopps, ed., *Byron's Ghosts: The Spectral, the Spiritual, and the Supernatural* (Liverpool: University of Liverpool Press, 2013). See Hopps's "Introduction" (8–18), where he writes of "postmodern re-enchantment [where] *skepticism* ... dilates the parameters of the possible and underwrites the hospitality towards the spectral" (8). Byron is the emblematic executor of a skepticism that "undermines, even as it carries to its logical conclusion, the Enlightenment project of 'radical doubt'" (8).

13. This is from Henry Crabb Robinson's diary notes on his 1825–1826 conversations with Blake as Robinson later (1852) organized them for his *Reminiscences*. My text is from G. E. Bentley Jr., ed., *Blake Records*, second edition (New Haven, CT, and London: Paul Mellon Centre and Yale University Press, 2004), 692–706. Bentley prints the text of the original diary notes at 420–438 *passim*. The Voltaire passage is at 703.

14. In Kant's signature essay "What Is Enlightenment?" (1784). Daring or not daring to think is a recurrent issue in *Manfred*. See *Manfred* II. 2. 195–204, when Manfred chooses *sapere aude* in face of his greatest fear, as well as the opposite move taken by the Abbot at the end of the action when he says "I dread to think" about Manfred's afterlife.

15. Jesus, Blake told Robinson, "took much after his mother [the law], and in that respect was one of the worst of men" (705). Blake generalized his criticism of Jesus's action against the money changers by remarking that "He should not have attacked the govern[men]t. He had no business with such matters" (696). For good commentary on Blake's view of vicarious atonement, see Michael Ferber, *The Social Vision of William Blake* (Princeton, NJ: Princeton University Press, 1985): 77; Jennifer Jesse, *William Blake's Religious Vision: There's a Methodism in the Madness* (Lanham, MD: Lexington Books, 2013): 117–120. Also see Michael Farrell, *Blake and the Methodists* (New York: Palgrave Macmillan, 2014), 55; for a different view, see J. G. Davies, *The Theology of William Blake* (New York: Oxford University Press, 1948), 116–122.

16. Blake told Crabb Robinson, "If another man pay your debt, I do not forgive it" (271), meaning vicarious atonement prevented the key

Blakean action of mutual forgiveness of sin. As for Byron, see *Manfred* III. 1. 98–99, where Manfred repudiates the "necessity" of atonement declared by the Abbot. See also his letter to Francis Hodgson of September 13, 1811: the sacrifice of Jesus "no more does away with man's guilt than a schoolboy's volunteering to be flogged for another would exculpate the dunce from negligence, or preserve him from the rod" (*BLJ* II. 97).

17. Blake's famous apothegm, "One Law for the Lion & the Ox is Oppression" (*The Marriage of Heaven and Hell* plate 24), is probably his antinomian reading of Jesus's declaration recorded in Mark 2: 27 ("The Sabbath was made for man, not man for the Sabbath").

18. Blake's and Byron's criticism of the doctrine of atonement aligns itself with what Gregory Chaplin, discussing Milton's doctrinal views, calls "the classical friendship tradition" (see his essay "Beyond Sacrifice: Milton and Atonement," *PMLA* 125.2 [2010]: 365. Chaplin argues that Milton himself opposed "penal-substitutionary," or vicarious, atonement. But Samuel Smith has recently disputed Chaplin's view ("Milton's Theology of the Cross: Substitution and Satisfaction in Christ's Atonement," *Christianity and Literature* 63.1 [2013]: 5–25). See my discussion of Blake's *Milton*, which argues that Smith's judgment of Milton was also Blake's. But Blake also thought that Milton was actually "of the Devil's party without knowing it" and hence that *Paradise Lost* ought to be read, so to speak, against its own grain – ought to be read, in other words, the way Chaplin reads Milton.

19. See Robinson, *Reminiscences*, 700, where Blake endorses "the cultivation of the fine arts & the imagination." Philosophy only "holds a candle in [the] sunshine" of imaginative expression (*The Marriage of Heaven and Hell* plate 22); see also *On Homers Poetry*: in poetry, "Unity & Morality, are secondary considerations & belong to Philosophy & not to Poetry."

20. Harold Bloom shrewdly described Blake's *Milton* with this phrase, which applies as well to Byron's famous "Dramatic Poem." Blake's crisis came at Felpham in 1803, when *Milton* was begun, and Byron's came in 1816–1817, when he wrote *Manfred*.

21. See in particular his letter to Hayley (May 28, 1804), where he dismisses "the French ... the English [and] the Americans" for their commitment to the "Grecian, or rather Trojan, worship" of war (*Erdman* 749–750).

22. For analyses of the significance of Felpham, see Paul Mann, "Apocalypse and Recuperation: Blake and the Maw of Commerce," *ELH* 52.1 (1985): 1–32; *Blake, Politics, and History*, ed. Jackie DiSalvo, G. A. Rosso, and Christopher Z. Hobson (London: Routledge, 1998), in particular Eric V. Chandler, "The Anxiety of Production: Blake's Shift from Collective Hope to Writing Self," 53–79, and my "Did Blake Betray the French Revolution?" especially 129–135 (in *Presenting Poetry: Composition, Publication, Reception*, ed. Howard Erskine-Hill and Richard A. McCabe (Cambridge: Cambridge University Press, 1995), 117–137.

23. Though I have a different view of the Forgiveness Curse stanzas, I recommend the recent essay by Jonathan Shears, "'In One We Shall be Slower': Byron, Retribution, and Forgiveness," *Christianity and Literature* (2016): 1–28. See also Clara Tuite's fine study *Lord Byron and Scandalous Celebrity* (Cambridge: Cambridge University Press, 2015).

24. Compare Emerson: "the discovery ... that we exist ... called the Fall of Man" ("Experience"). Emerson's transcendentalism gives a strongly benevolent inflection to his thought.

25. The second fall is the subject of Shelley's late uncompleted poem. Its truncated condition leaves uncertain whether he intended to finish it with a movement that would run counter to the fearful pageant that constitutes the verses as received.

26. The Peninsula War and the Levantine wars of the European powers are Byron's focus in Cantos I and II, as Cantos III and IV meditate in the long French Revolution and the history of Rome.

27. This is the Prayer Book translation of Psalm 105: 18 that became proverbial for bitter despair. The iron had entered the soul of Eve when she delivered her staggering curse on her son Cain in Byron's play, which seems to me the piteous emotional focal point for the entire work.

28. And he acquiesced, as he agreed to rewrite Act 3 of *Manfred*. But when Murray and his editorial circle edited *Don Juan I–II* against his explicit prohibition, he was so furious that the break with Murray became inevitable.

29. That view is summarily presented in the commentary and notes to the *Ghost 1993* volume of the Blake Trust volumes, *op. cit.*: see here 220–237, 254–263, and especially "there is no agreement among critics about what specifically in Byron's play Blake is responding to or whether Blake is criticizing or praising Byron" (222).

30. See *The Poems of William Blake*, ed. W. H. Stevenson, text by David Erdman (London: Longman, 1971), 860–864, and Leslie Tannenbaum, "Lord Byron in the Wilderness: Biblical Tradition in Byron's *Cain* and Blake's *The Ghost of Abel*," *Modern Philology* 72.4 (1975): 350–364. See also S. Foster Damon, *A Blake Dictionary: The Ideas and Symbols of William Blake*, with a new foreword and bibliography by Morris Eaves (Hanover, NH: Brown University Press, 1988), the entry for "Elijah." Damon says Blake "hail[s] Byron as a true poet while correcting his ideas" (118). Essick and Viscomi disagree with that reading (224–226). Three other important discussions of the Blake/Byron nexus in *The Ghost of Abel* are Kerry Ellen McKeever, "Naming the Name of the Prophet: William Blake's Reading of Byron's *Cain. A Mystery*," *Studies in Romanticism* 34.4 (1995): 615–636, and Matthew J. A. Green, "Voices in the Wilderness: Satire and Sacrifice in Blake and Byron," *The Byron Journal* 36.2 (2003): 117–129, and Morton D. Paley, *The Traveller in the Evening: The Last Works of William Blake* (Oxford: Oxford University Press, 2003).

31. Against Tannenbaum/Stevenson, Viscomi and Eaves argue that the answer to Blake's question is not no, but both yes and no.

32. Julia Wright, "The Medium, the Message, and the Line in William Blake's *Laocoön*," *Mosaic*. 33.2 (2000): 101–124.

33. These are the dates established for the engraving: see The Blake Archive: www.blakearchive.org/work/laocoon.

34. Wilde's remark comes in *The Critic as Artist* (1891). On Byron's masks and masquerades, see my essays "'My Brain Is Feminine': Byron and the Poetry of Deception" and "Hero with a Thousand

Faces: The Rhetoric of Byronism," both reprinted in my collection *Byron and Romanticism*, ed. James Soderholm (Cambridge: Cambridge University Press, 2002), chapters 3 and 7.

35. This tag from the top of the *Laocoön* plate is jotted as well into *The Notebook of William Blake* (aka *The Rossetti Manuscript*): www .bl.uk/collection-items/the-notebook-of-william-blake.

6 THE STUBBORN FOE: BAD VERSE AND THE POETRY OF ACTION

1. *The Edinburgh Review* 36 (1821–1822): 413–452.
2. *The Letters of Percy Bysshe Shelley*, ed. F. L. Jones (Oxford: Clarendon, 1964) 2:57–58; see also Cochran, "Byron and Shelley: Radical Incompatibles": www.erudit.org/en/journals/ron/1900-v1-n1-ron1383/013589ar.
3. For "the seat of all dissoluteness," see Byron's epigraph to *Beppo*.
4. Shelley, *Letters*, II. 323.
5. I quote from the Internet Archive's facsimile edition of the first edition (https://archive.org/details/revoltofislamooshel/page/n11/mode/2up).
6. For a useful discussion, see Kathryn Gutzwiller, *Theocritus' Pastoral Analogies: The Formation of a Genre* (Madison: University of Wisconsin Press, 1991), 125–126.
7. Wordsworth to John Scott, April 18, 1816, *The Letters of William and Dorothy Wordsworth: The Middle Years*, ed. Ernest de Selincourt (Clarendon: Oxford, 1937), 2:734–735.
8. From *Table Talk*, December 29, 1822, *Coleridge's Miscellaneous Criticism*, ed. Thomas M. Raysor (Cambridge, MA: Harvard University Press, 1936), 401.
9. The closing section of Canto 15 explicitly forecasts the virtually slapstick comedy of Canto 16.
10. Since the "reality" that was most burning and distressing was his discovery of his love for Augusta, it tilts the mind to think how, of all poems, *The Bride of Abydos* should have helped distract him.
11. Donald A. Low, ed., *Robert Burns: The Critical Heritage* (London: Routledge and Kegan Paul, 1974), 259–260.
12. *The Merry Muses of Caledonia*, ed. James Barke and Sydney Goodsir Smith (New York: G. P. Putnam Sons, 1964), 181.

13. *The Art of Sinking in Poetry: Martinus Scriblerus.* A Critical Edition. Ed. Edna Leeke Steeves (New York: Columbia University Press, 1952), 10.

14. For a good discussion, see D. M. R. Bentley, "Dante Gabriel Rossetti's 'Inner Standing-Point' and 'Jenny' Reconstrued," *University of Toronto Quarterly* 80.3 (2011): 680–717.

15. Shelley gives the Greek original as the epigram to *Adonais.* Mary Shelley published his translation after Shelley's death.

16. Isaac Nathan, *Fugitive Pieces* (London: Whittaker Treacher and Company, 1829), 42–43.

17. In his useful online edition of the *Hebrew Melodies*, Peter Cochran regularly notes what he sees as a kind of contradiction between Byron's hatred of Jewish moneylenders and what he judged the "proto-Zionist" features of various poems. See www.newsteadabbeyby ronsociety.org/works/downloads/hebrew_melodies.pdf.

INDEX

Aeschylus, 137, 164, 180
  works
    Prometheus Unbound, 97, 137
Alighieri, Dante, 20, 37, 60, 62–63,
    97, 164
Ariosto, Ludovico, 15, 164, 186
Aristotle, 115, 121
Arnold, Matthew, 48, 162

Baudelaire, Charles, 44, 79
Beatty, Bernard, 2
Beatty, James, 39
Benjamin, Walter, 110
Bernstein, Charles
  works
    Recalculating, 64
Blake, James, 128
Blake, William, 1, 17, 40, 63, 165
  works
    Everlasting Gospel, The, 124

Four Zoas, The, 121, 132,
    134, 158
Ghost of Abel, The, 119, 130,
    143–150
Homers Poetry, On, 119,
    150, 202
Jerusalem, 1, 120, 121, 124,
    126, 129, 147
Laocoön (יה [Yod] & his two
    Sons Satan & Adam), 143,
    148–153
*Marriage of Heaven and Hell,
    The*, 123, 124, 125, 126,
    129, 147, 152, 165, 202
*Milton. A Poem in Two
    Books*, 121, 124, 128–130,
    141, 145, 148, 151, 152
Notebook, 124
Songs of Innocence
The Divine Image, 100
To The Accuser Who Is
    The God of This World
    (engraving), 147

Blake, William (cont.)
    *Urizen, The [First] Book
      of*, 122
    Virgil, On, 126, 150, 192
Bowles, William Lisle, 17, 18
Brougham, Henry, 41, 43, 159,
    160, 168
Browning, Robert
  works
    Sordello, 151
Bukowski, Charles, 154
  works
    Style, 154
Burns, Robert, 22, 107, 114,
    165–168, 175
  works
    Ken Ye Na Our Lass, Bess?,
      167, 177
Butler, Samuel, 170
Butts, Thomas, 128
Byron, George Gordon, 1, 107
  and the Jews, 180
  his Years of Fame, 3, 40, 72, 137
  on Cant, 2, 17, 38, 59, 101, 105,
    134, 136, 153, 164, 168, 176
  works
    Age of Bronze, The, 112,
      130, 150
    Beppo, 4, 15, 17, 28–31, 55,
      89, 101, 103, 105, 156, 157
    Bride of Abydos, The, 46, 54,
      62, 164
    Cain. A Mystery, 63, 76, 103,
      106, 119–132, 133, 143,
      147, 155, 175

Childe Harold's Pilgrimage, 1,
  12, 41, 45–47, 69, 75, 78,
  95, 101, 109, 115, 116, 122,
  130–142, 148, 156, 158,
  160, 161, 168–175,
  176, 202
Corsair, The, 58, 60–63, 69,
  96, 117
Deformed Transformed, The,
  49, 106
Don Juan, 1, 9–37, 55, 81,
  87, 94, 101–102, 103,
  114–118, 120, 121, 126,
  133, 134, 137, 139, 140,
  142, 150, 152, 157, 158,
  162, 165, 168, 175, 176
Dedication, 16, 17, 19, 20,
  35, 112
*English Bards and Scotch
  Reviewers*, 40–44, 55, 114,
  126, 133, 159, 160
Epistle to Augusta, 131, 138
Fare Thee Well, 67, 70,
  161, 175
Giaour, The, 4–8, 47, 49–51,
  59, 64–68, 79, 82, 91, 94,
  96, 102, 115, 122, 175
Heaven and Earth, 121
Hebrew Melodies, 180–181
Magdalen, 180–181
She Walks in Beauty, 175
Sun of the Sleepless!, 81,
  178–179
Hours of Idleness, 41, 159
Damaetas, 159–160, 168
Journal, 163, 166
L'amitié, c'est l'amour sans
  ailes, 53

Lament of Tasso, The, 108
Lara, 3, 52, 55–58, 60–63, 70, 96, 136, 164
Manfred, 1, 63, 68, 82–102, 103, 105, 115, 118, 122, 123, 128, 130–131, 133, 151, 160, 175
Marino Faliero, 106
Memoirs, 166
Oriental Tales, 1
Parisina, 61, 71–72, 75
Prisoner of Chillon, The, 105
Prometheus, 62, 97, 110, 137, 161, 173
Sardanapalus, 106, 120
Siege of Corinth, The, 19, 47–48, 60, 72–81, 175
Stanzas for Music, 175, 177
Stanzas to Augusta, 89, 142
To the Po, 12
Two Foscari, The, 120, 121, 144
Vision of Judgment, The, 86
Written Beneath a Picture, 68, 91

Campbell, Thomas, 107
Cavalcanti, Guido, 31
Celan, Paul, 103
Cervantes, Miguel de, 164
Chaucer, Geoffrey, 21
Cicero, 109
Cochran, Peter, 60, 117, 180, 193
Coleman, Ornette, 31

Coleridge, Samuel Taylor, 11, 16–21, 94, 111, 114
works
Biographia Literaria, 16, 17, 18, 19, 27
Christabel, 19
Friend, The, 17, 19
Kubla Khan, 19
Lyrical Ballads, 11
Rime of the Ancyent Marinere, The, 19, 54
Table Talk, 162
Crabb Robinson, Henry, 123, 124, 126, 147
Crabbe, George, 24, 108
Crane, Hart, 11, 173

Darwin, Erasmus, 107
Davies, Alan
works
Private Enigma in the Opened Text, 82
Dickens, Charles
works
Tale of Two Cities, A, 118
Dickinson, Emily, 137
Drummond, Sir William, 110
Dryden, John, 13, 114

Eckermann, Johann Peter, 48, 99
Elijah (prophet), 120, 143, 147, 150

Eliot, Thomas Stearns, 9, 24–25, 27, 35, 37, 116, 140, 162
  works
    Byron, 9
    Four Quartets, 190
    Burnt Norton, 13
    East Coker, 13, 175
    Little Gidding, 12, 14
    Waste Land, The, 6, 41
Erdman, David, 120

Frost, Robert, 116

Gay, John, 170
Genesis, Book of, 63, 125, 143, 152
Gibbon, Edward, 61
Gifford, William, 55, 79, 164, 175
Goethe, Johann Wolfgang von, 2, 44, 48–49, 81, 95, 97, 106, 162
  works
    Faust, 82, 95, 97, 101
Guiçcioli, Teresa, 160

Hardy, Thomas, 116
Hayley, William, 128, 129
Hazlitt, William, 108
Hegel, Georg Wilhelm Friedrich, 122
Homer, 6, 26, 50, 52, 53, 175, 192
Hopkins, Gerard Manley, 115
Hoppner, Richard, 101, 192

Horace, 17, 26, 42
Hunt, John, 104, 164

Jackson, Laura (Riding), 10
Jarry, Alfred, 28
Jeffrey, Francis, 71, 155–159, 162
Jesus, 121, 124–126, 128, 129, 145–147, 180–181
Johnson, Samuel, 55
Jones, David
  works
    Compleat History of the Turks, A, 75, 78
Jones, Sir William, 107
Joyce, James, 187, 188
  works
    Dubliners, 35
    Finnegans Wake, 35
    Ulysses, 69

Kant, Immanuel, 63, 89, 123, 138
Keats, John, 1, 3, 192
  works
    Cap and Bells, The, 42
    Endymion, 4, 177
    Fall of Hyperion, The, 50, 54
Kinnaird, Douglas, 165
Kleist, Ewald Christian von, 164
Knight, George Richard Wilson, 2, 184
Kraus, Karl, 110

Lamb, Charles, 20
Lamb, Elizabeth, 163, 178

language, 34–35, 37, 139,
    184
  English, 37, 175
    commonplaces, 26–27, 34, 36,
        53, 163, 176
    vernacular, 11, 14–15, 20,
        25–27, 34, 39, 40
  in general, 34
  Italian, 15, 101, 106
  Latin, 171
  philology, 45, 46, 50, 108
  Scots, 22, 52, 89
Laocoön (Vatican), 148, 150, 152
Leigh, Augusta Maria, 62, 83,
    177
Lenin, Vladimir, 79
Leviticus, Book of, 144
Lewis, Matthew Gregory, 47
Longinus, 38, 170
Lopez, Barry, viii
Lovejoy, Arthur Oncken, 108, 121
Lucretius, 184

Macpherson, James, 109, 186
Mallarmé, Stéphane, 154
  works
    Le Tombeau d' Edgar Poe,
        154
Manning, Peter, 12, 96
Melville, Herman, 58, 97
Milton John, 26, 55, 114, 124
  works
    Paradise Lost, 129, 130, 152

Montaigne, Michel de, 109
Monty Python, 102
  works
    Life of Brian, The, 118
Moore, Marianne, 25
Moore, Thomas, 104, 107, 111,
    112, 114, 166
Mozart, Wolfgang Amadeus
  works
    Don Giovanni, 101, 187
Murray, James, 34
Murray, John, 16, 101, 102, 103,
    105, 106, 107, 111, 114,
    163, 164

Nathan, Isaac, 180
  works
    Fugitive Pieces, 180
Nietzsche, Friedrich, 82, 91,
    97, 118

Paine, Thomas, 123
Partch, Harry, 54
Paul, Saint (apostle), 97, 121,
    124
Pausanias, 94
Peacock, Thomas Love, 156
Percy, Thomas, 47
  works
    *Reliques of Ancient English
        Poetry*, 109
Plato, 63
Plutarch, 94

Poe, Edgar Allan, 27, 44,
        54–55, 154
    works
        City in the Sea, The, 27
        Rationale of Verse, The, 54
poetics
    address, 2, 10, 38, 40, 42, 45, 50,
        54, 59, 80, 106, 119,
        133–134, 138–139, 142,
        152, 158, 170, 175, 176
    Byronism, 44, 64
    carelessness, 61, 162, 163
    diction, 14, 27, 34, 39, 42,
        44–48, 79, 191
        vulgar, 22, 40, 47, 89, 91, 162
    grammar, 54–58, 62, 66, 69–73,
        136, 176, 193, 194
    prosody, 54, 57, 58
        couplet verse, 50, 55, 59
    rhetoric, 38, 44, 49, 52, 56, 81,
        104, 109, 120, 137, 143,
        176, 192
        address, 10
    subtractions, action of, 70
    syntax, 66, 70–75, 81, 91–94,
        142, 173
        knotted, 70
        torqued, 99, 142
        tortured, 71, 178
    usage, 34, 39, 45, 47–48, 70,
        90, 191
    verse
        bad, 182
        doggerel, 169

    didactic, 39, 45
    free, 40
    lyrical, 45, 131, 133, 169,
        180
    medley, 28, 82, 103, 105,
        190, 196
    mixed, 59
    narrative, 39, 63
    perversification, 80, 93,
        136, 163
    pointing, 57
    recitation, 55
Pope, Alexander, 17, 26, 39, 49, 59,
        69, 107, 113, 114, 150,
        155, 192
    works
        Dunciad, The, 41, 116
        Essay on Criticism, An, 17, 111
        Essay on Man, An, 17, 111
        Imitations of Horace, 42
        Peri Bathous, 170
Pound, Ezra, 115
Prior, Matthew, 170
Pythagoras, 20

Reznikoff, Charles, 11
Richards, Ivor Armstrong, 112
Rimbaud, Arthur, 173
Rogers, Samuel, 108
Rossetti, Dante Gabriel, 170
Roth, Philip
    works
        Sabbath's Theater, 181
Rousseau, Jean-Jacques, 134
Rukeyser, Muriel, 11

Scott, Sir Walter, 1, 39, 44–48,
	107, 155, 166
	works
		Ivanhoe, 119, 141
		Marmion, 52
		Rokeby, 44, 52
Seneca, 109
Shakespeare, William, 21, 26, 33,
	100, 136, 192
Shelley, Percy Bysshe, 1, 37, 110,
	156, 157–158
	works
		Cloud, The, 37
		Revolt of Islam, The
		Preface, 157
		The Triumph of Life, 132
		To Stella, 179
Socrates, 109, 134
Sophocles, 164
Southey, Robert, 9, 16, 25, 26, 29,
	35, 47, 114, 115, 155
Stein, Gertrude, 11, 15, 83
Stevens, Wallace, 11
Stevenson, W. H., 143, 144
Swift, Jonathan, 80, 170
Swinburne, Algernon Charles, 113

Tannenbaum, Leslie, 143, 144
Tasso, Torquato, 164
Tennyson, Alfred Lord, 7, 116
	works
		Lady of Shallot, The, 116
		Maud, 151

Thelwall, John, 15
Theocritus, 160
Tobin, James, 19

Valéry, Paul, 154
Voltaire, 111, 123

West, Paul, 36, 43
Whitman, Walt, 11, 15, 33
Wilde, Oscar, 150
Williams, Raymond, 184
Williams, William Carlos, 11,
	15
Wittgenstein, Ludwig
	works
		*Philosophical
		Investigations*, 82
Woolf, Virginia, 9
Wordsworth, William, 1, 3, 11, 27,
	38, 54, 85, 107, 114, 122,
	160, 161
	works
		Elegiac Stanzas, 4, 161
		Excursion, The, 16, 17,
		35
		Intimations Ode, 15, 16,
		161
		Lyrical Ballads, 11, 13–15,
		111, 160, 168, 169
		Idiot Boy, The, 114, 167
		Michael, 4, 54, 114
		Preface, 13, 160
		Tintern Abbey, 16, 122
		Poems (1815)

Wordsworth, William (cont.)
    Essay Supplementary, 17
    Preface, 17
    Prelude, The, 4, 12, 79, 116,
       139, 161, 167
    Recluse, The, 16
    Resolution and
      Independence, 4
    Solitary Reaper, The, 4, 175

    To the Cuckoo, 168
    White Doe of Rylstone, The, 4
Wright, Julia, 148, 150

Yeats, William Butler
  works
    Circus Animals' Desertion,
      The, 36, 79